School Choice Myths

Setting the Record Straight on Education Freedom

School Choice Myths

Edited by Corey A. DeAngelis and Neal P. McCluskey

CATO INSTITUTE
Washington, DC

ISBN: 978-1-948647-90-8
eISBN: 978-1-948647-92-2

Library of Congress Cataloging-in-Publication Data

McCluskey, Neal P., 1972- editor. | DeAngelis, Corey A., editor.
School choice myths : setting the record straight on education freedom / Corey A. DeAngelis and Neal P. McCluskey, Eds.
p. cm.
Washington, DC : Cato Institute, [2020]
Includes bibliographical references and index.
LCCN 2020024864 (print) | LCCN 2020024865 (ebook)
ISBN 9781948647908 (hardback) | ISBN 9781948647922 (ebook)
1. School choice—Social aspects. 2. Educational equalization.
3. Democracy and education.

LB1027.9 .S352 2020
DDC 379.1/11—dc23 2020024864

Jacket design: Jon Meyers.
Printed in Canada.

Cato Institute
1000 Massachusetts Avenue NW
Washington, DC 20001
www.cato.org

CONTENTS

LIST OF ILLUSTRATIONS

Figures

Tables

ABBREVIATIONS AND ACRONYMS

ACLU	—	American Civil Liberties Union
CPE	—	Committee for Public Education (Charlottesville, Virginia)
CPS	—	Chartered public school
DCOSP	—	District of Columbia's Opportunity Scholarship Program
ESA	—	Education savings account
ICSP	—	Indiana Choice Scholarship Program
IDEA	—	Individuals with Disabilities Education Act
IEP	—	Individualized education program
LSP	—	Louisiana Scholarship Program
NAACP	—	National Association for the Advancement of Colored People
NAEP	—	National Assessment of Educational Progress
PISA	—	Programme for International Student Assessment
RCT	—	Randomized controlled trial
SCSF	—	School Choice Scholarships Foundation
SFO	—	Scholarship funding organization
TPS	—	Traditional public school
VEA	—	Virginia Education Association

INTRODUCTION

Corey A. DeAngelis and Neal P. McCluskey

It should be no surprise that there is substantial opposition to school choice. Disapproval is probably not from the majority of Americans, with survey responses depending a lot on the specific choice mechanisms discussed and wording of the questions, but opposition is nonetheless appreciable. This question-driven volatility reflects the existence of many reasons that people might oppose choice—we need uniform schools to treat all kids equally, tax dollars should not go to religious schools, and quite a few others—but all can likely be justified in some rational way. Unfortunately, though there are many understandable reasons to oppose school choice, far too often myths—beliefs that never had a factual basis or that have been disproven—are trotted out to fight educational freedom.

This is not to say that choice opponents are all wanton purveyors of dishonesty. It is hard to know why people repeat myths, but probably most do not purposely try to deceive. Some of these myths are intuitively appealing or require some semi-deep analysis to penetrate, and the average person with a job, family, and social life simply does not have time to delve deeply enough into education policy to dismiss them.

On one level, for instance, it is clear that private school choice programs, if they use funds that would have otherwise gone to public schools, take money away from public schools. But as Ben Scafidi and Marty Lueken explain in Chapter 6, just because the money follows the student doesn't mean the district—or more important, *the students in it*—are worse off financially. If only part of the total per-pupil expenditure follows the child into a private school, which is usually the case, there is actually more money per child in the public school. And while districts do have some fixed costs that curb their ability to direct more resources to remaining kids, Scafidi and Lueken show that those are limited and that in the long run even buildings can be sold.

How about whether kids whose parents do not choose private schools must suffer as they are "left behind"? (For those who remember the No Child Left Behind Act, that's a big rhetorical no-no in education policy.) Intuitively it would seem that they would: more engaged and savvy families would be more likely to move, and families with less political and social capital would remain. But as Matt Ladner points out in Chapter 7, competition benefits everyone. It pushes the schools that are losing students to do better, just as competition from FedEx and UPS forces the U.S. Postal Service to deliver packages on Sundays.

Of course, it is quite possible that some who inveigh against school choice know perfectly well that they are propagating untruths, or at least half-truths, and that is too bad. But no matter why people say the things they say, it sure would be nice to have a guide on your desk, bookshelf, Starbucks table, backyard patio furniture—wherever you do your education policy reading or writing—that you could grab whenever a myth rears its fantastical head. Such a guide is what this volume aims to be. It tackles 12 of the biggest myths out there—a dirty dozen, if you will—and arms you with facts and logic to combat mythology wherever and for whatever reason it pops up.

The chapters start with the notion that school choice would "Balkanize" the country, allowing Americans to scatter into insular—and warring—communities. It's a fear that even former Supreme Court Justice John Paul Stevens expressed in his dissent in *Zelman v. Simmons-Harris*, a 2002 ruling that school vouchers eligible for use at religious schools do not violate the U.S. Constitution's First Amendment. It's a fear that makes intuitive sense, writes the Cato Institute's Neal McCluskey, but one that also ignores reality: Americans are already highly stratified by race, income, and myriad other factors according to where they live, and, hence, what public schools they attend. Moreover, what research exists (more is needed) suggests that choice, not compulsion, holds the greatest potential, at least in education, to bridge divides.

An extreme, and more repugnant, subset of the Balkanization myth is that school choice began explicitly—and will be used again—for racial segregation of the Jim Crow variety. We've seen this accusation leveled against choice many times, and there is some factual basis for it: some people did try to escape public school integration after *Brown v. Board of Education* via public funding to attend "segregation academies." But as the American Institute for Economic Research's Phil Magness explains, not only did the idea of educational freedom long predate *Brown*, but some segregationists *opposed* choice on the grounds that it would grease the skids for eventual school integration, subverting "massive resistance" and potentially opening additional seats in public schools that African Americans would occupy, thereby accelerating integration.

Closely connected to the notion that school choice is a natural divider is the belief that government-run schools are necessary for democracy. The underlying idea is that common schools will create among all students a common identity and, even more concretely, that they will inculcate the attitudes and knowledge needed for a democracy to thrive, including a desire to volunteer in one's community and an understanding of how a bill becomes a law. But a funny thing happened on the way to education for democracy, writes Patrick Wolf, Distinguished Professor and 21st Century Chair in School Choice at the University of Arkansas: a comprehensive review of the civic outcomes research indicates that private and other chosen schools have done a much better job of instilling democratic knowledge and values than government-run schools. It might have a lot to do with what freedom enables educators and families to do together.

Of course, there is a great question of what we actually mean by "democracy," and whether the United States is such a thing. What we can all agree on is that the country has a Constitution and that some people say school choice, especially if it allows the selection of religious schools, violates that document. In Chapter 4, Tim Keller, who leads the Educational Choice Team at the Institute for Justice—"the National Law Firm for Liberty"—opposes the conclusion that choice violates the federal Constitution. There may be specific things a choice law either must have or must omit to be constitutional, but choice broadly violates no constitutional provisions.

Moving from the social and legal, the book heads into the economic and financial. And there is no bigger economic—or, at least, quasi-economic—myth than that education is a "public good." In other words, because a well-educated populace benefits society overall, and because children are not mere products, schooling cannot possibly be left to the market. In Chapter 5, the Reason Foundation's director of school choice Corey DeAngelis dismantles this accusation, explaining that not only does public education not actually meet the definition of a "public good" but that even if it did, in practice it may well be a public "bad." It fuels inequality—what you get depends on where you can buy a home—and, by its one-size-fits-all, factory-like nature, essentially *requires* that kids be treated as identical widgets.

In Chapter 6 Ben Scafidi of Kennesaw State University and Marty Lueken of EdChoice give the lie to the belief that school choice "siphons" money from public schools. Yes, money follows kids, but rarely the full amount. And honestly, where other than states with school choice programs does someone get paid to deliver a service to a customer who has taken her business elsewhere?

Chapter 7, by Matt Ladner, director of the Arizona Center for Student Opportunity, knocks to the ground the idea that choice hurts kids left behind in public schools by reviewing both the broad empirical research and diving into the experience of his own, choice-rich state of Arizona. Choice, and the resulting competition, gives powerful incentives for public schools to get better, and it spurs the sort of innovation that can put education on a permanent trajectory for improvement.

In Chapter 8, Albert Cheng, an assistant professor in education policy at the University of Arkansas, grapples with the assertion that choice will mainly help the rich get richer and that the wealthy and well-connected will be better able to exercise choice than the poor. Cheng argues that that depends on how one defines "choice." If we mean the predominant form of choice—choose a home to choose a school—yes, the rich win. If we are talking about school choice programs as they currently exist in the United States—aimed at poor families or families that include kids with special needs—the answer is that the rich get no richer, while the poor get greater access to previously out-of-reach schools because they increasingly do not have to pay for a home to get a school.

In the final third of the book, we look at the bounds of school choice. Does it need to be highly regulated to keep it from going off the rails? Can there be such a thing as too-compromised choice? Must federal rules for children with disabilities, currently geared to force public schools to treat such kids equally, be applied to schools of choice? And can poor people really be expected to choose effectively?

That private school choice needs to be accompanied by thick red tape—testing mandates, open-admission requirements, and more—is the myth tackled in Chapter 9 by Lindsey Burke of the Heritage Foundation and Jason Bedrick of EdChoice. Comparing and contrasting the regulation-heavy and regulation-light choice approaches of Louisiana and Florida, respectively, and dissecting the many "equalitarian" prescriptions to regulate choice, Burke and Bedrick readily acknowledge the good intentions of the equalitarian crowd—which seeks to equalize educational opportunity by providing school choice only for the poor—but explain that their regulations appear to end up hurting much more than they help, especially by encouraging the best private schools to stay on the school choice sidelines lest their recipes for success be destroyed, ironically, in the name of "quality."

In Chapter 10, John Merrifield, emeritus professor of economics at the University of Texas, San Antonio, goes after a myth that emanates from *within* school choice circles: that any program furnishing any additional choice is worthy of support. Merrifield finds this myth hard to dispel (If even one child can be helped, shouldn't we try?), but he determines that some policy combinations are "toxic." In particular, combining profit with "priceless-ness" is a deadly mix that enables charter schools to take shortcuts because people are waiting in droves to get in. Basically, the inability to charge a price keeps the best schools from expanding in order to make more money, and it keeps competitors, who would also like to make a profit, from entering the market. That artificial shortage leads to big waitlists for the most in-demand charters and enables them to rest on their laurels, or even decrease quality to increase profits, comfortable that they will always have plenty of demand. Long waitlists are often a sign that a "toxic mix" is brewing, which is bad both because of the shenanigans that attend it and because it can give real school choice—choice with broad freedom for both families and educators—a politically crippling bad name.

Perhaps the most understandable myth is that school choice will fail to serve students with special needs. Such children are often more expensive to educate than other kids—sometimes *much* more—because they require additional, specialized interventions that can often be pricey. But here again, troubling public school reality butts up against school choice imperfections. As Inez Feltscher Stepman, a senior policy analyst at the Independent Women's Forum, explains in Chapter 11, public schools have had a very poor track record of serving special-needs students. While the federal Individuals with Disabilities Education Act says that disabled students are entitled to a "free and appropriate public education," what that means in practice is constantly contested in courts, with families having to pay for litigation from their own pockets in pursuit of the services their kids need, while districts have expertise in the law and taxpayer dollars to pay for their fights. School choice, which puts money in the hands of parents, helps level the playing field between family and school.

Finally, we tackle one of the most enervating school choice myths: that low-income families will not make good choices, whether out of ignorance, misplaced educational priorities, or other potential failings. Dispelling this myth in our final chapter is Virginia Walden Ford, who has been a school choice activist for decades and who was a driving force behind enactment of the District of Columbia's Opportunity Scholarship Program. She is also the subject of the major motion picture *Miss Virginia*, which depicts her crusade for better education in the nation's capital. Drawing on the research of others and her own experience helping countless low-income families, Walden Ford shows that far from being inept choosers, poor people "reach for that brass ring. They make good choices."

There are certainly reasonable, important arguments that can be made against freedom in education. But the discussion should be an honest one. Whether the myths that haunt school choice seem reasonable or not, disproven or exaggerated accusations should not be allowed to stand in the way of greater educational freedom.

CHAPTER ONE

MYTH: SCHOOL CHOICE BALKANIZES

Rather than pulling us apart, choice is the key to building bridges.

Neal P. McCluskey

It is easy to understand the fear that society would splinter if people could choose private schools on an equal footing with public. If everyone could select the education they wanted for their children, many would choose different things. People of diverse religions might cloister their kids in schools sharing their convictions. Families of different ethnicities might stick to "their kind" out of comfort or of hostility toward others. The rich might remain with people of wealth and away from the riffraff.

This fear cannot simply be chalked up to a ruse to defeat school choice. The evidence is powerful—overwhelming, even—that human beings have a strong inclination to self-segregate.[1] Many people with choice likely *would* associate with others like themselves.

But that also happens *without* school choice programs such as vouchers or scholarship tax credits, both in American society generally and in the public schooling system that has long enrolled the vast majority of children. Public schools have accounted for roughly 90 percent of K–12 enrollment for decades,[2] and while in 1950 only 34 percent of Americans 25 years of age and older had completed high school, by 2016 nearly

90 percent had.[3] Despite this fact, Americans today are starkly polarized and stratified. As Charles Murray observes:

> The American project . . . consists of the continuing effort, begun with the founding, to demonstrate that human beings can be left free as individuals and families to live their lives as they see fit, coming together voluntarily to solve their joint problems. The polity based on that idea led to a civic culture that was seen as exceptional by all the world. . . . [Yet] that culture is unraveling.[4]

To challenge the fear of Balkanizing school choice, we must ask two questions: Is greater choice likely to lead to greater *physical* stratification relative to what we have today. And will choice lead to stronger bridges connecting different groups psychologically? The answers may not be what we expect.

Public Schools, Poor Unifiers

How have Americans come together over the centuries, first as colonists and then as countrymen? What role did public schooling play? There is insufficient space to explore this comprehensively, but the contours of American educational history are powerful: there is little evidence that public schooling unified Americans, and it may very well have been an obstacle.

From the 1607 landing of British settlers in Virginia to the 19th century's common-school crusade, education was a matter left primarily to private and civil society—free people working voluntarily together. There were attempts to create government-run schools, including the Massachusetts Bay Colony's famous 1647 "Old Deluder Satan Act," which required towns of various sizes to maintain either a teacher, or a teacher and schoolhouse. This effort disintegrated. Authorities regularly wrestled with towns flouting the law, and by the Revolutionary War none complied.[5] Other colonies did not even go that far. The idea that government should control education was largely foreign to people of British extraction, and the schooling was insufficiently useful to marshal broad support.[6]

This did not mean there was a learning vacuum. As historian Bernard Bailyn has written, all of colonial life was educational, as transplanted Europeans learned to live in a new, largely wild land.[7] But they also undertook more formal education focused on reading, mathematics, and religion, in homes and various types of private schools. The result was, by the dawn of the common-school era, a literacy rate among white adults of about 90 percent—blacks were often forbidden by law to be educated.[8] "Before Americans generally accepted the idea that schooling should be publicly controlled and financed they clearly believed in education of the public," concludes historian David Tyack.[9]

Between the end of the colonial era and the beginning of the common-school movement, typically pegged to the 1837 appointment of Horace Mann as the first Massachusetts education secretary, several crucial things occurred that almost certainly reflected increasing American unity. These include claiming independence; doing so through a declaration establishing the nation's philosophical foundation; erecting a federal system solidified by the Constitution; electing the nationally revered George Washington president; fighting a second war with England; and having an Era of Good Feelings. A civil war would come, but even it likely reflected a big chunk of people no longer seeing themselves as citizens of separate states but wanting to be one nation.

Despite this, the common-schooling movement was substantially driven by fear that people were not sufficiently unified—or, perhaps, not sufficiently *uniform*.[10] As Horace Mann wrote in his 1845 annual report, "The children of a republic [must] be fitted for society as well as for themselves."[11]

In this effort, Mann was often frustrated. Opposition sprang up almost immediately. The overwhelmingly Protestant Massachusetts population saw Christianity as central to education, but there were major cleavages among Protestant denominations. The result was substantial disagreement over what Christian doctrines would be taught.[12] Mann, who needed the schools to be nonsectarian to be broadly accepted, devoted a large section of his last annual report rebutting accusations that he would remove the Bible from the schools. A transformation that enabled the movement to somewhat overcome these impediments was mass Irish

Catholic immigration—the Roman Catholic Church was a common enemy—yet conflicts persisted among Protestants. Presbyterians, for example, had established only four parochial schools prior to 1846, but dissatisfied with the common schools, they created 260 between 1846 and 1869.[13]

Conflicts between Protestants and Catholics eventually occupied the center of the arena. Notable political battles were fought in New York City, where Catholics struggled for years to access public school funds for their own schools, which used the Catholic version of the Bible and none of the lessons hostile to Catholics sometimes found in public schools. In Philadelphia, literal warfare erupted with the 1844 "Bible Riots." The riots, sparked by policies regarding the place and version of the Bible in public schools, ended with dozens dead, hundreds wounded, and massive property damage.[14]

It is hard to see this as unifying, except perhaps in the sense that conquering is unifying. And we know from the Balkans themselves that "conquered" does not necessarily mean "unified." For three-quarters of a century Yugoslavia existed as one country, but as dictatorial power waned the country split, initiating years of calamitous warfare as numerous ethnic groups and regions fought for independence. It was separation that ultimately brought peace.

The same held true for American education. Prior to common schooling it was not unusual for diverse religious schools to receive public money, which largely came under scrutiny only when Catholics sought funds.[15] Peace was further maintained by schools tending to serve small, homogenous communities. The earliest national count of school districts dates to just the 1937–1938 school year. In that year there were 119,001 districts in the United States serving a population of 128,824,829, or 1,083 people on average. The average district almost certainly served even fewer people before that. Today there are only 13,584 districts serving a population of 321,418,820, or 23,662 people per district.[16]

When a district did serve diverse communities in the latter 19th century, it would sometimes split schools, either by time or physical buildings, so different groups would have their own schools.[17] And some groups just split, especially Catholics, who set up their own institutions.

By their 1965 peak, Catholic schools enrolled 5.5 million students, or nearly 12 percent of all school-aged children.[18]

A more egregious way than chosen separation in which public schooling failed to unify was by *forbidding* togetherness. For decades many public schools were racially segregated by law. And government-orchestrated segregation was not restricted to the South or to African Americans. Some states segregated Hispanics from whites, and some separated Asians. In most Northern states, at least through 1860, African Americans were either excluded from public schools or given separate institutions.[19] And while de jure segregation in the South was under legal siege after the 1954 *Brown v. Board of Education* decision, many Northern governments maintained segregation more stealthily, including by placing new schools in heavily white housing areas, or busing whites to white-dominated schools. The Supreme Court did not demand rectification of stealth segregation until the 1973 *Keyes v. School District No. 1* ruling, which declared Denver's placements unconstitutional because, though they were not on their face segregationist, the intent behind them was.[20] The very next year the Court established the limit of coerced integration, in *Milliken v. Bradley,* forbidding mandatory desegregation across district lines unless all affected districts had had segregationist policies.[21]

Desegregation was seemingly effective, especially in the South, but the story is largely one of retrenchment, and as we will see, little "bridging." As of 1968, the beginning of federal courts seriously demanding desegregation, 78 percent of African American students in the South attended schools identified by the Civil Rights Project as "intensely segregated," meaning 90 to 100 percent minority.[22] By 1980 that share had plummeted to 23 percent, but it bounced back up to 36 percent by 2014. Other regions saw a similar decrease-and-rebound, except the Northeast, where intense segregation *increased* after 1968, from 43 percent of black public school students attending intensely segregated schools to 51 percent doing so in 2009–2010.[23] Nationally, 64 percent of black students attended intensely segregated public schools in 1968–1969, hitting a low of 33 percent in 1991–1992, then rebounding to 38 percent in 2009–2010.

"Intensely segregated" school counts can obscure average racial mixes. Looking at the exposure of the average white public school student to

African Americans and vice versa, we again see greater integration since the late 1960s. In 1968, 15 percent of public school children were black and 79 percent "majority white," meaning non-Hispanic white. In that year the average black public school student attended a school that was only 22 percent white. The average white public school student attended a school that was only 4 percent black. By 1972 that had changed considerably: the average African American public school student went to a school that was 34 percent white, while the average white student had 7 percent black schoolmates.[24] In the 2009–2010 academic year, the average black public school student was in a school that was 29 percent white—about half of the 55 percent white share of the total national population aged 5 to 17—and the average white student was in a school that was 9 percent black, or 63 percent of the black share of the total population aged 5 to 17, which was roughly 14 percent.[25]

Where Kids Are Going

A common explanation that fuels the Balkanization myth is that private schools have encouraged it, and this is not totally baseless.[26] After *Brown*, there were efforts in the South to escape integration by closing public schools and giving people money to pay for private education, and the share of Southern students in private schools rose during the height of desegregation, from 6 percent of elementary students in 1960 to 9 percent in 1979, and from slightly below 6 percent of high school students to somewhat above.[27] Those are notable upticks, but hardly a mass exodus from public schools. Nationally, private schooling's share actually dropped during this period, from 14 percent of elementary students to 11 percent, and from 11 percent to just 7 percent of high school enrollees. In the Northeast, which saw integration fall between 1968 and 1972, private schooling's share also declined between 1960 and 1979, from 23 percent to 14 percent of elementary schoolers and from 18 percent to 10 percent of high schoolers. Over a longer term, private schooling's total share of students fell from 14 percent in 1959 to 10 percent in 2009.[28]

Far more to blame for frustrated desegregation was housing. As Judge Stephen J. Roth attested in the case that led to the Supreme Court's

Milliken decision, it would be impossible to desegregate Detroit schools without incorporating the many districts that surrounded the city, because white people had moved to them in droves. White flight was not primarily a response to forced busing—the ultimate and most controversial form of mandated integration. It occurred in many places regardless of school assignment policies.[29] But school assignment did matter. Christine H. Rossell and David J. Armor found that the degree of flight was significantly affected by whether a district was countywide or central city—it is harder to leave county districts—and whether desegregation was mandatory, such as busing, or voluntary.[30] And even if school desegregation did not ultimately increase flight, it likely hastened it in many districts.[31]

Given the huge disruption and fear busing created, it was, not surprisingly, extremely unpopular. Polls between 1972 and 1984 consistently found white support in the mid-single digits, and among African Americans it never exceeded 44 percent.[32] This was true even as white support for the *principle* of integrated schools reached near unanimity.[33] Polling since has made clear that white people happily express support for school integration, but they won't prioritize it over "neighborhood schools."[34]

By the 1980s, busing was in retreat, and today even districts considered paragons of peaceful coerced integration such as Wake County, North Carolina, are moving away from it. A mid-2000s plan would have necessitated more busing, which led to a sea change on the school board in 2009, with a new majority championing a return to neighborhood schools. After a bruising and nationally watched battle ensued, the insurgent majority was booted, but the district did not return to the coercion even as of 2009, with "stability" being the school-assignment watchword.[35]

Bridge Building

Likely a major reason that coerced integration has proven unsustainable is that it does not appear to foster bridge building between different groups. Improving race relations has not been a primary goal—that's been equal access to quality education—but it was certainly hoped for.

As Justice Thurgood Marshall wrote in *Milliken*, "Unless our children begin to learn together, there is little hope that our people will ever learn to live together."[36]

In addition to white flight, integration has been stymied by segregation *in* schools, both formally—through ability tracking—and through social grouping, rendering much school-level integration hollow. Classrooms are often much more segregated than a school's total population, with white and Asian students tending to be tracked into advanced classes, and Hispanic and African American students not. Much research has found that this has a negative effect on bridging,[37] though at least one researcher has posited that such tracking may be necessary to prevent further flight.[38]

Socially, physical integration leads to far less bridge building, as measured by friendly intergroup interactions than if friendships were formed in proportion to group presence. High-quality research on bridge building during peak desegregation was scarce, with studies failing to collect good pre- and post-integration data, and lacking rigorous comparisons of children in affected and unaffected schools. Ticking off these shortcomings, in 1978 John B. McConahay reported, "Reading this literature leaves one impressed with how little is known. . . . The need for research is truly impressive in this case."[39]

That said, what research existed in 1978—and what relatively little has been produced since—has generally found scant improvement in expressed attitudes about blacks by whites and whites by blacks; nor has it demonstrated much bridging, such as increased interracial play or more integrated seating at lunch.[40] And Moody found the dearth of mixing worst in the South, where there was the greatest building-level integration.[41] Of course, as McConahay pointed out, any bridging beats no bridging, which would have presumably been the case had schools remained segregated.

It is very difficult to determine the extent to which coerced integration built bridges nationwide, but an interesting analysis of wedding parties suggests little progress overall. After searching the internet for photos, Berry assessed the racial makeup of thousands of wedding parties (i.e., bridesmaids and groomsmen), with controls for wealth and other potentially confounding factors, reasoning that wedding parties would demonstrate mixes of truly close friends. He found in 2006 that only 3.7 percent of whites had black members in their parties, and only 22 percent of black parties included whites.[42]

Enter Choice

If we cannot force togetherness, can choice help? It seems counterintuitive, but it is consistent with a respected theory. In 1954, social psychologist Gordon Allport formalized contact theory in *The Nature of Prejudice*.[43] He hypothesized that members of separated groups needed to come into contact to see the error of their prejudices. He did not stop at mere contact, however, but offered four conditions, the first two essential, for success:

> Prejudice . . . may be reduced by *equal status contact* between majority and minority groups in the *pursuit of common goals*. The effect is greatly enhanced if this contact is *sanctioned by institutional supports* (i.e., by law, custom or local atmosphere), and provided it is of a sort that leads to the *perception of common interests and common humanity* between members of the two groups.[44]

Coerced integration meets neither of the first two provisos: it is clear who is of superior and who is of inferior social status, and it sets up zero-sum turf wars for school control. And while forced integration is sanctioned by law, it often creates a perception of *opposing* interests.

One response to the backlash against forced integration has been magnet schooling, which generally refers to specialized public schools in which people enroll by choice. The idea is that members of different races, often living in different parts of a district, will choose to attend because the schools offer something special that all want. This is more in line with equal status contact: all are there voluntarily, and there are common goals if all students want to become better musicians or engineers, for example.

Even with those things, magnets still diverge from Allport's provisos. African Americans might be perceived as lower status if the explicit goal of magnet schooling is desegregation. To the extent that seats are scarce, they can also make people competitors based on race. This recently roiled African American, Hispanic, and Asian communities in

New York City, where the latter are vastly overrepresented, and the former two vastly underrepresented, in selective public high schools.[45]

Controlled choice is even more restrictive, bounding selections by racial or economic floors and ceilings and creating race-based competition. The 2007 *Parents Involved in Community Schools v. Seattle School District No. 1* case, in which the Supreme Court curtailed racial balancing policies, was touched off in part by an African American family whose daughter was denied a spot at the school nearest her home because she would have tipped the scales "too black."[46]

Theoretically, the ideal system to achieve sustainable, bridging integration is one in which educators are free to establish schools as they see fit—religious, arts based, and so on—and families are free to choose among them. This would largely fit all of Allport's provisos:

- **Equal status.** All freely choose to attend, without presumption that choice is intended to benefit any particular group.
- **Pursuit of common goals.** This is maximized by different groups having to work together to achieve something mutually beneficial, and schooling in general tends to be more about individual than group gain. But chosen schools can do more to build shared identities—everyone wants to be there—and for religious, military, performing arts, or other schools, interdependent, teamlike striving can be integral to the culture.
- **Sanctioned by institutional supports.** With programs such as vouchers, the law is enabling equal choice.
- **Perception of common interests and humanity.** People in chosen educational communities would very likely share common interests and beliefs.

Choice Research: Physical Integration

Whether private school choice programs appear to exacerbate physical segregation depends on the country and the rules of the program and can be difficult to tease out from housing decisions. Chile, for instance, has extensive school choice, with more than 51 percent of students attending government-aided private schools and another roughly 10 percent at fully private institutions.[47] In contrast, about 10 percent of U.S. pupils attend private schools, and less than 1 percent do so through government choice efforts.

Research suggests that Chilean students might be more segregated under choice than residential assignment, but families may well have chosen even more segregated housing without choice, enabling them to access institutions preferable to local schools. Chang-Tai Hsieh and Miguel Urquiola found that between 1982 and 1996 stratification by income grew, with wealthier people more likely to sort into private schools (wide-scale Chilean choice started in 1981).[48] Gregory Elacqua, Mark Schneider, and Jack Buckley found that parents in metropolitan Santiago sought student bodies socioeconomically similar to themselves first, though middle-class families considered achievement next.[49] However, Sapelli found that wealth stratification resulted in large part from voucher amounts that were determined by a formula unweighted by income,[50] a policy that was changed in 2008; subsequently Elacqua[51] and Mariano Narodowski[52] found that stratification decreased. Research in Sweden has found that while choice coincided with increased segregation, most was due to housing patterns.[53]

Research in the United States has been more positive, showing that private schools in choice programs tend to be better integrated by race than traditional public schools in affected districts.[54] More telling, assessments of student moves have typically found neutral-to-small net integrative effects.[55] One study in New Orleans found that 82 percent of voucher transfers rendered their departed public schools less segregated, though 55 percent made their receiving private schools more segregated.[56] What might drive these outcomes is that U.S. programs are essentially means-tested by income, applicable only to children in "failing" public schools or to kids with disabilities.

The Research on Choice: Bridging

The bridging findings are more encouraging but also sparser. They include positive assessments of racial climate by teachers and observations of children's choices of lunch seatmates.[57] One study, specifically about religious schools, found that compared to public institutions, religious schools were less likely to experience racially motivated fights and somewhat more likely to see interracial friendships.[58] A 1991 survey asked Detroit-area residents how they would rank seven criteria to assess schools were choice available. The first was safety; the second, values.[59] Finally, a 2019 federal study found that students in private schools were much less likely than those at public schools to see hate-related graffiti at school and slightly less likely to be targeted with hate-related words.[60]

What is the effect of school choice programs? A 1970 study looking at a voluntary busing program for Chicago-area Roman Catholic schools found a positive effect on intergroup relations.[61] Analyzing privately funded choice in New York City, Paul E. Peterson and David E. Campbell found that African Americans attending private schools had more intergroup friendships than black students in the public schools who applied for vouchers but did not receive them. They were also more likely to eat lunch with a student of another race, though neither result was statistically significant and, hence, could have been a result of chance.[62] Using quirks in the timing and applicability of a law requiring wealthy private schools in India to admit 20 percent of their students from poor families, Guatam Rao found that contact made wealthy students more willing to socialize with poor students.[63] Finally, M. Danish Shakeel and Corey DeAngelis, and DeAngelis and Marty Lueken, found that private school principals are significantly more likely to report "never" experiencing racial tensions in their schools than public school principals after controlling for schools' racial makeup, nationally and in Indiana, respectively.[64]

This literature is thin. But what there is attaches real-life education experience (there is much more outside of education[65]) to what contact theory would predict: bringing diverse people together is essential to building bridges, but contact should be equal status and in pursuit of common goals—it should be chosen—to succeed.

Conclusion

Fear that school choice will lead to Balkanization is understandable. People *do* self-segregate. But for worsened Balkanization to occur, choice would have to be more stratifying than the current system and have less potential for building bridges. On the former, the research suggests that U.S. private choice programs decrease physical segregation. On the latter, choice likely fosters greater intergroup bridging. Of course, more research on wider choice is needed to solidify these conclusions, but what research exists indicates that school choice in the United States helps to bring people together.

CHAPTER TWO

MYTH: SCHOOL CHOICE HAS RACIST ORIGINS

The charge that vouchers have white supremacist roots is premised upon an intentional misreading of the evidence.

Phillip W. Magness

Are school vouchers historically linked to segregation in the United States? If so, does this sordid link ethically taint vouchers in the present day? Both claims entered the arsenal of political arguments against choice with fervor in recent years, aided by a 2017 Center for American Progress study proclaiming the "racist origins of private school vouchers."[1] In this telling, the modern voucher movement owes its genesis to the segregationist backlash against the landmark 1954 U.S. Supreme Court ruling in *Brown v. Board of Education.* In response, a handful of Southern states enacted tuition grant subsidy programs that allowed white parents to send their children to private, racially segregated schools as a means of circumventing integration. The most developed of these efforts by far occurred in Virginia, accompanied by the state's notorious "Massive Resistance" policies against *Brown.* These tuition grants directly presaged the modern voucher movement, thereby linking it to racism, or so the argument goes.

The historical appeal of this claim has gained a substantial amount of intellectual currency among voucher critics, despite being premised upon a genetic fallacy—the use of a tainted origin story to discredit a policy in the present day. In this instance, the proposed origin story is not even situated in the correct historical period. The voucher concept dates back at least a century before *Brown*, having been proposed in

John Stuart Mill's 1859 book *On Liberty*. Earlier precursors to vouchers may be seen in the writings of Adam Smith and Thomas Paine. It also has antecedents in the town tuitioning programs of rural Vermont and Maine, dating to the 1870s. Nonetheless, attempts to tie vouchers to historical racism have become a frequent talking point against the concept in recent years.

The argument's purpose is to contend that segregationist historical antecedents preclude the ability of vouchers to help racial minorities, even if modern empirical results show otherwise.[2] To this end, Randi Weingarten, president of the American Federation of Teachers, labels vouchers as "slightly more polite cousins of segregation" and strongly implies they are sustained in the present by similar racial motives.[3] In addition to advocacy sources, scholarly research has increasingly embraced the same narrative. One recent article contends that "vouchers buttressed white supremacy during public school desegregation" and only owe their current form to an intentional "reinvention" that obscures this past.[4] Pressing this line of argument even further, several historians, education scholars, and policy analysts have sought to specifically charge libertarian voucher theorists such as Milton Friedman with willful "complicity" in white supremacist objectives from the *Brown* era.[5] Voucher advocates, they contend, allowed their cause to be used for segregationist ends in the hope that it would advance simultaneous libertarian objectives such as school privatization, neglecting any harmful effects upon African American students in the process.

A closer examination of this argument shows that it is built upon slipshod historical research and even intentional misrepresentations of evidence. An examination of the history of the modern voucher movement, starting with Friedman's landmark article "The Role of Government in Education," actually reveals an acute attentiveness to the ethical complications posed by the racist resistance to *Brown*. Friedman in particular believed that vouchers would help to undermine segregation in schooling. Furthermore, recent attempts to advance a genetic argument against vouchers on racial grounds have neglected ample evidence of segregationist *opposition* to school vouchers in the civil rights era—particularly among white public school teachers' unions. Evaluated as a whole, the historical case against vouchers falters as a mixture of oversimplification and politically motivated mythology.

Vouchers and Segregation in Theory

Although it has classical antecedents in the work of Adam Smith, John Stuart Mill, and several 19th-century education theorists, the modern concept of vouchers traces its origin to a 1955 article by Milton Friedman proposing the introduction of economic competition into schooling.[6] Friedman drafted his article independently of the political fallout from the *Brown* decision but became aware of the Southern tuition grant schemes through correspondence with his editor Robert Solo shortly before the article's publication. Far from complicit acquiescence, Friedman took the moral gravity of this development seriously and addressed it in an extended footnote on the complications posed by segregation.

Acknowledging that voucher-like tuition grants had "recently been suggested in several southern states as a means of evading the Supreme Court ruling against segregation," Friedman admitted his initial reservations. He feared "that this possible use of the proposal was a count against it" and even a "striking case of the possible defect" of social class separation under a voucher system. As a personal principle, he "deplore[d] segregation and racial prejudice." "So long as the schools are publicly operated," he conceded, "the only choice is between forced nonsegregation and forced segregation; and if I must choose between these evils, I would choose the former as the lesser." Friedman also valued the general ethical principle of governing human behavior through voluntary choice, even while acknowledging that some people would make ethically noxious choices, including voluntarily separating themselves from persons of a different race. Yet further contemplation of the issue led him to conclude that a robust voucher system would actually serve the cause of racial integration: "The appropriate activity for those who oppose segregation and racial prejudice is to try to persuade others of their views; if and as they succeed, the mixed schools will grow at the expense of the nonmixed, and a gradual transition will take place."[7]

Since segregation itself was a feature of state intrusion into education, educational competition would necessarily break its uniformity at the expense of the previous status quo.

Leo Casey, one of the only voucher critics to engage Friedman's argument on this point, misrepresents it as a "strange posture of neutrality" on *Brown*. Incredulous at the suggestion that vouchers could ever break down segregation, he simply dismisses Friedman's arguments as "on their face incongruent" and implausible.[8] Yet ample evidence shows that Casey, not Friedman, is in historical error. Friedman left no uncertainty that he would "undoubtedly choose nonsegregation" if faced with these two options, as he elaborated in a June 1955 lecture. Rather than staking a position of neutrality, he reframed the question as one of achieving desegregation with a moral rather than political instrument. "Attempting to get people to come to [desegregation] from persuasion is a different line of approach than coercion," he stated, and in his mind it was a more enduring solution.[9]

While voucher critics such as Casey would likely dismiss this observation as naïve and overly wishful, Friedman's argument actually drew on the insights of cutting-edge social science from the time. Friedman was almost certainly invoking the work of his PhD student Gary Becker, whose dissertation on the economics of racial discrimination provided the basis for a groundbreaking book on the subject in 1957.[10] One of Becker's key insights held that institutionalized racial discrimination also carries certain economic costs with it, including both the maintenance of the discriminatory barrier and the constraints on economic opportunity incurred from adhering to racist beliefs. While Becker's analysis primarily examined employment discrimination, his thesis implied that—under certain conditions relating to the nature of the activity and the relative sizes of affected racial groups—the introduction of competition to a previously noncompetitive market could make discriminatory social practices costly to maintain. Becker specifically rejected the illusion that competition functioned as a magic bullet solution to discrimination and documented many instances to the contrary. But he also saw legalized discrimination in education as both a contributing cause of race-based employment disparities in the Southern

United States and considered them a symptom of a state-monopolized educational market.[11]

Friedman reiterated and expanded upon the voucher concept in his 1962 book *Capitalism and Freedom,* making specific reference to the problem of segregation and the possible implications of the Becker model. Segregation in schooling originated with state monopolization of educational provision, although Friedman openly conceded once again, "If one must choose between the evils of enforced segregation or enforced integration, I myself would find it impossible not to choose integration." Writing amid the heated political rancor of school desegregation, he proposed a combination of vouchers and moral suasion as suitable market tools to undermine the pre-*Brown* status quo in time.[12]

The benefit of hindsight allows us to recognize that Friedman likely underestimated the political entrenchment of segregationist interests, yet the context of his argument here is revealing. Friedman observed that the tuition grant program in Virginia had "many features in common" with his own voucher plan, even though the Virginia system was originally adopted "to avoid racial integration." Despite this origin, Friedman predicted that "the ultimate effects of the law will be very different after all," allowing that "the difference between result and intention is one of the primary justifications of a free society." If permitted to operate freely, he expected the program to bring about "an increase in [the] diversity" of racial attendance at Virginia public schools.[13]

Friedman did not make these comments in a vacuum. Virginia's tuition grant experiments began in 1956 as a conscious feature of the state's segregationist Massive Resistance laws against *Brown.* The original program permitted white parents to remove their children from a public school facing court-ordered integration. The state then shuttered the integrated public school by way of a legal trigger that empowered the governor to withdraw its funding, effectively leaving black children without an educational option. Crucially, this original program did not offer educational choice; it actually removed choice through school closures. An important reversal occurred in January 1959, though, after dual rulings by state and federal courts struck down the Massive Resistance program, including its tuition grant system.

Resisting calls to shirk the courts by segregationist hardliners in the political machine of U.S. senator Harry Flood Byrd Sr., a segment of the state's political establishment began to moderate its course toward gradual acquiescence to *Brown* and the court rulings. Rejecting the school closure strategy, the breakaway faction successfully revamped the tuition grant program on race-neutral grounds to comply with the court rulings and paired it with the reopening of the shuttered schools. Although framed as a "safety valve" to allow segregationist parents to voluntarily remove their children from integrated schooling, the new statute's race neutrality required grants to be offered for any reason a parent of any race provided. Friedman accordingly pointed to early evidence of grant applicants who sought transfers from segregated to integrated schools "simply because the integrated school happened to be the better school educationally."[14] Foreshadowing this development, Friedman's voucher concept actually admitted the propriety of establishing "minimum requirements" for program eligibility. As he stated in his 1955 lecture, the government "might make one of those minimum requirements non-segregation."[15]

Friedman's interest in advancing desegregation through vouchers was genuine. As he confided in a letter to his former student G. Warren Nutter, an economist at the University of Virginia, resistance to desegregation was "an ill wind that blows no good." He nonetheless encouraged Nutter and his colleague James M. Buchanan to publish a paper of their own advancing the argument for vouchers in the state. In doing so they could "try to convert the situation into a positive good."[16] A year later, Friedman advanced a similar argument in a visiting lecture at the University of Virginia, expressing cautious optimism that the state's new tuition grant program would have the effect of breaking down racial barriers through competition.[17]

The 1959 iteration of Virginia's tuition grants warrants additional mention for its connection to an oft-cited example of the alleged segregationist roots of the voucher movement. From 1959 until 1964, segregationist local officials in Prince Edward County, Virginia, shuttered their entire public school system in an extreme attempt to evade court-ordered desegregation. White students transferred into a local privately operated "segregation academy," while black students were left without any schooling options.

Prince Edward County officials originally intended to take advantage of the revamped tuition grant program to finance private segregated education. Predictably, this circumstance has led numerous voucher opponents to accuse Friedman, as well as the Virginia economists Nutter and Buchanan, of providing the intellectual architecture for the Prince Edward segregationists' scheme. The charge itself is entirely specious, with no evidence connecting any of the economists' arguments to the Prince Edward officials or suggesting they influenced the school closures in any way.[18] In fact, the race neutrality found in the 1959 statute actually allowed a federal court to permanently enjoin Prince Edward from participating in the tuition grant program until the U.S. Supreme Court overruled the county entirely in 1964.

The 1961 ruling by federal district judge Oren Lewis noted that "a 'freedom of choice' between public and private schooling is clearly contemplated" in the enacting statute of 1959. Referring to its rules as "plain and unequivocal" in their mandate of this choice, Lewis held that "scholarships are not available to persons residing in counties that have abandoned public schools." As per this finding, Lewis continued,

> an order will therefore be entered restraining and enjoining the County Superintendent of Prince Edward County, the Superintendent of Public Instruction, their agents and employees, and all persons working in concert with them, from receiving, processing or approving any applications for state scholarship grants from persons residing in Prince Edward County so long as the public schools of Prince Edward County remain closed.[19]

The increasingly common attribution of the Prince Edward County episode to school vouchers is thus premised on a fundamentally mistaken historical claim.

Historically, situating the voucher movement's relationship to segregation nonetheless requires a more nuanced exploration of the tuition grant program's motives and operation. Friedman's voucher proposal was rooted in the practical realities of the political system that existed in 1955, including a deeply entrenched policy of segregated schooling across the South and in other parts of the United States. His eschewing of a top-down solution evinced a genuine belief that educational markets would dislodge that policy more effectively than any government-imposed program. "Let schools specialize, as private schools would," he argued in a 1973 article, "and the pull of common interest will overcome the pull of color, leading, I believe, to far more rapid integration than is now in process."[20]

The underlying theory of Friedman's argument may actually be sounder than either its opponents or supporters have thus far realized. To illustrate how, we may turn to one of the most famous critiques of Friedman's voucher proposal, originally offered independently of the segregation issue. In 1970 political scientist Albert O. Hirschman famously observed that educational competition could induce an exit-voice trade-off in schooling, with the potential to undermine the promised competition-induced gains from a voucher system.

Briefly summarized, Hirschman noted that vouchers are premised upon the tool of economic exit, the threat of which induces schools to improve their educational products as parents depart declining schools in favor of higher-quality offerings for their children. Exit is a double-edged sword, though, as the parents who utilize the voucher also happen to be the most quality-conscious attendees of the previous school, the type of parents who participate in PTA meetings, vote in school board elections, and exercise other tools of voice to pressure for improvement. As these parents depart an existing school system on a voucher, they take that pressure mechanism of voice with them. The unintentional effect predicted by Hirschman is the hastening of the prior school's decline, as it no longer has any parents willing to apply internal pressures for quality improvement.[21]

Hirschman's critique remains an important complication to the theory behind vouchers, but it also assumes that the most active parents are using the tools of voice for good—that they are advocating for higher standards, more funding, more teacher and administrator accountability, and a broader range of programs and activities for their children. The implications of the Hirschman model radically change when we relax or replace this assumption. Imagine a scenario where the voice-engaged parents at an existing public school are advancing a harmful and exclusionary cause. Such a scenario existed in the 1950s United States, where some of the most vocal parents in public schooling were segregationists. These parents also constituted numerical majorities in cities and towns across the South. Instead of seeking better educational offerings, these parents mobilized their PTA against *Brown,* voted for school board candidates who pledged themselves to Massive Resistance, and in some cases even physically harassed black students who attempted to register at majority-white schools.

Note how this change in assumptions fundamentally alters the outcomes of the Hirschman critique. Rather than withdrawing positive voice from an existing public school, the departure of a segregationist parent on a tuition grant actually *removes* an unambiguous source of harm from the public school system. He may take that harm elsewhere, including choosing self-isolation in one of the private "segregation academies" of the post-*Brown* era. But a pronounced source of resistance to integration in the public school is now gone. The outcome, at least according to this modification of the Hirschman theory, bears a striking resemblance to Friedman's original argument wherein educational competition induces a dwindling away of segregated institutions over time.

The Virginia Case and Anti-Voucher Segregationism

We need not dwell in the abstractions of voucher theory to see the significance of the exit/voice model to the school desegregation debate. One such scenario played out in 1959. Although a slowly moderating portion of Virginia's segregationist political class turned to the race-neutral tuition grant statute under the aforementioned "safety valve" argument, a neglected body of evidence shows that several segregationist hardliners in the state came to recognize this voucher-like mechanism as a Trojan horse against the old political order.

The earliest signs of this shift occurred amid the upheaval of the January 1959 court rulings that struck down the Massive Resistance laws, clearing the way for integration to proceed. Two important political developments followed as segregationists scrambled to preserve racially separated schooling.

First, a handful of intransigent hardliners in the Byrd machine vowed to press on with Massive Resistance, including by ignoring the courts and proceeding in violation of their orders. This strategy exposed a rift in the state's Democratic Party between Byrd loyalists and an insurgency of moderate segregationist "cushioners"—those who accepted the inevitability of *Brown* and consigned themselves to a strategic retreat that permitted limited integration. The safety-valve argument for tuition grants had obvious appeal to the latter group, which included the state's governor, J. Lindsay Almond, and his lieutenant governor, A. E. S. Stephens. In early February 1959, this faction effectively abandoned the school closure strategy and shifted their support to the race-neutral version of the tuition grants, drawing heavily upon a 1958 proposal submitted by retired newspaperman Leon S. Dure.[22]

Those vowing to resist the courts aligned behind Blackburn Moore, Speaker of the House of Delegates and Byrd's chief lieutenant in state government. Moore actually saw the revamped tuition grant scheme as a threat to holding the line of Massive Resistance after the January 1959 court rulings against his policies. Since the proposal mandated educational choice between public and private options, its enactment would necessarily clear the way for the reopening of closed public schools. As Lt. Gov. Stephens later confided to Dure, Moore, lacking the votes to defy the courts outright, "attempt[ed] to block the reenactment of the tuition grant after our massive resistance laws had been stricken down" by running down the legislative clock and thereby impeding the enactment of a court-compliant replacement policy. Stephens used parliamentary rules to outflank Moore, clearing the way for a special legislative session to enact a revised tuition grant based on Dure's proposal.[23] Although Stephens's cushioner approach plainly intended to slow the pace of integration, including with the tuition grant safety valve, it also utilized the same program to outmaneuver the hardline Massive Resistance strategy of Moore. Rather than serving as the segregationist tool of their critics' simplistic depiction, vouchers actually triggered a complex and historically important political rift within the segregationist ranks that gave the moderates the advantage. Notably, this development was welcomed by state National Association for the Advancement of Colored People (NAACP) officials E. B. Henderson and Oliver Hill, even as both personally opposed tuition grants on the ground that they could still be used to finance private "segregation academies."[24]

The second political development in the wake of the January 1959 rulings revealed growing awareness among segregationists of their own vulnerability to Friedman's arguments. Recognizing the futility of maintaining Massive Resistance, a number of segregationist hardliners shifted toward a conscious legal strategy of containment against *Brown*. In Virginia, its primary legal architect was John Battle Jr., a politically prominent attorney who served as the segregationists' main litigator against several post-*Brown* NAACP lawsuits. Battle's scheme, which he presented to the Charlottesville school board after the 1959 court rulings, entailed using a combination of geographic zoning constraints and enrollment caps to severely limit the number of black registrants at previously all-white schools.[25]

The containment strategy had an Achilles heel, though, as it depended on the sustained enrollment of white students to work. The new tuition grant program threatened to upend public school enrollment and assignment patterns. If any white students took advantage of a voucher for any reason, their departure from a school would open up a space for black students to register.

Battle dubbed this process the "negro engulfment" of the public school system, a term he likely borrowed from Hardy Cross Dillard, a law professor at the University of Virginia. Dillard first predicted the engulfment threat while analyzing the aftermath of the January 1959 rulings. Although case law in the wake of *Brown* made some integration inevitable, Dillard seized on the narrow application of another recent federal court ruling in Alabama to argue the constitutional validity of containment measures such as those proposed by Battle. He identified "available room and teaching capacity," transportation resources for students relative to geography, and a list of criteria pertaining to academic preparedness as legally defensible grounds to prevent "both engulfment and the threat of engulfment."[26]

Dillard was a moderate segregationist, whereas Battle was a hard-liner who simply accepted the impracticality of continuing Massive Resistance. Yet both recognized tuition grants as an existential threat to the containment strategy. "Now if a large number of the patrons of the public schools leave . . . and enter new private schools," Battle explained in a widely circulated speech at a Charlottesville elementary school, "it will have the effect of leaving many classrooms practically vacant, and that will immediately suggest and permit the introduction of far more integration" than the containment plan intended. "No Negro child is going to force any white child out of his desk," he continued, "but for every white child who vacates his desk there is a great risk that a Negro child will occupy it.[27]

Battle's ominous warnings about a voucher-fueled "negro engulfment" of the public schools spread like wildfire in segregationist circles. "John Battle, Jr. has made a big point," explained Dillard in a letter to the chair of the state assembly's education committee. Private tuition vouchers "would accelerate engulfment by making it more difficult to administer a student assignment plan."[28] Newspapers across the state reprinted excerpts of Battle's speech, and press wires carried it as far as Mississippi, which was debating the tuition grant system amid its own desegregation fight.[29] Three days later the University of Virginia law school hosted a public debate on tuition grants, pitting Battle and Dillard against the revamped plan's author—Leon S. Dure. While Dure pled the safety-valve case for the voucher-like system, Dillard and Battle stressed its tensions with the containment plan.[30]

Although offered from a staunchly segregationist vantage point, Battle's arguments found some of their strongest support among public school interest groups. The Charlottesville Committee for Public Education (CPE) presented itself as neither an integrationist nor a segregationist organization, claiming only to have an interest in ensuring that the public schools were reopened and well funded. Battle's anti-voucher message resonated within their ranks though, effectively bringing them into a strategic alliance with segregation. To this end, a March 1959 internal memorandum from the group outlined a publicity campaign to oppose the Dure proposal. The document suggested it was a mistake to view tuition grants as a "solution to the segregation probelm [*sic*]." It continued: "[While] great publicity has been given to the possibilities of private state-supported schools," there was almost no attention being given to "the possibility of containing integration, as outlined by John S. Battle, Jr." Tuition grants ensured that "integration will be as extensive as possible, thus making public schools unacceptable to as many people as possible." To rectify this situation, the memo outlined an extensive publicity campaign aimed at "holding integration to the barest minimum possible."[31]

After the Dure plan passed in April 1959, the CPE shifted its strategy to restricting tuition grant use. They printed and distributed thousands of copies of an even more bombastic speech by Battle at a Lynchburg high school, pleading with parents to refuse the voucher. In this longer set of remarks, Battle made a clear appeal to the relationship between defeating the tuition grants and their own primary concern—school funding:

> Let us therefore assume that in the event of the mixing of races in the schools of Lynchburg either voluntarily or under court order a thousand students elect to apply for the scholarships for the purpose of attending private schools. This would cost the city $176,820.00 each year and unless it resulted in a closing of one or more of your present public schools or the discharge of a substantial number of teachers there would be no substantial reduction in the operating costs of this public school system as you now have it.[32]

The only solution, he concluded, was for white parents to collectively refuse the tuition grants. Provided that they did so, "a full enrollment of white pupils" and "a conscientious school board and teaching staff" would ensure that "integration can be controlled and probably so discouraged in the long run that ultimately segregation can be achieved in many cities on a voluntary basis."[33]

Battle's speeches did not convince all segregationists, and a number of parents availed themselves of the tuition grants to remove their children from court-ordered integration. The 1959 statute's race-neutral language nonetheless expanded its uses well beyond segregation, much as

Friedman predicted. A 1962 survey of grant applicants by the *Richmond Times-Dispatch* suggested that a majority of respondents opted into the program for nonsegregationist reasons such as school quality and convenience of location. Some participants even transferred from segregated to integrated public schools, as economists Nutter and Buchanan verified in a statistical study of the program in 1964.[34]

As a revealing point of contrast, we may also look to the process of racial integration through the Virginia public school channels in the same period. The case of Arlington County is illustrative, as its school system came under a federal desegregation order prior to the adoption of the school closure policy used elsewhere by the Massive Resisters. Arlington officially began integrating its schools on paper in 1958; however, the school board promptly rejected all thirty of the African American students who applied for transfers into a white middle school. School board chairman Barnard D. Joy, a moderate segregationist aligned with the "school saver" movement, defended the rejections in court by asserting that the applicants were psychologically "unfit" and academically subpar, even as the NAACP presented counterevidence that several of the black applicants' test scores exceeded those of white students who currently attended the same school. The federal court ultimately overturned the school board's rejection of four applicants and ordered them admitted by the spring semester of 1959.[35]

Even in nominally integrated locales such as Arlington, a pattern of "passive" resistance became the norm for containing integration. Board chairman Joy rejected another 20 of 31 black transfer applicants in advance of the 1960 school year, sparking a repeat of the federal court battle. A year later the same school board took advantage of a population-induced need to open a new and legally integrated elementary school by funding an expansion project at an existing historically black school, where most black students could then be zoned. The renovated Drew Elementary would be packed with almost 1,200 black students, whereas the typical white elementary school at the time housed only 200.[36] The federal court would not certify Arlington's compliance with the *Brown v. Board* decision until 1972, almost two decades after the original decision was handed down.

It is in this point of comparison that we see a crucial fault of genetic arguments attempting to link vouchers to segregation. As Virginia's turn toward obstructionist tactics after nominally desegregating its public school system illustrates, the political channels of the public school system were often an extremely ineffective means of carrying out the task of integration—if not something worse. Whereas the 1959 tuition grant program catered to a mixture of motives, with some parents attempting to avoid integration but many more using vouchers for reasons unrelated to race, the public school system's policy was uniformly discriminatory against excluded persons. That public school system continued to discriminate through administrative tactics long after the Supreme Court repudiated its ability to do so by statute.

Not coincidentally, some of the most vocal political opposition to vouchers in that era also came from segregation-aligned forces within the public school system. The much-overlooked partnership between anti-voucher school interests and segregationists, such as Battle, persisted well beyond the legislative fights of early 1959 and became a mainstay argument in subsequent political fights over education funding. Battle's "containment" strategy found an enthusiast in Robert F. Williams, the executive secretary of the Virginia Education Association (VEA). In late April 1959, the head of the state's largest teachers' union distributed a copy of Battle's Lynchburg speech to every public school superintendent in Virginia.[37]

For the next five years, the VEA positioned itself as a persistent critic of tuition grants. Although financially motivated by the potential loss of public school income, the union (which remained all-white until 1964) also made recurring segregationist appeals intended to limit the scope of the program. In November 1960 the union adopted a resolution calling on the state to tighten restrictions on the program's use by limiting it only to families seeking to escape court-ordered integration.[38]

In 1964, the union formally called on "state, district and local associations to take appropriate action to ensure the repeal of legislation providing for tuition grants from public money." Williams explained the organization's rationale in staunchly segregationist terms. The program's intent, he maintained, "was not to subsidize private education generally" but rather to provide an alternative to integration. Recent statistics showed that "parents are using the grants to send their children to integrated schools which the entire purpose of the legislation was to avoid." In doing so, the program cost public schools $2,931,455 the previous year. Williams's comments quickly turned to the usual litany of anti-voucher arguments: Is it fair "to finance private education out of public funds"? "Is it wise to drain away from our local public schools . . . funds so urgently needed?" Are private schools of sufficiently high quality? To the VEA, these problems compounded the "abuse" of the program for nonsegregationist purposes.[39]

To be certain, others still opposed tuition grants on anti-segregation grounds, and the program certainly had motivated participants. The NAACP adapted its own legal strategy to argue that the program did not sufficiently safeguard against the use of public money for segregationist purposes—a point that the federal courts sustained in 1969, effectively ending the program.[40]

At the time of Williams's article, though, the strongest pushback against the VEA's overt segregationist posturing actually came from the voucher supporters in Friedman's camp. Nutter and Buchanan updated their own article the same year to endorse the propriety of barring voucher use "in the case of private schools that exclude pupils on the basis of race." An accompanying report prepared by their research center attacked the VEA's position, noting that the union intended to exclude "any use of scholarships except to avoid racial intermixing." The enacting statute, however, contained no such restrictions by design, and subsequent reapprovals of its budget all took place while "the use of grants in integrated situations grew steadily."[41]

The dispute with the VEA played out against the backdrop of increasing court scrutiny over lingering resistance to desegregation. In 1964, the Supreme Court struck down the entire Prince Edward County school closure policy, noting the propriety of enjoining the county from accessing the tuition grants in the lower court's ruling from 1961. The following year a federal district court barred the use of tuition grants when they constituted "the greater part of the cost of operation of a segregated school."[42]

While both cases restricted the use of voucher-like mechanisms in segregated schooling, many voucher advocates actually welcomed and encouraged this development. An amicus brief filed by Citizens for Educational Freedom, a national voucher advocacy group founded in 1959 with Friedman's encouragement, noted the importance of the race-neutral Virginia statute as a step toward educational competition. Yet insofar as local authorities sought to enlist the grants to segregationist ends, the result was "no real freedom of choice" and thus a violation of equal protection. The organization accordingly announced its unequivocal support for the "injunction against State and County tuition grants . . . until such time as all racial, religious, and regional restrictions thereon are removed."[43] Although the complex political dynamics around *Brown,* subsequent court rulings, and tuition grants remain an important part of the school voucher origin story, the claim of a segregationist voucher alliance simply does not withstand scrutiny.

CHAPTER THREE

MYTH: PUBLIC SCHOOLS ARE NECESSARY FOR A STABLE DEMOCRACY

The evidence suggests that private schools produce superior civic outcomes.

Patrick J. Wolf

> "Public governance of our schools matters for the health of our democracy."
>
> —Diane Ravitch and Carol Burris, *Washington Post*, November 4, 2018

Only four in ten Americans can pass a basic civics quiz. That dispiriting finding, from a recent national survey of 41,000 of our fellow citizens, is merely the latest in a long line of results suggesting that most Americans are ill-equipped to fulfill their responsibilities for active and informed self-government.[1] Although some commentators point their fingers at private schooling for undermining American civil society,[2] it seems a stretch to blame a sector that educates only 10 percent of our citizens for a dearth of knowledge about, or commitment to, basic civic values. Government-run public schools are necessary for a stable democracy, these commentators contend.[3] Our civic life would be better informed and more vibrant if all American children were forced to attend their neighborhood, government-controlled public school.

The claim that only government-run schools can promote civic practices and ideals is arguably the biggest myth in the school choice debate. Though commonly repeated, it is such a whopper because the actual evidence proves it to be false. The private school advantage over public schools in nurturing the democratic values of young Americans is far greater than any advantage private schools have in boosting students' test scores. The myth that public schools are necessary for a stable democracy is not only unfounded, but the data suggest it is perverse. Access to private schooling is more conducive to civic flourishing.

What Values Are Necessary for a Stable Democracy?

The United States is a democratic republic. Adult citizens engage in self-government by electing their representatives and urging them to adopt specific policies or take specific actions. The government cannot provide everything that a society needs, of course, so another requirement of self-government is community involvement. Finally, self-government tends to pit different factions of society against each other, with each side convinced it is right. Tolerance of opposing groups and their alternative perspectives is therefore vital. The various attitudes and behaviors that contribute to a stable democracy and, in turn, civic flourishing can be categorized as political tolerance, political participation, civic knowledge and skills, and voluntarism and social capital.

Political tolerance is the willingness to extend constitutional and legal protections to political groups one abhors. It is best captured by a statement that first appeared in a biography of Voltaire though probably was not actually uttered by him: "I disapprove of what you say, but I will defend to the death your right to say it."[4] To measure political tolerance, researchers first ask respondents to identify their least-liked political group and then ask them a series of questions regarding what rights they would extend to a member of that detested group.[5] The more rights and privileges a person would extend to the least-liked group, the higher that person's score on the political tolerance scale.

Political participation is a behavioral measure of a person's willingness to engage in the activities of self-government. Measures can involve something as basic as voting in the previous election, or they can involve more demanding political actions such as contacting a political representative or participating in a political rally. Most data on political participation come from self-reports on surveys and therefore are vulnerable to socially conditioned response bias, but some evidence on the question comes from voter registration databases.

Civic knowledge and skills constitute a set of understandings and abilities widely viewed as conducive to self-government. The list includes basic facts regarding the U.S. constitutional system, including separate branches of government, federalism, and how a bill becomes a law. The set also can include self-reports regarding a person's ability to write a persuasive letter or give a public speech.

Voluntarism and social capital are measures of one's involvement in activities that benefit the broader community and the depth of one's community attachments. Voluntarism usually is measured by questions such as "Did you volunteer more than an hour of your time, without pay, in any service activity in the past month?" or "How many hours of volunteer service did you provide in the past year?" Social capital is measured in scales based on indicators of shared social norms, networks, and cooperation.

Propagators of the choice-hurts-democracy myth claim that government-run public schools are far superior to private schools in fostering these attitudes and behaviors thought necessary or conducive to a stable democracy.

Sources of the Myth

At least five assumptions undergird the myth that public schools are necessary for a stable democracy: (1) education is a public good, (2) government organizations focus on public goals while private organizations focus on private goals, (3) public schools are more accountable than private schools, (4) public schools create unity from diversity, and (5) exit weakens voice. All five of these assumptions are highly questionable.

First, K–12 education clearly is not a public good, at least as delivered through actual schools. Public goods by definition must be nonexcludable, meaning no one can be denied access to them.[6] Public goods also must be nonrivalrous, meaning access by one person does not limit access by others.[7] A prime example of a public good is a lighthouse.[8] All ships benefit equally from its beacon, and there is no use fee.

At first blush, K–12 schooling might appear to be a public good. Every child aged 5 to 18 is guaranteed access to some public school, at no direct charge. Unlike ships traveling the sea lanes illuminated by a lighthouse, however, children are not guaranteed free access to any particular public school. The public school system uses a variety of mechanisms—including strict residential boundaries, ability-based admission to magnet schools, and expulsions—to exclude students from the specific schools their parents want them to attend. Parents even have been jailed for enrolling their children in schools that they were not permitted to attend, based on governmental rules.[9] Traditional public schools are not just *excludable*—most of them are *exclusive* because of residential assignment. Access to specific public schools also is rivalrous, as a person who buys the last available house within a residential school boundary or who claims the final spot on a charter school waitlist denies everyone else access to that public school.

Elementary and secondary education are definitively not public goods. They are, at best, merit goods, with some features of a public good, such as spillover benefits to society, and some features of a private good, such as excludability at the point of provision.[10]

Second, defenders of the myth that public schooling is required for a stable democracy claim that government organizations prioritize public goals but that private organizations prioritize private ones. This assertion is also clearly false. The academic literature on "regulatory capture" confirms that government organizations commonly operate in ways that serve private interests.[11] For example, the Securities and Exchange Commission informed corporations that their businesses would be absolved of regulatory liability if they permitted "independent" consultants to decide how proxy votes should be allocated on corporate governance matters, advancing the private opinions and financial interests of those consultants.[12] Public schools, in particular, are notoriously responsive to powerful private interests, such as teachers' unions and the most influential families served by the school.[13]

Private schools are responsive to the parents whose loyalty they must have to continue operating. Parents have particular interests, to be sure, including the desire that their children be kept safe and nurtured in a variety of ways during the school day. Parents tend to demand that schools teach "the whole child"—mind, body, heart, and soul.[14] They pressure private schools to instill in their children habits of hard work, personal responsibility, and a concern for society.[15] These character skills that are the focus of the education delivered in many private schools serve the public goals of promoting self-government and the common good. American Catholic schools, in particular, have a reputation for emphasizing the preparation of effective citizens.[16] There is no broad evidence that public schools necessarily privilege the public interest over private interests any more than private schools do.

Third, peddlers of the myth that public schooling is necessary for democracy claim that public schools are more accountable to the public. Public schools are governed by elected school boards that direct them to serve the general needs of the community.[17] Private schools operate based on market values and are not accountable to the people, they assert.[18] Both aspects of this claim are suspect. A deep literature documents the political shortcomings of public school boards.[19] Most board members are elected in separate elections at odd times of the year, such as May, with voter turnout below 10 percent. District employees turn out in great numbers because they naturally have a larger personal stake in a board election than the average citizen—their livelihoods are in the balance. Once elected by interested parties, school boards tend to take a hands-off approach to the public schools they are supposed to direct, leaving most decisions to superintendents.[20] This reality hardly fits the model for democratic accountability that we learned about in civics class. Private schools, in contrast, are accountable to parents empowered to take their money elsewhere—a more highly leveraged form of accountability than the low-leverage form exhibited by public school boards. Private schools also are subject to an extensive set of government laws and regulations, whether or not they participate in school choice programs.[21] Private schools are thus more accountable to government, and public schools less so, than the myth suggests.

Fourth, defenders of the myth of public schooling's necessity for a stable democracy argue that traditional public schools advance our nation's motto of *E pluribus unum*, "From the many, one." Public schools are "common schools" that serve as a melting pot for children from diverse backgrounds, instilling similar values and skills to all so as to promote social cooperation and comity.[22] Every aspect of that submyth has been disproven, however. Public schools are not and never have been "common schools," equally welcoming of students of all backgrounds.[23] The leaders of the common-school movement in the 19th century explicitly sought to convert Catholics and conservative Protestants into more socially acceptable mainstream Protestants.[24] The public schools have continued to be mechanisms for promoting one particular view of the good life over all others, to create a unity of beliefs, but they have failed to do so. There have been at least 2,133 disputes involving people's basic values and identities in public schools nationally since roughly 2005.[25]

Choice opponents claim that these thousands of public schooling disputes are actually good. Citizens will be more motivated to participate in politics if their children go to public schools, since the collective decisions of the polity determine the form and content of that education.[26] But that claim is illogical. Public school parents either have majority or minority opinions on public school disputes. If their perspective is in the majority, then they have an incentive to free ride on their like-minded fellow parents' work and not participate in the debate. If their perspective is in the minority, then they will be discouraged from participating because they will always lose. "What's the point?" they will repeatedly ask themselves and will certainly feel little to no ownership in the decisions of the collective that bind them.

Finally, the assertion that conflict in public education is a good thing is grounded in a naïve and incorrect understanding of the relationship between "exit" and "voice." In his seminal work *Exit, Voice, and Loyalty*, economist Albert O. Hirschman theorizes that the dissatisfied clients of an organization, such as a public school, have three options.[27] They can exit quietly for an alternative provider, they can complain vocally, or they can remain meekly loyal. Hirschman argues that generally, and specifically in the case of school choice, exit and voice are contrary forces. The more parents who exercise their power to exit, the fewer who exercise their voice, and the disappointing public schools they leave do not improve because few outspoken parents remain to pressure administrators to change.

Hirschman's argument that exit options weaken voice and thus diminish the prospects for organizational improvement has been heavily questioned and criticized.[28] If parents cannot transfer their child to another school, no matter how unsatisfied they are with their child's education, why would school leaders be affected by their voice? Far from diminishing the positive effects of voice, increasing exit options via choice policies is certain to enhance the influence and practice of parental voice. Hirschman eventually admitted as much:

> I had originally insisted on the seesaw character of exit and voice interventions in these fields. Education and health systems especially seemed exposed to the danger that premature exit—of the potentially most influential members—would undermine voice. The opposite relation may also occur, however, for the opening up of the exit perspective may serve to strengthen voice: parents who have been passive because they were feeling powerless and fearing reprisal may feel empowered for the first time once they are given vouchers that can be used "against" the schools currently attended by their children, and they will be readier than before to speak out with regard to desirable changes.[29]

Contrary to the claims of myth supporters, the traditional public school system that denies parents exit options is likely to diminish their practice of the civic skill of voice, whereas school choice systems that provide parents with serious exit opportunities create greater incentives for them to exercise voice and for their voices to be heard.[30] Why would we expect young people to internalize the key lesson that "the people" govern the United States if their first civics lesson is the government telling them where they must go to school?

Previous Reviews of the Evidence

Four prior reviews of the literature on the effects of private schooling on civic outcomes exist. Two of them are limited to studies of the civic effects of private school choice programs. The other two are more expansive, including studies of private schooling in general in addition to private school choice initiatives.

Jay Greene titled a chapter of his 2005 book *Education Myths* "The Democratic Values Myth: Private schools are less effective at promoting tolerance and civic participation."[31] Drawing from a handful of studies on the topic that existed at the time, he concluded, "Studies consistently show that private schools are actually better at conveying the democratic values of tolerance, participation, and volunteerism than public schools."[32]

Corey DeAngelis published a systematic review of 11 evaluations of the effects of private school choice on civic outcomes in 2017.[33] Six of the studies measured the effects of private school choice on student levels of political tolerance, with three concluding that the results were positive and the other three finding that students in private school choice programs were neither more nor less politically tolerant than their public school peers. Five of the evaluations examined civic engagement, which included political or voluntary activity. Three of those studies concluded that private school choice programs increased civic engagement, while the other two found that they had no effect on it. Finally, DeAngelis included a study of the generally positive effect of private school choice on social order in the form of criminal activity, a civic outcome that is not part of the current review. He concluded that access to private schools through choice policies either improves or has no significant effects on the civic outcomes of young people.

The advocacy organization EdChoice largely replicated DeAngelis's review in 2019.[34] The EdChoice authors identified a slightly different set of 11 studies of private school choice and civic values than DeAngelis had. They classified the studies as reporting (1) any significant positive effects of school choice, (2) no significant differences between the choice and public school students, or (3) any significant negative effects of choice. The EdChoice authors concluded that six studies reported positive effects of private school choice on civic outcomes, five found only nonsignificant differences in outcomes between the choice students and their public school peers, and none of the studies reported that access to private schooling through school choice had a negative effect on civic values or behaviors.

Finally, I conducted a systematic review of the findings regarding school choice and civic values in 2007.[35] I included all studies of the effects of private schooling, private school choice programs, or public charter schools on student civic outcomes. Since most of the studies included multiple findings regarding the effects of choice on specific civic outcomes, and sometimes those individual findings differed, I classified 36 individual findings from 21 different studies. Twenty-one findings showed that school choice had positive effects on civic values or behaviors, 13 were that school choice had no significant effects, and only 2 findings supported the notion that traditional public schooling produced significantly better civic outcomes than the alternatives.

Data and Methods

This chapter updates my 2007 systematic review of the findings regarding school choice and the civic outcomes necessary for a stable democracy, limiting the results to studies either of private schooling in general or private school choice in particular. Findings of the civic effects of public charter schools were excluded from the update, as the myth focuses on the difference between public and private schools, not alternative forms of public schools. The review includes each statistical finding from any quantitative study of the effects of private school choice or private schooling compared to public schooling in the United States on any civic value. In all, I located 34 studies (see the list of studies reviewed at the end of this chapter) containing 86 total findings, an increase of 50 findings from my 2007 review.

I classified a finding as supporting a "public advantage" if the outcomes for public school students were higher on the measure than those of private school students by a statistically significant amount. I used the minimum level of statistical significance the original researchers employed, which was either 90 percent or 95 percent confidence that the difference was real and not merely a product of statistical noise. I classified a finding as "neutral" if the outcomes for the public and private school groups were not significantly different from each other. Finally, I classified a finding as supporting a "private advantage" if the outcomes for private school students were significantly higher than those for their public school peers. The three categories considered together were mutually exclusive and exhaustive.

The findings in the review are organized into four subcategories of civic outcomes: political tolerance, political participation, civic knowledge and skills, and voluntarism and social capital.

Findings

If government-run public schooling is necessary for a stable democracy, then we would expect most of the findings from the research on school sector and civic outcomes to appear in the "public advantage" category. In the bar graphs below, myth supporters would lead us to expect that the far left bar, which signals the number of findings of a public school advantage, would be dramatically higher than the far right bar, which signals the number of findings of a private school advantage. Instead, the reverse is the case.

When we consider all 86 findings from the 34 studies regarding all of the civic outcomes central to a stable democracy, only three indicate that public schooling outperforms private schooling (Figure 3.1). A whopping 50 statistical findings indicate that private schooling produces significantly better civic outcomes than does public schooling. The remaining 33 findings detect no difference between the two. If this score were from a rec-league softball game, the officials would end the contest under the

Figure 3.1
All findings on private school choice and civic outcomes

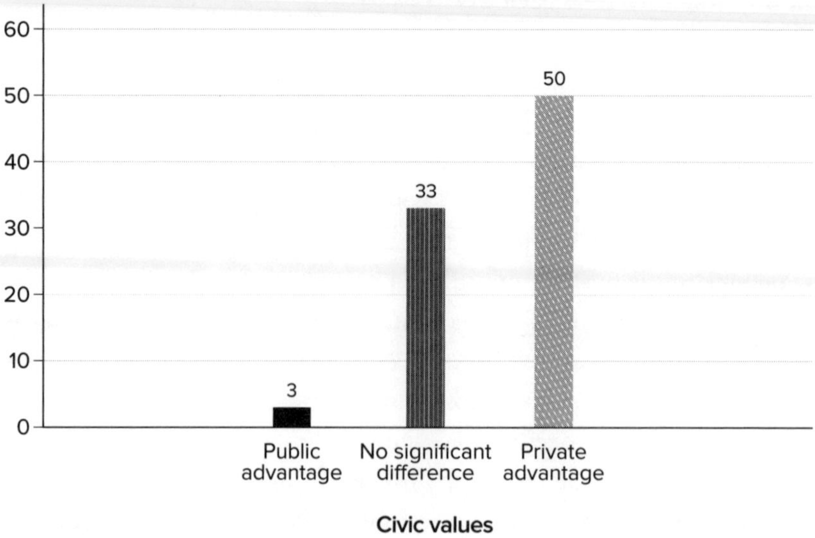

Sources: See list of studies reviewed at end of chapter.

"mercy rule." When it comes to generating the values and behaviors supportive of a stable democracy, private beats public schooling in a rout.

Myth supporters might object that private schools only enroll students with advantaged backgrounds. It is student background, and not better private school performance, that is generating all of these positive effects, they might say. While every study in the review used some variables to control for student background, a total of 27 of the findings come from especially rigorous studies that use random assignment, instrumental variables, or reliable student matching methods to ensure that student selection is not biasing the results. When we limit the review to just those more sophisticated studies, the pattern is the same (Figure 3.2). Only one finding indicates a public school advantage, while 14 results indicate a private school advantage regarding instilling vital civic values in students, with 12 findings suggesting no significant differences between

Figure 3.2

Findings on private school choice and civic outcomes from methodologically rigorous studies

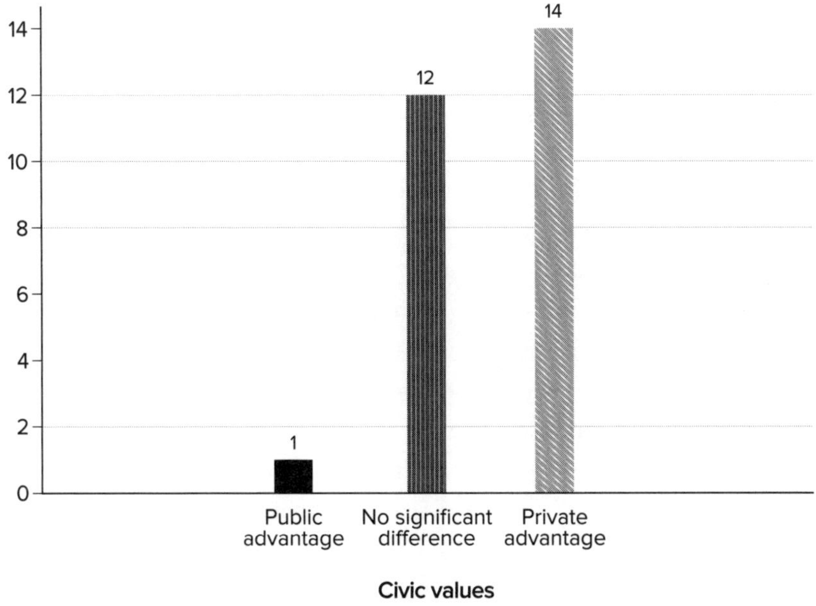

Sources: See list of studies reviewed at end of chapter.

Figure 3.3

Findings on private school choice and political tolerance

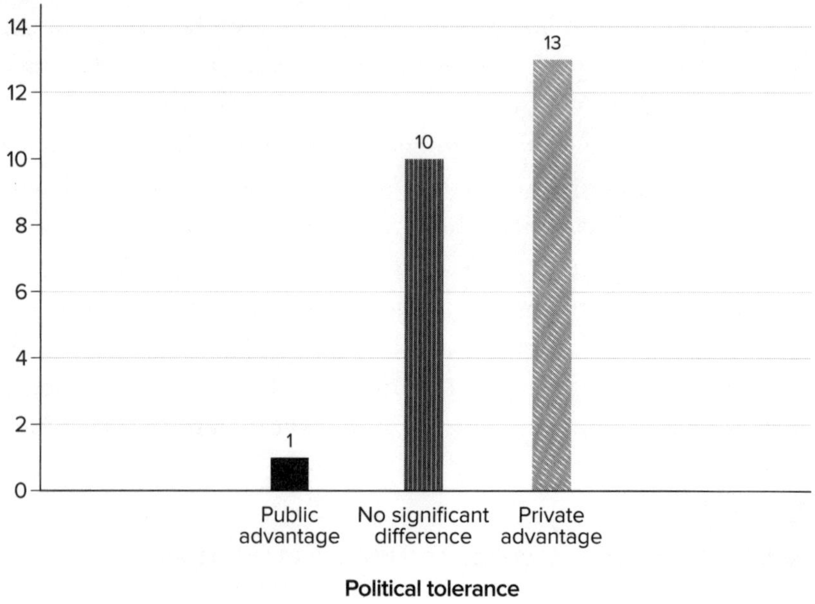

Sources: See list of studies reviewed at end of chapter.

the two groups. With a 14-to-1 score, private schooling again clearly beats public schooling at generating the outcomes necessary to support a stable democracy.

Now let us examine the results for specific conceptual groupings of civic outcomes. When we look at the results for the vital outcome of political tolerance, we see just one finding of a public schooling advantage but 13 findings of a private schooling advantage, with 10 findings of no significant difference between the groups (Figure 3.3). Private schooling has a strong empirical record of outperforming public schooling in producing tolerant citizens.

The record is even stronger regarding the private schooling advantage in promoting political participation. There are no findings of a public school advantage, but there are eight results supporting a private school benefit, with six statistical results indicating parity between the two groups (Figure 3.4).

Figure 3.4

Findings on private school choice and political participation

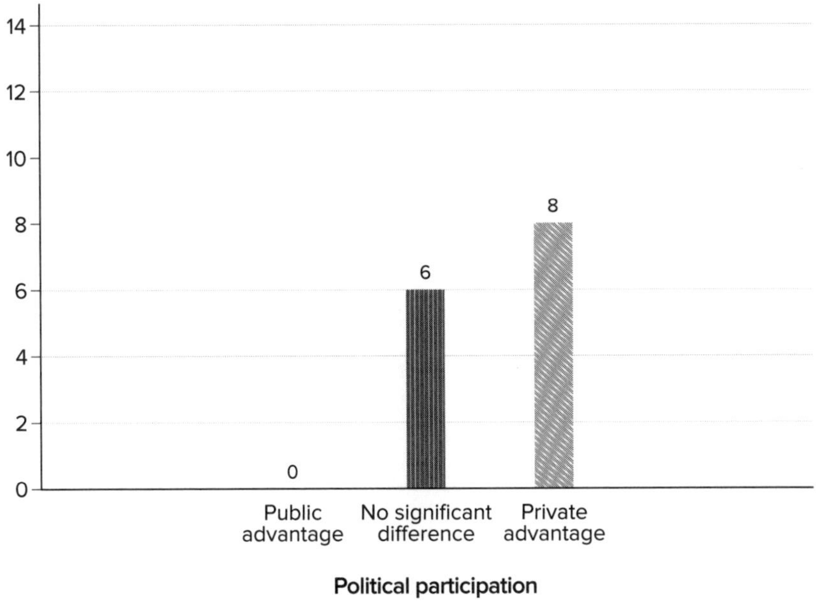

Sources: See list of studies reviewed at end of chapter.

Private schooling also outperforms government-run public schooling in imparting civic knowledge and the skills required of active citizenship. As with political participation, there is not a single finding that public schools provide an advantage over private schools in teaching civics and the skills of persuasive communication (Figure 3.5). There are, however, 10 findings of a private school advantage in imparting civic knowledge and skills, with the remaining six findings indicating no difference between the two groups.

The record is even more favorable for private schooling regarding voluntarism and social capital (Figure 3.6). While two findings support the claim that government-run public schools are superior to private schools in inspiring young adults to volunteer in their communities and develop active social networks, private schooling demonstrates an advantage in promoting voluntarism or social capital according to 19 findings, with 11 findings of no difference between the two school sectors.

Figure 3.5
Findings on private school choice and civic knowledge or skills

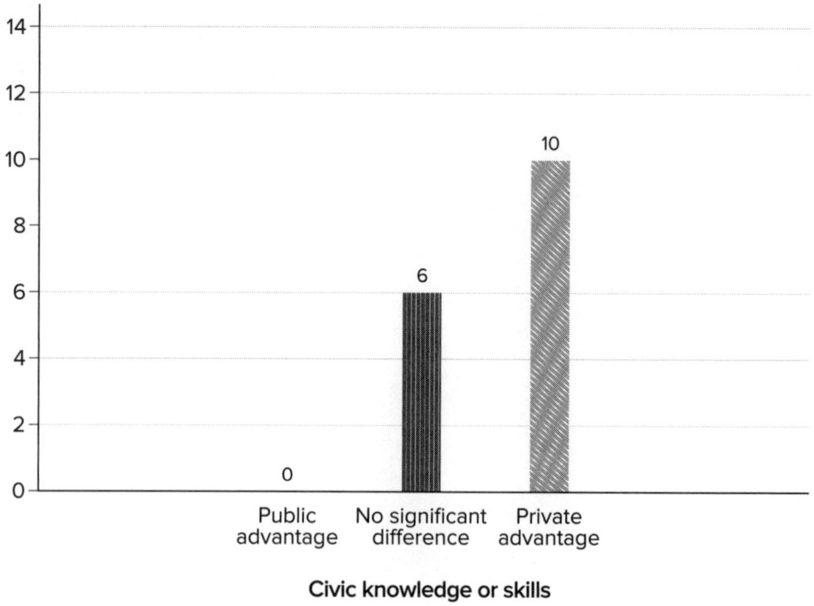

Sources: See list of studies reviewed at end of chapter.

Across the board, private schools have demonstrated themselves to be much better than public schools at equipping young people with the dispositions and skills to support a stable democracy.

Conclusion

How could a widely held myth be so demonstrably wrong? Three tendencies explain the disconnect between what is generally thought about the importance of public schooling to democratic values and the reality that private schooling better promotes democracy. First, none of the scholars and commentators who propagate the myth of private schooling being a threat to democracy actually put their claims to the test. There are scholars who claim that public schooling is essential to democracy, and there are scholars who have carefully examined the relationship between school sector and civic outcomes, and never have

Figure 3.6
Findings on private school choice and voluntarism or social capital

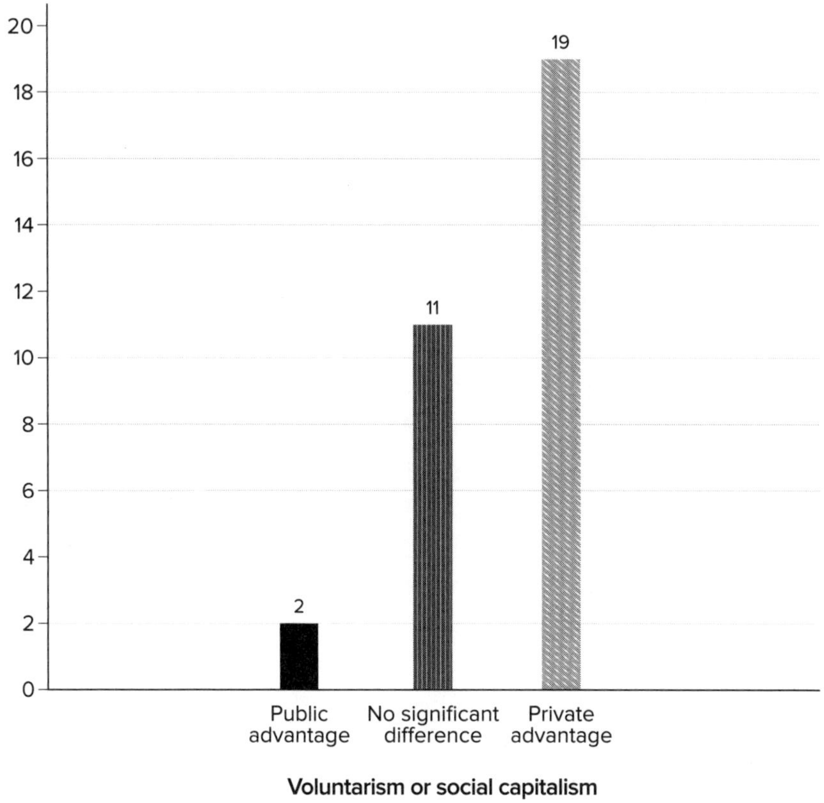

Sources: See list of studies reviewed at end of chapter.

the twain met. Thus, there are two separate literatures regarding the effects of private schooling on civic outcomes: a nonempirical myth-making literature and the empirical myth-shattering one I present here. Opponents of private school choice overwhelmingly emphasize what *may* happen to democracy if choice expands, while supporters of private school choice overwhelmingly emphasize what actually *does* happen to civic outcomes when more parents are able to choose private schooling for their children.

Second, defenders and critics of the centrality of public schooling to democratic outcomes are arguing about different things. Opponents of private school choice speak of how it harms the condition of public institutions. Supporters of private school choice overwhelmingly emphasize how it improves the civic outcomes of actual people. Opponents of school choice care primarily about what government-run schools *are to society*, while choice supporters care primarily about what any type of school *does for society*. In philosophical terms, opponents of private school choice view government-run public schools as an intrinsic good, regardless of the effects they have on people. Supporters of private school choice view government-run public schools as an instrumental good, meaning they are only beneficial to the extent that they produce positive outcomes. Compared to private schools, when it comes to civic outcomes, public schools do not demonstrate a performance advantage. To the contrary, private schools clearly outperform public ones in fostering student outcomes supportive of a stable democracy.

Recently I attended two events at different high schools in my community. The first event was an open house at the new Catholic high school. Visitors, mostly parents of prospective students, were greeted at the door and provided with snacks and bottles of water. Just before the formal presentation began, it was clear there were more parents than seats, so the school staff set up additional chairs to accommodate the parents, and some staff members stood at the back of the room so that parents could have seats. Students at the private school had major speaking roles in the formal program, even though the oldest student was only 16. At the end, parents were given information packets about the school and well wishes as they left.

The second event was a school board meeting at my son's residentially assigned government-run public high school. As at the first event, a large crowd of parents showed up. The accommodations were different, though. The elected school board members sat in leather chairs on a raised dais, seated like rulers on their thrones. The prime seats up front and along the sides of the room were reserved for school staff, in some cases with their names and formal titles on nameplates, like a regal coat-of-arms. Some parents were able to fight for the few open seats in the back. Less fortunate parents were forced to stand, uncomfortably, at the back of the room. Some parents were completely excluded from the room and had to hang out in the hallway and try to listen to what was happening in the inner sanctum.

Those attendees privileged enough to secure a spot in the room were able to witness the honoring of the school's National Merit Scholar Finalists. The students were announced, paraded before the school board, and given certificates. This spectacle was the public high school celebrating itself, in front of itself, with many parents and other members of the public excluded because there just was not enough room for them. The students, all high school seniors of extraordinary accomplishments, were allowed to be seen but not heard. I used to wonder why private schooling, as opposed to traditional government-run public schooling, tends to improve civic values and community involvement. I don't anymore.

Studies Reviewed

Abernathy, Scott Franklin. *School Choice and the Future of American Democracy.* Ann Arbor: University of Michigan Press, 2005.

Bettinger, Eric, and Richard Slonim. "Using Experimental Economics to Measure the Effects of a Natural Educational Experiment on Altruism." *Journal of Public Economics* 90, no. 8 (2006): 1625–48.

Campbell, David E. "Civic Education: Readying Massachusetts' Next Generation of Citizens." White Paper 17. Boston: Pioneer Institute for Public Policy Research, 2001.

———. "The Civic Side of School Reform: An Empirical Analysis of Civic Education in Public and Private Schools." *Brigham Young University Law Review* 2008, no. 2 (2008): 487–523.

———. "Making Democratic Education Work." In *Charters, Vouchers, and Public Education*, edited by Paul E. Peterson and David E. Campbell, pp. 241–67. Washington: Brookings Institution, 2001.

Carlson, Deven, Matthew M. Chingos, and David E. Campbell. "The Effect of Private School Vouchers on Political Participation: Experimental Evidence from New York City." *Journal of Research on Educational Effectiveness* 10, no. 3 (2017): 545–69.

Cheng, Albert. "Does Homeschooling or Private Schooling Promote Political Intolerance? Evidence from a Christian University." *Journal of School Choice* 8, no. 1 (2014): 49–68.

Cheng, Albert, and David Sikkink. "A Longitudinal Analysis of Volunteerism Activities for Individuals Educated in Public and Private Schools." *Youth and Society* (2019).

Coleman, James S., and Thomas Hoffer. *Public and Private High Schools: The Impact of Communities*. New York: Basic Books, 1987.

DeAngelis, Corey, and Patrick J. Wolf. "Will Democracy Endure Private School Choice? The Effect of the Milwaukee Parental Choice Program on Voting Behavior." *Journal of Private Enterprise* 34, no. 2 (2019): 1–21.

Dee, Thomas S. "The Effects of Catholic Schooling on Civic Participation." *International Tax and Public Finance* 12 (2005): 605–25.

Dill, Jeffrey S. "Preparing for Public Life: School Sector and the Educational Context of Lasting Citizen Formation." *Social Forces* 87, no. 3 (2009): 1265–90.

Fleming, David J. "Learning from Schools: School Choice, Political Learning, and Policy Feedback." *Policy Studies Journal* 42, no. 1 (2014): 55–78.

Fleming, David J., William Mitchell, and Michael McNally. 2014. "Can Markets Make Citizens? School Vouchers, Political Tolerance, and Civic Engagement." *Journal of School Choice* 8, no. 2 (2014): 213–36.

Godwin, R. Kenneth, Zen Deng, Patrick J. Wolf, and Sandy Wood. "Comparing Tolerance in Public, Private, and Evangelical Schools." Working paper. Center for the Study of Education Reform, University of North Texas. 1999.

Godwin, R. Kenneth, Carrie Ausbrook, and Valerie Martinez. "Teaching Tolerance in Public and Private Schools." *Phi Delta Kappan* (March 2001): 542–46.

Godwin, R. Kenneth, and Frank R. Kemerer. *School Choice Tradeoffs: Liberty, Equity, and Diversity*. Austin: University of Texas Press, 2002.

Greene, Jay P. "Civic Values in Public and Private Schools." In *Learning from School Choice*, edited by Paul E. Peterson and Bryan C. Hassel, pp. 83–106. Washington: Brookings Institution, 1998.

Greene, Jay P., Joseph Giammo, and Nicole Mellow. "The Effect of Private Education on Political Participation, Social Capital, and Tolerance: An Examination of the Latino National Political Survey." *Georgetown Public Policy Review* 5, no. 1 (Fall 1999): 53–67.

Greene, Jay P., Nicole Mellow, and Joseph Giammo. "Private Schools and the Public Good: The Effect of Private Education on Political Participation and Tolerance in the Texas Poll." *Catholic Education* (June 1999): 429–43.

Hill, Jonathan P., and Kevin R. den Dulk. "Religion, Volunteering, and Educational Setting: The Effect of Youth Schooling Type on Civic Engagement." *Journal for the Scientific Study of Religion* 52, no. 1 (2013): 179–97.

Howell, William G., and Paul E. Peterson, with Patrick J. Wolf and David E. Campbell. *The Education Gap: Vouchers and Urban Schools*. Washington: Brookings Institution, 2002.

Kingsbury, Ian. "Silencing the Seventh Trumpet: Analyzing the Effect of Private Schooling on Voting Behavior." *Education, Citizenship and Social Justice* 14, no. 3 (2019): 199–210.

Mills, Jonathan N., Albert Cheng, Collin Hitt, Patrick J. Wolf, and Jay P. Greene. *Measures of Student Non-cognitive Skills and Political Tolerance after Two Years of the Louisiana Scholarship Program*. Louisiana Scholarship Program Evaluation Report 2. School Choice Demonstration Project, University of Arkansas, Fayetteville. Education Research Alliance, Tulane University, New Orleans. 2016.

Niemi, Richard G., Mary A. Hepburn, and Chris Chapman. "Community Service by High School Students: A Cure for Civic Ills?" *Political Behavior* 23, no. 1 (2000): 45–69.

Peterson, Paul E., and David E. Campbell. "An Evaluation of the Children's Scholarship Fund." Working Paper 01–03. Program on Education Policy and Governance, Harvard University, 2001.

Peterson, Paul E., David E. Campbell, and Martin R. West. "An Evaluation of the Basic Fund Scholarship." Working Paper 01–01. Program on Education Policy and Governance, Harvard University, 2001.

Schneider, Mark, Paul Teske, Melissa Marschall, Michael Mintrom, and Christine Roch. "Institutional Arrangements and the Creation of Social Capital: The Effects of Public School Choice." *American Political Science Review* 91, no. 1 (1997): 82–93.

Sikkink, David. "Religious School Differences in School Climate and Academic Mission: A Descriptive Overview of School Organization and Student Outcomes." *Journal of School Choice* 6, no. 1 (2012): 20–39.

Smith, Christian, and David Sikkink. "Is Private Schooling Privatizing?" *First Things* 92 (April 1999): 16–20.

West, Martin R., Paul E. Peterson, and David E. Campbell. "School Choice in Dayton, Ohio, after Two Years: An Evaluation of the Parents Advocating Choice in Education Scholarship Program." Working Paper 01–04. Program on Education Policy and Governance, Harvard University, 2001. Available by request of the lead author, martin_west@gse.harvard.edu.

Wolf, Patrick J., et al. "Democratic Values in New York City Schools." Report of the Workshop in Applied Policy Analysis, School of International and Public Affairs, Columbia University, 1998.

Wolf, Patrick J., Paul E. Peterson, and Martin R. West. "Results of a School Voucher Experiment: The Case of Washington, D.C., after Two Years." Working Paper 01–05. Program on Education Policy and Governance, Harvard University, 2001.

Wolf, Patrick J., Jay P. Greene, Brett Kleitz, and Kristin Thalhammer. "Private Schooling and Political Tolerance." In *Charters, Vouchers, and Public Education*, edited by Paul E. Peterson and David E. Campbell, pp. 268–89. Washington: Brookings Institution, 2001.

CHAPTER FOUR

MYTH: PRIVATE SCHOOL CHOICE IS UNCONSTITUTIONAL

The U.S. Supreme Court disagrees.

Tim Keller

The constitutional battle surrounding private school choice programs has been raging for three decades. It began with the enactment of the Milwaukee Parental Choice Program in 1990, a publicly funded scholarship program that gave eligible families a grant, or voucher, to attend the eligible private school of their choice.[1] Even though the original program did not permit families to choose religious schools, "various school administration organizations" and the National Association for the Advancement of Colored People (NAACP) mounted an unsuccessful constitutional challenge to the choice program.[2] And when the program was expanded to permit families to choose religious schools, it was again challenged unsuccessfully—this time by the National Education Association, the Wisconsin Education Association, the American Civil Liberties Union (ACLU), and Americans United for Separation of Church and State.[3] Throughout the 1990s, litigation followed in each state that passed a private school choice program.[4]

After 30 years of litigation, choice proponents may not be able to declare complete and total victory—but they can confidently state that they are winning the legal war. The U.S. Supreme Court and at least nine state supreme courts, one state appellate court, and the territorial Supreme Court in Puerto Rico have rejected constitutional attacks against school choice programs on the merits.[5] The U.S. Supreme

Court, two state supreme courts, and one state appellate court have also declared that taxpayers do not have legal standing to challenge private school scholarship programs that are funded by incentivizing private donations to nonprofit scholarship-granting organizations through tax credits. This is because taxpayer-plaintiffs are not harmed when individuals or corporations are permitted to claim tax credits for donations that fund scholarships.[6] In fact, since the Wisconsin Supreme Court victories affirming the constitutionality of the Milwaukee Parental Choice Program, not one court decision has ever completely foreclosed a state legislature's ability to adopt a private school choice program.[7] And as of January 2019, 29 states, the District of Columbia, and the territory of Puerto Rico were operating 65 different programs that empower nearly a million families to choose private schools.[8]

This chapter briefly discusses the constitutionality of school choice programs under the federal Constitution, as well as the U.S. Supreme Court's two landmark decisions on school choice. It then addresses the various state constitutional provisions that opponents of private school choice have invoked, with little to no success, to try to halt the spread of private school choice programs.

Properly Designed Private School Choice Programs Do Not Violate the Federal Constitution

In 2002, in *Zelman v. Simmons-Harris*,[9] the U.S. Supreme Court rejected an Establishment Clause[10] challenge to a publicly funded scholarship program that allowed Cleveland parents to send their children to private schools, including religious ones. The Court upheld the program because it had a "valid secular purpose of providing educational assistance to . . . children" and did not have the "the forbidden 'effect' of advancing . . . religion," even though the vast majority of families chose religious schools.[11] As the Court explained, the program was (1) "neutral with respect to religion, . . . permit[ting] the participation of all schools within the district, religious or nonreligious"; and (2) a program of "true private choice," providing a benefit "to a broad class of citizens who, in turn, direct government aid to religious schools wholly as a result of their own genuine and independent private choice."[12] So long as the touchstones of neutrality and private choice are satisfied, any private school choice program should survive an Establishment Clause challenge.

Moreover, the U.S. Supreme Court's landmark decision in *Espinoza v. Montana Department of Revenue* held that it would violate the U.S. Constitution to exclude religious schools from a private school choice program.[13] In *Espinoza*, the Court concluded that Montana violated the U.S. Constitution when it relied on a clause in its state constitution to strike down a school choice program because students were permitted to use their scholarships to attend religious schools. Chief Justice John Roberts explained that the "supreme law of the land condemns discrimination against religious schools and the families whose children attend them. They are members of the community too, and their exclusion from the scholarship program here is odious to our Constitution and cannot stand."[14] It is now clear that the U.S. Constitution will not tolerate the exclusion of religious options from private school choice programs. As the Court said in *Espinoza*, "A State need not subsidize private education. But once a State decides to do so, it cannot disqualify some private schools solely because they are religious."[15]

After the U.S. Supreme Court's decision in *Zelman*, the National Education Association's chief counsel promised that choice opponents would "continue to challenge voucher and choice programs under state constitutions on whatever grounds are available to us—from lofty principles such as church-state separation, to 'Mickey Mouse' procedural issues like the single-subject rule."[16] And indeed, school choice opponents have continued to challenge choice program under myriad state constitutional provisions.

State Constitutions Are No Bar to Private School Choice Programs

A truly comprehensive review of state constitutional provisions is beyond the scope of this chapter, but there are three categories of clauses worth a brief overview: religion clauses, education clauses, and the most common "Mickey Mouse," or miscellaneous, provisions used by private school choice opponents.

State Religion Clauses

Many state constitutions contain religion clauses that are worded differently than the federal Establishment Clause. These provisions often speak in terms of prohibiting appropriations of public funds "in aid of" or "for the benefit of" "sectarian" institutions.[17] The overwhelming majority of state courts that have considered legal challenges to modern educational choice programs have concluded that such programs "aid" or "benefit" students, not religious institutions. In fact, in nearly every state some form of private school choice will pass muster under these state religion clauses.[18] The two most common types of religion clauses are Blaine amendments and compelled support clauses.

BLAINE AMENDMENTS

Blaine amendments are characterized by their restriction on the "use" or "appropriation" of public funds "in aid of" or "for the benefit of" "sectarian" schools and are found in 37 state constitutions.[19] The name "Blaine" refers to James G. Blaine, a politician from Maine who served as both a U.S. senator and Speaker of the U.S. House of Representatives in the late 1800s.[20] Blaine proposed an amendment to the federal Constitution in 1876 to prohibit states from appropriating public money to "sectarian" schools.[21] The term "sectarian" was widely understood at that time to mean "Catholic."[22] It was not a synonym for "religious," as it is often understood today.

The proposed federal Blaine amendment arose at a time when public schools were not the thoroughly secular institutions we know today.[23] Public schools were often overtly religious, promoting a generic, nondenominational Protestantism that most Protestant sects found unobjectionable, or at least tolerable.[24] Large numbers of Catholic families were unhappy with the Protestant orientation of the public schools and, after opening their own schools, began campaigning for a proportional share of public school funds.[25] These efforts outraged the Protestant majority.

Blaine, eager to secure the 1876 Republican presidential nomination, introduced his amendment in a "transparent political gesture against the Catholic Church."[26] The proposed amendment failed to garner the required supermajority in the U.S. Senate to send it to the states for ratification, but many states thereafter (and a handful before) adopted similar state constitutional language to rebuff the efforts by Catholics to acquire institutional assistance for their parochial schools. Congress also sometimes required new states, including Montana, Washington, and the Dakotas, to incorporate Blaine amendments in their state constitutions as a condition of admission.

Thankfully, under *Espinoza*, Blaine amendments are no longer a barrier to educational choice programs that empower parents to choose religious educational options alongside nonreligious options. Of course, even before *Espinoza*, most state courts had concluded that it is the students themselves—not religious schools—who are the true beneficiaries of educational choice programs. Many of these decisions have been in the context of traditional voucher programs.[27] In *Espinoza*, the U.S. Supreme Court has mostly laid to rest any interpretation of state Blaine amendments that would resurrect the anti-Catholic animus that animated their adoption or allow that animus to be extend to all religions. Of course, it has yet to be seen whether opponents of choice will in fact abandon Blaine-based arguments the same way that they abandoned the Establishment Clause. We now know that parents cannot be denied religious educational options simply because they are religious. But choice opponents may try—in a desperate (and ultimately doomed) bid to keep Blaine amendments alive as a means to attack educational choice programs—to assert that Blaine amendments do not permit states to fund religious instruction or tolerate religious schools that seek to inculcate religious values.

Even before *Espinoza*, two types of school choice programs were especially resistant to Blaine amendment attacks. It is worth exploring why.

Scholarship Programs Incentivized by Tax Credits

Scholarship programs that rely on private donations incentivized by tax credits have proven largely immune to Blaine amendment challenges. This is because such programs do not involve any appropriation or use of public funds, and thus the textual analysis of most Blaine amendments, which apply only to uses or appropriations of "public funds," ends before the question of whether private school programs "aid" or "benefit" parents or schools is even reached. With only one recent exception, every court, including the U.S. Supreme Court, that has considered whether programs that offer tax credits to taxpayers who donate money to private charities are funded with public or private dollars (or whether tax credits constitute an appropriation of public funds) has concluded that the donated dollars are private funds and thus do not constitute an appropriation.[28] Tax credits allow taxpayers to keep more of their own money. At no point does the state own the donated money legally or ever possess it physically. To find otherwise would mean that the state essentially has a claim over every cent of taxpayers' money.[29]

Education Savings Account Programs

Education savings account (ESA) programs have twice proven immune from Blaine amendment challenges, though they are a relatively new type of private school choice program.[30] ESAs are flexible, parent-controlled accounts from which parents may draw funds to tailor their child's education, whether it be in the form of home educational materials, private tutoring, private school tuition, online education, or any combination thereof. ESAs thus differ from traditional voucher and scholarship programs by permitting parents to spend their child's education dollars on more than just private school tuition.

ESAs originated as a response to the Arizona Supreme Court's 2009 decision invalidating two publicly funded private school scholarship programs.[31] The court rejected the argument that the programs appropriated funds "in aid of" families and not "in aid of" private schools because parents had "no choice" but to use the scholarship money at private schools.[32] However, the court concluded its opinion by stating that there "may well be ways of providing aid to these student populations without violating" Arizona's Blaine amendment.[33]

Arizona policymakers found one of those ways by reviewing the oral argument in *Cain*:

> *Justice*: Do you agree that the state could pick this population of worthy parents and say to them, "Here's a grant for each of you for $2,500 to be used in pursuit of your children's education. Spend it as you wish"?
>
> *Union lawyer*: Yes.
>
> *Justice*: And if they spend it on a private or parochial school, or on a public school transfer, that would be okay?

> *Union lawyer*: Yes. I think the dividing line is how much the state constrains the choice.
>
> *Union lawyer*: Under the [Blaine amendment], that funding is for the most part only going to be used to pay one of two prohibited recipients. So the choice is constrained to the point that the odds are overwhelming that it's going to go to a prohibited recipient.
>
> *Justice*: So then why wouldn't that make illegal the program I just described, where we said to each parent, "Here's money to use for your child's education"? Those who are going to public school would have no expenditure in any case.
>
> *Union lawyer*: My assumption is that you can hire a tutor with it; you can do all kinds of things with it other than paying a private or religious school.[34]

This colloquy was the inspiration for Arizona's ESA program.[35] The two distinguishing features of this program are that (1) participating families are not required to enroll their children in a private school, and (2) they can use the funds deposited in their child's ESA for a wide array of educational goods and services. To no one's surprise, the ESA program was immediately challenged in court. The outcome was quite different. The Arizona Court of Appeals upheld the ESA program because account funds were not "pre-ordained" for any particular use.[36]

COMPELLED SUPPORT CLAUSES

Another source of objection has been compelled support clauses. These clauses prevent—and in some relatively early cases they ended—the establishment of an official state religion. Most states modeled their compelled support provisions after Pennsylvania's 1776 Constitution, whose Declaration of Rights reads in part,

> That all men have a natural and unalienable right to worship Almighty God according to the dictates of their own consciences and understanding: And that no man ought to or of right can be compelled to attend any religious worship, or maintain any ministry, contrary to, or against, his own free will and consent.

With only one exception, state courts have not invoked compelled support clauses to prevent parents from choosing religious schools for their children while participating in a private school choice program.[37] This is because compelled support language prohibits states from providing direct financial support for and/or requiring attendance at churches. They say nothing about providing religiously neutral financial aid to families to enroll their children in the school of their choice.

Education Provisions

Just about every state constitution contains language addressing public education. Most contain a mandate to establish and maintain a public school system. There are three lines of argument that educational choice opponents tend to make when relying on public education mandates to challenge private school choice programs. The first is that the imposition of a duty to operate and fund a public school system limits the authority of state legislatures to fund any educational alternatives outside of that system. In other words, opponents claim that the public school system is and must remain the *exclusive* means of educating the state's students with public funds. But nothing in the plain language of such provisions suggests an intent to set forth the exclusive means of delivering publicly funded education. Instead, such provisions merely set a floor upon which states may add alternative educational options.

Second, opponents argue that choice programs impermissibly impede the ability of state legislatures to maintain a system of public schools by draining resources from the state treasury.[38] But private school choice programs in no way impede a legislature's ability to meet its obligation to provide for a constitutionally mandated system of public schools. After the adoption of private choice programs, public schools remain firmly in place and fully available to parents who wish to send their children to them.

Finally, opponents argue that if the programs are permissible, then the private schools that parents choose must be considered part of the public school system—and thus be subject to the same legal requirements as public schools. But private school choice programs do not transform private schools into public schools. Private schools remain private.

Thankfully, every state supreme court that has considered these arguments has rejected them, except Florida's, which relied on an education provision to strike down a statewide voucher program while distinguishing programs that serve students with disabilities.[39] Of course, Florida remains home to some of the nation's largest private school choice programs, including the Florida Tax Credit Scholarship Program, which serves over 107,000 students and was upheld in a separate legal decision because it is funded with private dollars[40]; the McKay Scholarship for Students with Disabilities Program, which serves over 30,000 students; and the Gardner Scholarship Program for severely disabled pupils, which serves over 10,000 students.[41] The state also enacted a new voucher program in 2019, which had not been challenged in court as of this writing.

Miscellaneous Provisions

The foregoing does not exhaust the realm of miscellaneous provisions that might be found in state constitutions, but it does address the three most common provisions used to date to try to strike down private school choice programs. Here are some others.

Restricted funding provisions. Many state constitutions restrict certain pots of money exclusively for use on public schools. Often the interest and investment income generated from federal lands granted to a state at the time of statehood is set aside to fund public schools.[42] Publicly funded private school choice programs are permissible in states with such provisions so long as the programs are funded from nonrestricted revenue streams.[43]

Anti-gift/anti-donation clauses. Anti-gift or anti-donation clauses, which generally state that governments cannot give financial subsidies to private organizations and were intended to prevent gratuitous giveaways to private individuals and corporations, are sometimes cited in opposition to private school choice programs.[44] Programs have been upheld against legal challenges under these clauses because they further a valid public purpose (education) and benefit the state through increased educational options for parents, increased competition, and encouraging innovation in the educational marketplace, as well as saving the state money by not having to educate program participants in the public school system.[45]

Single-subject provisions. Single-subject provisions prevent disparate and unrelated subjects from being included in the same legislation.[46] The Ohio Supreme Court struck down the Cleveland voucher program on single-subject grounds,[47] but the Ohio General Assembly immediately repassed the program as stand-alone legislation. While the precise legal test for single-subject provisions varies from state to state, courts generally ask whether the subjects contained in the challenged bill possess a common purpose or whether there is a legitimate reason for combining multiple subjects in a single bill. There is, of course, a simple, straightforward way to avoid single-subject challenges: pass programs in stand-alone bills.

Special and local law provisions. Special and local law clauses require the adoption of laws that are of general applicability, rather than special or local laws applicable only to certain individuals or limited jurisdictions.[48] Opponents have invoked such provisions to challenge private school choice, such as the Milwaukee program, which was geographically limited. These claims tend to fail if there are valid, nondiscriminatory reasons for limiting the scope of the legislation or the class of beneficiaries.[49]

Local control provisions: Local control provisions may vest control over certain aspects of public education at the local level.[50] In 2004, the Colorado Supreme Court relied on a local control provision to invalidate a statewide school choice program because it directed school districts to turn over a portion of their locally raised funds to nonpublic schools over whose instruction the districts had no control.[51] Local control provisions can be avoided by not intruding on any prerogatives preserved for local school boards or districts. In some instances, this will mean ensuring that no local funds are utilized.

Conclusion

After nearly three decades of constitutional litigation, policymakers can confidently expect that properly designed private school choice programs will pass both federal and state constitutional muster.

CHAPTER FIVE

MYTH: CHILDREN ARE NOT WIDGETS, SO EDUCATION MUST NOT BE LEFT TO THE MARKET

Of course children aren't widgets. That's why education mustn't be left to the government.

Corey A. DeAngelis

Government-schooling advocates frequently argue that education is not something that ought to be left to the market because education is somehow different from any other good or service. The reality is that education is a service that is currently provided by the government for about nine out of every ten kids in the United States. And it isn't cheap. According to the Digest of Education Statistics, we currently spend over $15,000 per child per year, or more than $195,000 for each child's K–12 education.[1] Even though all families must pay a share of these large costs for government schools—whether their children attend them or not—about 10 percent of all students receive a private education. The presence of private schooling demonstrates that education can be provided by the market even when American citizens are compelled to allocate about $738 billion each year toward government schooling.[2]

The heart of the argument for government-run schooling is that children are not widgets, so education shouldn't be left to the market. For example, American Federation of Teachers president Randi Weingarten recently said, "Education is not a business to be run on a profit margin."[3] Similarly, *Times Union* columnist Chris Churchill proclaimed, "Children aren't widgets and schools aren't factories."[4]

Of course children aren't widgets. This is precisely why education must not be left to *government.* If children were all identical it would be much easier to educate all of them the same way in uniform factory-like schools, which is what government schooling tends to provide. If children within a certain ZIP code and age group were all the same, we could simply assign them to one government school and it would likely work well for them all, assuming government were competent with delivering uniform education. But there's just one problem: children are unique. They all have unique interests, abilities, and needs. They are not widgets, so we shouldn't expect that placing them on the government assembly line will lead to long-run success.

Public and private school choice programs allow children to opt out of their one-size-fits-all government school to attend whatever school works best for them based on their individual needs.[5] School choice also gives schools financial incentives to serve all children well.[6] After all, private and charter schools must attract families, which requires addressing their needs if they want to keep their doors open.[7] On the other hand, people are forced to pay for government schools through property taxes and other taxes whether they are happy with them or not.

The political process tends to produce uniform systems and rules based on the will of the majority and the politically powerful.[8] But that's only the beginning of the problem. As Bryan Caplan and Ilya Somin point out, each individual voter correctly understands that their vote has a near-zero chance of determining the outcome of a given election.[9] They also know that researching candidates and understanding their preferred policies is very costly. Because becoming an informed voter has high expected costs and low expected benefits, it is completely rational for citizens to be uninformed voters. Because these rationally ignorant voters determine which uniform education policies and rules are implemented, the resulting education system tends to fail. Perhaps this at least partially explains why we have increased inflation-adjusted per pupil education funding by 280% since 1960 with no discernable student achievement improvements overall.[10]

Some members of the public call for standardized testing requirements as a form of top-down accountability for taxpayer-funded schools.

The problem is that these measures tend strongly to be uniform so that all schools can be measured consistently and the public can gauge whether dollars are being used "efficiently." But uniform measures don't work well for people with unique needs, which are basically all people. Some children may benefit from focusing on standardized math and reading tests, but others may need more character or behavioral education. Still others may benefit from additional hours of mental health counseling or specialized therapies. The opportunity costs of focusing too much on uniform measures may explain the recent evidence that test scores are weak predictors of long-term outcomes such as high school graduation and college enrollment.[11] In fact, Colin Hitt, Michael McShane, and Patrick Wolf found that effects on math test scores did not successfully predict high school graduation rates 61 percent of the time, and reading test scores failed to predict graduation rates 50 percent of the time. But that's not all. Other causal studies have found that effects on standardized test scores do not correlate with other long-term outcomes such as crime, earnings, labor force participation, physical health, altruism, and even happiness.[12] Focusing too much on standardized tests—which "accountability" for a uniform system naturally leans toward—threatens to inflict unintended deleterious effects on the character skills necessary for flourishing in the long run.

It really shouldn't surprise us that the government schooling system treats children like widgets. Our current system of residentially assigned government schooling largely mirrors the Prussian school system. The compulsory system of schooling in Prussia started in 1819 with the clear mission of creating citizens that would be obedient miners, factory workers, and soldiers.[13] A system creating obedient factory workers may have sounded quite beneficial at the time of the Industrial Revolution, but treating kids like identical and replaceable cogs in a factory isn't very useful in today's economy.[14] Jobs have changed since the Industrial Revolution. Our education system should too. Unfortunately, the much-needed change is about two centuries overdue.

That children are not widgets is a foundational reason for grounding education not in government, as choice opponents believe, but in private choice.

Choice critics also offer other misguided assertions for why education shouldn't be "left to the market." These include (1) schooling is a public good, (2) schooling is good for the public, (3) education is too important to be left to the market, and (4) government-run schooling will lead to more educational equality. Let's go over each of these arguments to understand why none of them leads to the conclusion that the government ought to operate schools. On the contrary, most of these arguments actually strengthen the case to get the government out of the education business.

Schooling Is Not a Public Good

The economic argument for government using coercion to fund—and even provide—a specific good or service is strongest for a good or service deemed to be a public good. The formal definition of a public good is attributed to Nobel laureate economist Paul Samuelson. In a classic 1954 article, he explained that such a good satisfies two necessary conditions: it is nonexcludable, and it is nonrivalrous in consumption.[15]

The nonexcludability provision means that the producer cannot prevent nonpayers from using the good without bearing costs that exceed the benefit of payment. This provision is important because nonexcludability leads to a potential free-rider problem: individual consumers can enjoy the benefits of a product without directly paying for it. Consequently, the market may underprovide the good in question, or even fail to provide it at all. A feasible policy solution is to provide and produce the good publicly. In other words, the free-rider problem could be eliminated if all members of society were forced to pay for the service indirectly through taxes.

The nonrivalry provision simply means that one individual's consumption of the good does not diminish the abilities of others to consume it. A radio station can be thought of as a true public good, because it would be extremely difficult to prevent anyone with a radio from listening. And because one person's consumption of the service does not affect whether the rest of society can listen, the radio is considered nonrivalrous. One policy solution could be to have taxes fund local radio stations, but the market avoids the free-rider problem when radio stations use advertisements as a funding source.

If schooling were indeed a public good, there would perhaps be a stronger economic argument for government funding and operating schools. But schooling easily fails both parts of the economic definition. If one student occupies a seat in a classroom, another child is prevented from sitting in the same seat, meaning that educational services are rivalrous. Second and perhaps more important, because it is not difficult to exclude a person from a school—or any other type of institution with walls—schooling fails the nonexcludability condition. If someone does not pay me to educate the student, I can simply deny the student services. Fortunately, schools will never suffer from a true free-rider problem because they are not true public goods. That is precisely why private schools operate effectively without government operating or funding them.

Of course, schooling is but one channel to achieve an education. Could *education* be a public good, even if *schooling* clearly is not? It all depends on meeting the nonexcludability and nonrivalry conditions, but it is hard to imagine many nonschooling educational public goods. Homeschooling communities can easily exclude nonpayers from receiving the benefits of their services. The same goes for tutoring, or museums, or books.

Schooling as a Merit Good

When people, including prominent education scholars,[16] say that schooling is a public good, they likely mean that it is "good for the public." Or, as an economist would say, schooling is a "merit good" because it has net-positive externalities.[17] An economic externality occurs whenever a voluntary transaction between two parties affects an involuntary third party in a positive or negative way. The original argument regarding economic externalities has to do with pollution, a negative externality.[18] When I buy a car from a factory, the car manufacturer benefits from the transaction because it gets my money, and I benefit from the transaction because I get a car. Because the transaction is voluntary and not coerced, it would only occur if both parties perceived that expected benefits would exceed expected costs.[19] However, the rest of society could be involuntarily harmed by the transaction because they must breathe air that is less clean. Consequently, the market may produce a number of automobiles that is higher than the socially optimal level, where total social costs exceed total social benefits. As Arthur Pigou pointed out, one way to internalize the negative externality of pollution is to reduce consumption of automobiles toward the socially optimal level by taxing each unit of production—what is now called a Pigouvian tax.[20]

In the case of education, the externality is expected to be positive, which would make education a merit good. If I purchase an education through a school or otherwise, I benefit from the transaction because I will be able to command a higher salary in the future and will feel good about being an educated citizen. The education provider benefits from the transaction financially. The rest of society is better off because of the benefits I provide to it as a result of my education but for which I don't earn a market income. For instance, the educational blogs, lectures, and journal articles I post for free on the internet help society (I hope). Also, as an educated citizen, I am less likely to break the law and generally more likely to cast an informed vote on Election Day.[21] According to economists, leaving education to purely private transactions would result in education falling below the socially optimal level.[22] A feasible policy solution to move education levels up is a negative Pigouvian tax, also known as a Pigouvian subsidy. As Nobel laureate economist Milton Friedman concluded, government may have a role in funding schooling because of the theoretical positive externalities—he called them "neighborhood effects"—of education in general.[23]

While education itself seems to have net-positive externalities, the case is less clear for the system of traditional public schooling we have in the United States today. After all, if the traditional public schooling system is reducing overall levels of education, or producing education very inefficiently, it would be considered a demerit good—a good that has net-negative externalities.

The only existing analysis on the subject estimates that government schooling, relative to a universal private school choice system, has a net-negative effect on society of about $1.3 trillion dollars over each student cohort's lifetime.[24] This large negative effect is estimated using the most rigorous scientific evidence—experiments and quasi-experiments—linking private school choice programs to student achievement, taxpayer costs, and criminal activity in the United States. In other words, relative to a universal private school choice system, government schooling is likely a demerit good. However, because the scientific evidence on the prospect of a fully private system is severely limited, no studies exist that estimate whether schooling in general is a merit good relative to a fully private education system without any compulsory education laws or government-run schooling.

Nonetheless, even if schooling in general is a true merit good, that wouldn't mean that the government needs to operate the schools. As Milton Friedman pointed out, a good with a net-positive externality would only need additional funding—not government *provision*—to reach the socially optimal level of schooling.[25] Moreover, as even the founding theorist on externalities, Arthur Pigou, conceded long ago, "We cannot expect that any public authority will attain, or will even wholeheartedly seek, that ideal. Such authorities are liable alike to ignorance, to sectional pressure and to personal corruption by private interest. A loud-voice part of their constituents, if organized for votes, may easily outweigh the whole."[26] And as economist David Friedman argues, government interference may make us much worse off if we cannot confidently calculate the sign of the net externality.[27] Because of our severely limited knowledge of the true societal effects of different goods and services, we may end up subsidizing aspects of schooling that ought to be taxed, and vice versa.

Importance and Market Provision

Similar to the "good for the public" assertion, government schooling advocates argue that the societal benefits of education are too important to be left to the market. But there is a powerful argument that education is, in fact, too important to be left to the government. Many people agree that the government generally does a poor job with simple tasks such as delivering the mail or running the DMV. Then sometimes the same people turn around and argue that the government needs to perform complex tasks such as educating an extremely diverse population. But if the government cannot effectively perform simple tasks, we certainly shouldn't trust it to perform complex tasks. It is much better that government mess up mail delivery than education. As David Friedman said, "If the government is in charge of delivering the mail, all that means is that some of our letters get lost. If governments are in charge of running the schools, that means that some of our children never learn to read."[28]

If importance were a legitimate argument for government provision of a good or service, then we should also have government provide food. After all, food is much more important than schooling. People have a hard time throughout life when they don't receive a great education, but they don't have a life at all without food. If you think that education is so important that the government must run the schools, then you must also conclude that the government must run the farms and grocery stores.[29] But we all know how well that worked out for the USSR and Maoist China and how it is working out in current-day Venezuela.[30] It's likely that most public schooling advocates would agree that residentially assigned government-run grocery stores are a bad idea. But if they accept that having government-run grocery stores is a bad idea, they should also accept that government-run schooling is a bad idea. When government controls the food supply, children are starved of nutrients; when government controls the education system, children are starved of learning.

Let's look at it from a different angle. Religious institutions provide a form of moral education. Following the same "too important" logic, one could also argue that moral education is too important to be left up to the market; hence, all children ought to be compelled to attend government-run churches. I would imagine that to most public schooling advocates, making all citizens pay for and attend government-run churches would sound like a horrible idea. But if advocates accept the faulty logic that education in general is so important that everyone must attend government schools, they should also accept the argument that everyone must attend government churches for moral training.[31] If they don't accept the latter, they really need to rethink the former.

Educational Equality

Government is often seen as society's great equalizer. In education, nothing can be further from the truth. Indeed, it is nearly impossible to imagine an aspect of society with greater inequities than those that exist in the U.S. education system.

Because children are assigned to government-run schools based on their ZIP codes, and neighborhoods tend to be racially and socioeconomically segregated, traditional public schools are also highly segregated.[32] This is a huge problem given the scientific evidence suggesting that advantaged peer groups and diversity can improve outcomes for the least advantaged groups of students.[33] Of course, advantaged families can get their children into higher-quality government schools by purchasing expensive residences. In addition, the democratic process that determines what happens in schools is controlled by the most politically powerful members of society, meaning that government schools tend to ignore the needs of the least advantaged.

In addition to the problem of housing segregation, the best teachers are often promoted away from the least advantaged students. Teachers are paid based on years of experience rather than quality, and because the best teachers are not well rewarded financially, they are often rewarded with their choice of schools to work in instead. The best teachers tend to move to the schools with advantaged kids that are relatively easy to educate, leaving the least advantaged children with worse teachers.[34]

School choice provides the least advantaged students with more options. Choice allows them to escape schools that are not serving them well—for whatever reason—and to attend schools that better fit their unique needs. Rich people can escape the government school system far more easily than poor people because spending over and above their schooling tax dollars so that their children can attend a private school is a relatively far smaller hit for them. We should also enable the least advantaged to exercise choice by letting education funding follow them to whatever school serves them most successfully, public or private. Government schooling only exacerbates existing inequalities. School choice is an educational equalizer.

Conclusion

It is absolutely true that children are not widgets. They are all unique individuals. But this is precisely why a uniform system of schooling cannot meet their needs effectively. Educational failure is not the fault of government schoolteachers or administrators, because educating so many children of diverse needs is a job that is nearly impossible when they are crammed into classrooms based just on their ages and ZIP codes. The government-run school system incorrectly assumes that all kids will be served well by a largely uniform educational product. It assumes that children are interchangeable parts that can be placed into the government schooling machine and come out as successful human beings. It, and not the market, wrongly assumes that children are widgets, or at least it must function as if they are. A system of school choice, which frees families and educators alike, correctly assumes that one size does not fit all in the realm of education. And contrary to what education monopolists argue, school choice leads to more equality, not less, than a system in which only the rich have meaningful options.

CHAPTER SIX

MYTH: SCHOOL CHOICE SIPHONS MONEY FROM PUBLIC SCHOOLS AND HARMS TAXPAYERS

Actually, choice helps stayers and taxpayers.

Martin F. Lueken and Benjamin Scafidi

Taxpayer expenditures on public school students are typically much larger than taxpayer expenditures on students who utilize an education choice program. As an example, in the 2015–2016 school year, each Georgia public school student had an average of more than $11,000 spent on their education. Special-needs students who used a voucher to attend a private school under the Georgia Special Needs Scholarship had about half as much taxpayer funding devoted to their education as students enrolled in public schools—most of whom do not have special needs. Students who received a tax-credit scholarship in Georgia received about a third of the funding of students in public schools (see Figure 6.1).[1]

Among the 25 voucher and tax-credit scholarship programs launched before 2013 and in operation for at least three years, the average cost of awarding a voucher or tax-credit scholarship is just 40 percent of the average spending per public school student.[2]

Despite these dramatically lower funding amounts, opponents of more taxpayer-funded choice in K–12 education routinely claim that choice programs harm taxpayers and "siphon" money away from public

Figure 6.1

Taxpayer expenditures per student, Georgia, 2016

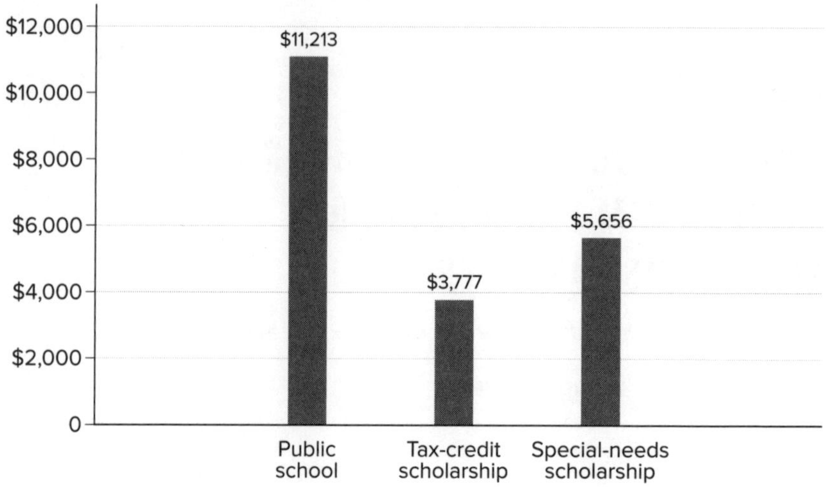

Source: Benjamin Scafidi, "Georgia 2020: Educational Opportunity for All Georgia Students," Georgia Public Policy Foundation, 2018.

schools.[3] It is rather easy—using elementary school mathematics—to show that choice programs can be (and almost always are) designed to save taxpayers money. As shown later in this chapter, a cautious estimate is that existing choice programs have saved state and local taxpayers at least $4.9 billion on a cumulative basis since 1998.

Regarding the claim that choice siphons money from public schools, opponents of choice are suggesting that students who remain in public schools will have fewer resources devoted to their education as some students leave via choice programs. Given that approximately 87 percent of American students attend public schools, this argument is very powerful in the political arena.[4] In this chapter we demonstrate, using both logic and the evidence from existing choice programs, that the claim that choice reduces resources for students who remain in public schools is a myth. Of course, the total budgets of public school districts decrease when they lose students for *any* reason, as is the case for universities, or any private sector business or nonprofit that loses customers or clients. But it is also true that costs go down when the number of students decreases.

While we show that public school students are not harmed financially, opponents of choice also claim that private school choice programs "leave behind" public school students and thus harm their learning. This claim is not backed by the large body of research that addresses this question: twenty-six empirical studies have examined the effects of eleven private school choice programs in eight states and Washington, DC, and nearly every one has found that students remaining in public schools after exposure to increased competition from private school choice programs experience modest gains on test scores.[5] This evidence suggests that not only are districts able to handle a smaller budget when they have fewer students, but they appear to be incentivized to improve academic outcomes for students who remain.

In this chapter, we first show how choice programs can be—and in practice are—designed to save taxpayers money. Next, using the basic mechanics of public school and choice program funding, and using elementary principles of accounting and economics, we explain the logic and evidence indicating that actual choice programs do not lead to fewer resources for students who remain in public schools.

Choice Programs Can Be Designed to Save Taxpayers Money

There is a direct cost to state governments when they have private school choice programs. They must fund vouchers and education savings accounts, and tax credits reduce the amount of revenues for the state. However, any net fiscal effect will be determined by a comparison between the fiscal cost to provide vouchers or scholarships and the fiscal savings from not having to pay the cost of enrolling students in public schools.

For students who switch from public to private schools as a result of a choice program, if the cost to provide a scholarship to them is less than the cost to fund their education in a public school, then those scholarship students will generate a fiscal benefit. Consider a situation where $10,000 per student is spent in the public schools. A school choice program that offers $9,000 scholarships to public school students to attend the private school of their choice would save taxpayers $1,000 per student.

It is realistic, however, that at least some voucher or scholarship students may not have enrolled in a public school if a choice program were not present. Given this likelihood, Robert M. Costrell has shown that it is straightforward to design school choice programs to save taxpayers money.[6]

Choice programs save money when the following is true:

$$\frac{\text{Money that follows the child to a school of choice}}{\text{Public school spending per student}} < \text{Percent of scholarship students who switch from a public to a private school as a result of the program}$$

(Hereafter, students who switch from a public to a private school as a result of a choice program are called "switchers.") The mathematical expression above shows that if the ratio of the taxpayer cost of the voucher or scholarship to the cost of educating a child in a public school is less than the percentage of program participants who are switchers, then the program will save money.

As an example, if the average cost of the scholarship is $9,000 and the average cost of educating a student in the public system is $10,000, then the break-even switcher rate will be expressed this way:

$$\$9{,}000 \ / \ \$10{,}000 = 0.90$$

In this example, 90 percent of the students who were funded under this hypothetical school choice program would have been enrolled in a public school, even if the choice program did not exist. Arithmetically, as long as the amount of taxpayer money that is redirected to schools of choice is less than 90 percent of the average amount that would have funded the student in a public school, this hypothetical example will generate savings for taxpayers.

This arithmetic leaves policymakers with a fiscal rule: *If the ratio of the average scholarship award to total spending per student in public schools is less than the break-even switcher rate, then the choice program provides a fiscal savings to taxpayers.*

Existing Choice Programs Have Actually Saved State and Local Taxpayers Money

While one can easily design a choice program to save taxpayers money using the elementary math described above, have actual programs done so?

According to the group EdChoice, there have been 50 separate fiscal analyses conducted on private school choice programs in the United States.[7] Importantly, only studies that account for both costs and savings from existing programs were included in the count. Of those, 45 found that programs generated net savings for taxpayers, and four found that programs were cost neutral. One very small Louisiana program for special-needs students had a minimal net cost.

In the next two subsections, we highlight a few of the studies that analyze the fiscal savings from voucher and tax-credit scholarship programs, respectively.

Voucher Programs

Two analyses of the Louisiana Scholarship Program (LSP) by Julie Trivitt and Corey DeAngelis estimated the fiscal effect on the state government and individual public school districts if this program were to be eliminated. The state government would experience a net savings for students who continue enrolling in schools outside the public system and incur net costs for students who return to public schools. Employing different assumptions about the types of schools in which students would enroll after the program's elimination, Trivitt and DeAngelis estimated that between 13.5 percent and 25.4 percent of students in the LSP would need to remain in private schools for the program's elimination to be cost neutral for the state.[8] DeAngelis and Trivitt estimated that if the LSP were eliminated, 62 to 67 of 69 Louisiana districts would incur a net financial cost, or about $1,500 for each voucher student returning to district schools.[9]

Costrell analyzed the differential fiscal impacts of the Milwaukee Parental Choice Program on state and local taxpayers.[10] His estimates suggest that, overall, Wisconsin taxpayers experienced net savings in

FY 2010 worth $46.7 million. However, he showed that these savings were unevenly distributed across taxpayers. Because of some peculiar rules governing how the program was funded, referred to by some as the "funding flaw," Milwaukee taxpayers were disproportionately affected and incurred a net cost, while non-Milwaukee taxpayers benefited.

Lueken estimated the fiscal effects of 16 voucher programs between their inceptions and FY 2015.[11] In addition to accounting for the costs of these programs, he estimated variable cost savings that these programs generated for public schools. Variable cost estimates were based on categorical expenditures for instruction, student support services, and instructional support services. His approach was more cautious than methods used by some economists, so estimated savings are likely conservative. This approach is also cautious because it treats administrative costs as fixed, where we show later in this chapter that at least a portion of these costs are variable.[12] After accounting for switchers and variable cost savings, these 16 voucher programs generated a lower-bound estimate of $3.2 billion in net savings for state and local taxpayers, or about $3,400 per voucher recipient (see panel A in Table 6.1).

Tax-Credit Scholarship Programs

Lueken estimated the fiscal effects of 10 tax-credit scholarship programs in 7 states by using a range of cautious assumptions about switchers and the number of students who receive multiple scholarships; his approach was very similar to his voucher estimates described just above. Panel B in Table 6.1 reports his most conservative estimates, indicating these programs generated cumulative net savings worth almost $1.7 billion, or about $1,400 for every scholarship awarded in the programs between 1998 and 2014.[13]

Combining results in panels A and B, the 26 voucher and tax-credit scholarship programs generated at least $4.9 billion in net savings for state and local taxpayers, or more than $2,000 per scholarship student.

Table 6.1

Fiscal effects estimates based on EdChoice analyses of voucher and tax-credit scholarship programs

	Year started	Cumulative number of students receiving vouchers	Estimated cumulative fiscal effect	Estimated cumulative fiscal effect per voucher
A. Voucher programs (through FY 2015)				
DC—Opportunity Scholarship Program	2004–2005	16,910	$36,250,786	$2,144
FL—John M. McKay Scholarships for Students with Disabilities Program	1999–2000	273,396	$1,513,277,535	$5,535
FL—A+ Opportunity Scholarships	1999–2000	2,848	$2,897,934	$1,018
GA—Georgia Special Needs Scholarships	2007–2008	20,468	$149,873,525	$7,322
IN—Choice Scholarship Program	2011–2012	62,007	$69,117,070	$1,115
LA—Louisiana Scholarship Program	2008–2009	24,348	$56,041,074	$2,302
LA—School Choice Program for Students with Exceptionalities	2011–2012	923	($83,806)	($91)
MS—Mississippi Dyslexia Therapy Scholarship for Students with Dyslexia Program	2012–2013	223	$1,443,329	$6,472
OH—Autism Scholarship Program	2004–2005	17,533	$108,363,412	$6,181
OH—Cleveland Scholarship Program	1996–1997	95,881	$400,450,680	$4,177
OH—Educational Choice Scholarship Program	2006–2007	113,538	$429,228,122	$3,780

(Continued)

Table 6.1

Fiscal effects estimates based on EdChoice analyses of voucher and tax-credit scholarship programs *(continued)*

	Year started	Cumulative number of students receiving vouchers	Estimated cumulative fiscal effect	Estimated cumulative fiscal effect per voucher
OH—Jon Peterson Special Needs Scholarship Program	2012–2013	6,865	$46,390,233	$6,757
OK—Lindsey Nicole Henry Scholarships for Students with Disabilities	2010–2011	983	$3,155,952	$3,211
UT—Carson Smith Special Needs Scholarship Program	2005–2006	5,573	$4,737,341	$850
WI—Milwaukee Parental Choice Program	1990–1991	285,504	$343,236,675	$1,202
WI—Racine Parental Choice Program	2011–2012	3,535	$2,900,024	$820
Subtotal		*930,535*	*$3,167,279,884*	*$3,404*
	Year started	**Cumulative number of scholarships**	**Estimated cumulative fiscal effect**	**Estimated cumulative fiscal effect per scholarship**
B. Tax-credit scholarship programs (through FY 2014)*				
AZ—Original Individual Income Tax Credit Scholarship Program	1997–1998	351,593	$115,245,374	$328
AZ—Arizona Low Income Corporate Tax Credit Scholarship Program	2005–2006	44,986	$103,672,167	$2,305
AZ—Lexie's Law for Disabled and Displaced Students Tax Credit Scholarship Program	2008–2009	1,020	$8,242,969	$8,081

Table 6.1

Fiscal effects estimates based on EdChoice analyses of voucher and tax-credit scholarship programs *(continued)*

	Year started	Cumulative number of scholarships	Estimated cumulative fiscal effect	Estimated cumulative fiscal effect per scholarship
AZ— "Switcher" Individual Income Tax Credit Scholarship Program	2011–2012	18,216	$23,343,635	$1,281
FL—Florida Tax Credit Scholarship Program	2002–2009	331,612	$372,187,624	$1,122
GA—Qualified Education Expense Tax Credit	2008–2009	54,371	$12,157,986	$224
IA—School Tuition Organization Tax Credit	2006–2007	77,893	$280,431,828	$3,600
IN—School Scholarship Tax Credit	2009–2010	19,540	$60,053,738	$3,073
PA—Educational Improvement Tax Credit Program	2001–2002	317,908	$721,694,759	$2,270
RI— Tax Credits for Contributions to Scholarship Organizations	2006–2007	3,268	$8,224,009	$2,517
Subtotal		*1,220,407*	*$1,705,254,089*	*$1,397*
Grand total		**2,150,942**	**$4,872,533,973**	**$2,265**

Sources: Martin F. Lueken, "The Fiscal Effects of Tax-Credit Scholarship Programs in the United States," *Journal of School Choice* 12, no. 2 (2018): 181–215; Martin F. Lueken, "Fiscal Effects of School Vouchers: Examining the Savings and Costs of America's Private School Voucher Programs," EdChoice, 2018.

Note: * Panel B reports the most conservative estimates for tax-credit scholarship programs from Lueken, "Fiscal Effects." The last column in panel B is adapted from the same article by reporting the cumulative effects on a per scholarship basis.

One reason that the savings are so much higher in voucher programs relative to tax-credit scholarship programs ($3,400 versus $1,400 per student) is that many voucher programs are targeted to students with special needs, and these programs provide significantly less funding per voucher relative to what the students would have spent on their education in public schools.

Two government agencies have documented the fiscal effects of tax-credit scholarship programs in their states. First, in a study by the Iowa Department of Revenue, Anthony Girardi and Angela Gullickson estimated that the Iowa School Tuition Organization Tax Credit Program generated between $10.3 million and $12.6 million in taxpayer savings each year between 2007–2008 and 2016–2017.[14] These estimates represent up to $1,380 per scholarship recipient and are predicated on the assumption that only 30 percent of program participants were switchers. If more than 30 percent of the scholarship students were switchers, then their estimates of cost savings would be higher, as the scholarships would be saving even more of the cost of educating children in the public schools due to more students being switchers. This 30 percent assumption is likely excessively cautious for a number of reasons. First, private schools surely care about their total revenue and have incentives to increase revenue by increasing enrollment. In addition, many private schools and scholarship organizations are also mission oriented and exist to serve as many students as they can. To achieve these goals, they will want to either fill empty seats or expand capacity by providing scholarships to students who are not enrolled in their schools. That is, they have a financial incentive, a mission calling, or both to provide scholarships to students switching from public schools.

Switcher rates tend to be high in private school choice programs, as demonstrated by recent randomized experiments of the Louisiana Scholarship Program and the District of Columbia's Opportunity Scholarship Program (DCOSP). During 2015–2016 of the LSP, about 90 percent of students who applied for a scholarship but who did not win the scholarship lottery enrolled in public schools. During both years of the most recent DCOSP evaluation, 9 percent of students who did not win the lottery either returned to the private school where they were previously enrolled before applying to the program or moved from a public school to a private school, even though they did not receive a scholarship in the lottery.[15] Both of these findings suggest that about 90 percent of those who desire to access a choice program are truly switchers from public to private schools and would be enrolled in a public school if the choice programs did not exist—far above the 30 percent estimate used in the Iowa analysis described above. If more students in choice programs are truly switchers, savings from these programs will be higher because the choice programs are pulling more students out of the relatively more expensive public schools via less expensive vouchers or scholarships.

The state of Florida's Office of Program Policy Analysis and Government Accountability estimated that in FY 2009, the Florida Tax Credit Scholarship Program generated a $1.44 benefit for the state's general fund for each dollar tax credit given.[16] Those savings for state taxpayers are equivalent to about $1,700 per scholarship.

Each of the above estimates of taxpayer savings—from both voucher and tax-credit scholarship programs—only consider fiscal savings. But there may be other benefits from choice programs to taxpayers as well. For example, Patrick Wolf and Michael McShane conducted a cost-benefit analysis of the District of Columbia's Opportunity Scholarship Program by accounting for the program's positive effect on high school graduation rates.[17] They estimated that the program generated benefits worth $2.62 for every dollar in expenditures on the program.

The fact that school choice programs tend to generate net savings for taxpayers should not be surprising, as the scholarship amounts represent just a fraction of the funds that public school districts receive for students, as shown in Figure 6.1.

Do Choice Programs Leave Fewer Resources for Students Who Remain in Public Schools?

In the prior section, we used evidence to demonstrate that education choice programs provide significant fiscal savings for taxpayers. Here we use evidence to analyze whether choice programs siphon money from public schools in a manner that leaves fewer resources for students who remain in public schools.

Some Basic Mechanics of Public School Funding

To address the question of whether choice programs lead to fewer resources for students who remain in public schools, it is first necessary to understand some basic mechanics regarding how public schools are funded and how dollars flow when students transfer in and out of public school districts.

Public school districts receive funding from state, local, and federal taxpayers. While the percentages vary significantly across states, public schools nationally receive 8 percent of their funding from the federal government on average and 45 percent from local sources. The remaining 47 percent comes from state governments (Figure 6.2).[18] Given that

Figure 6.2

Public K–12 revenue per student and percentage of total revenue by source, FY 2016

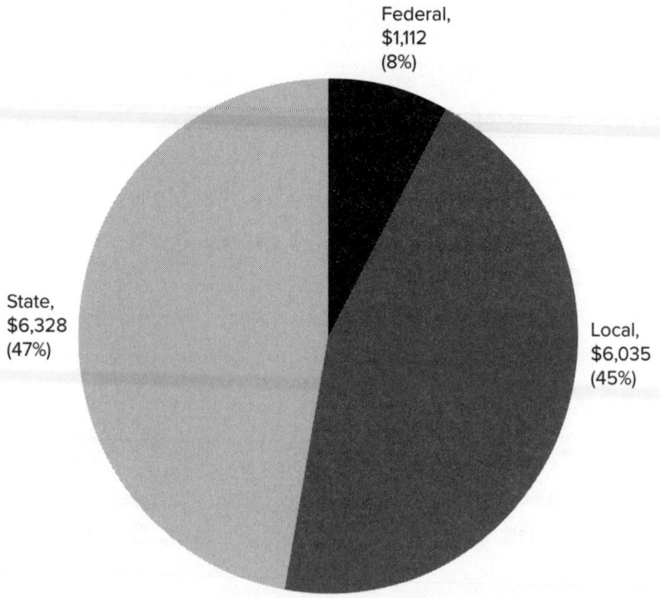

Source: Stephen Q. Cornman, Lei Zhou, Malia R. Howell, and Jumaane Young, *Revenues and Expenditures for Public Elementary and Secondary Education: School Year 2015–16 (Fiscal Year 2016): First Look (NCES 2019–301)*, (Washington: National Center for Education Statistics, 2018).

federal and state tax dollars flow to school districts, not to individual schools, the focus for this discussion is the district level.

It is important to understand that when students leave a public school district—for any reason—all dollars do not follow them. Funding from local and federal sources is usually not allocated on a per pupil basis. Typically, when public school districts lose students via choice—or lose students for any other reason—they get to retain their locally generated funding and a significant portion of federal funding.[19]

However, what matters for *resources* available for students who remain in public schools is not average revenue per student or even average expenditures. The answer to the question of whether students who remain in public schools have more or fewer resources available for their education when some students leave public school districts—for any reason, including via choice programs—depends on whether the revenue that public school districts actually lose is greater or less than the short-run variable cost of educating the students who left. To demonstrate this point, we now describe the relevant basic principles of accounting and economics.

School choice skeptics often cite high fixed costs in public schools as a reason to prevent choice programs from being introduced or expanded. The implication is that students would experience lower resource levels because districts are largely unable to reduce costs when students leave. Fixed costs are costs that do not vary with workload. Choice skeptics note that schools need electricity, air-conditioning, teachers, bus drivers, and assistant principals even though some students leave.

It is true that public school districts receive less funding when students leave—largely because of a reduction in state funds—but they retain local and most federal funds for students they no longer serve. It is also true that when schools serve fewer students they have lower costs. For example, when one or two students leave, the school needs fewer textbooks, supplies, or software licenses. If a large enough number of students leave, then schools can consolidate classrooms, reduce staffing, or take other cost-cutting actions.

The argument about substantial fixed costs is implicitly about the short run. An important and basic accounting and economic principle is that all costs are variable in the long run, and public school districts (along with any other economic entity) will adapt accordingly. No service provider that we are aware of keeps a portion of funds to cover fixed costs. For example, Kroger does not keep 20 percent of a customer's future grocery bill if the customer chooses to start shopping at Walmart.

Using the actual experience of school districts that lost students for non–school choice reasons, Scafidi estimated short-run fixed and variable costs in K–12 public schools by state, where the short run is defined as from one year to the next.[20] In general, this report found that in the short run, roughly two-thirds of all costs are variable and one-third are fixed. In terms of how public school districts actually adjusted their budgets when they lost students, a sizeable portion of short-run variable costs includes expenditures on instruction, of which a large majority is comprised of personnel compensation.

Scafidi showed that public school districts have behaved over the last several decades *as if* staff are variable by hiring personnel—both teaching and nonteaching staff—at rates that significantly outpace enrollment

Figure 6.3

Staffing surge in American public schools, 1992–2017

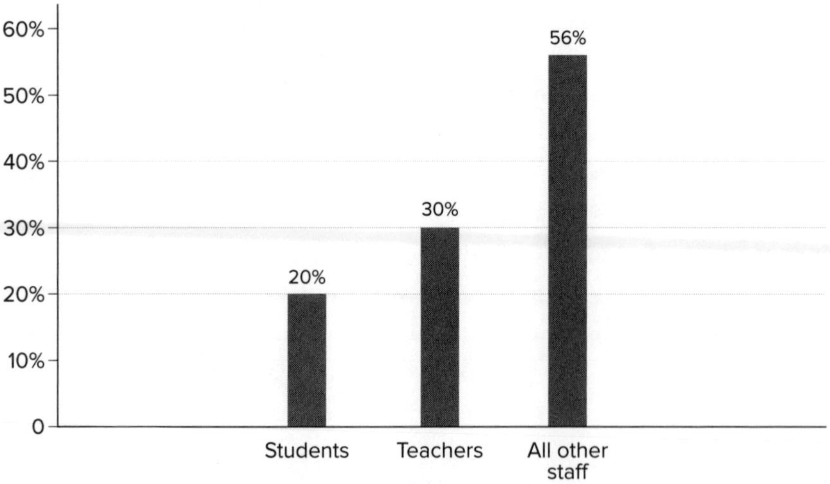

Source: Benjamin Scafidi, "Back to the Staffing Surge: The Great Teacher Salary Stagnation and the Decades-Long Employment Growth in American Public Schools," EdChoice, 2017.

growth (Figure 6.3).[21] Thus, it is reasonable to treat expenditures on a majority of personnel as a short-run variable cost.[22]

How Are Resource Levels Impacted for Students Who Remain in Public Schools?

The extent to which public school funding is based on student enrollment will influence the effects of private school choice programs on resources for students who remain in public schools. In fact, the fiscal effects of choice programs on students who remain in public schools are largely the same as when students leave public school districts for any other reason (e.g., transfer to another district, homeschool, move out of state, or enroll in a private school where their families pay the full cost). That is, the fiscal effect on school districts when students leave can be calculated like this:

$$\text{Net district fiscal benefit (cost)} = \text{Decrease in costs} - \text{Decrease in revenue}$$

When students leave a public school district, the district typically keeps all local funds and most federal funds, while just the state tends to move its portion of education funds. Consequently, when enrollment decreases, the district will end up with a lower total budget. But when enrollment decreases (as it may happen to some extent when a school choice program is introduced), the district ends up with more resources on a per pupil basis. This mechanism means that where funds don't completely follow students, a common by-product of private school choice programs is that districts end up with more resources per student.

But what about actual resource levels available to students who remain in public schools? Given the discussion of public school revenue sources, how dollars flow when students leave public school districts, and a basic understanding of fixed and variable costs, the golden rule is as follows: *Students who remain in public schools when some students leave via choice programs have more resources devoted to their education when the short-run variable cost of educating them is greater than the revenue lost when students leave to a private sc hool via choice.*

Figure 6.4

Change in enrollment and staffing in Indiana public district schools, 2012–2016

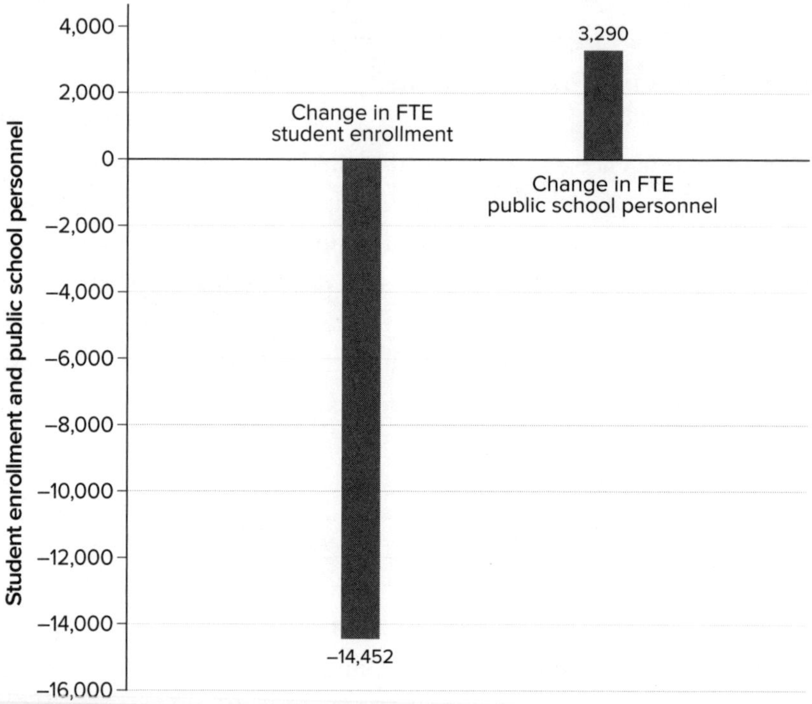

Source: Author calculations from data provided by the Indiana Department of Education. Charter and virtual schools are excluded.

Further, it is very likely that choice programs leave more resources for students who remain in public schools because:

- Choice programs typically have very low costs for scholarships or vouchers when compared to average per student costs in public schools.
- Estimates of short-run variable costs in public schools are typically about two-thirds or more of total per student expenditures in public schools.
- Public schools retain significant per student funding when students leave—namely, all local taxpayer funding and most federal funding.

As an example, in 2011 the state of Indiana began the nation's largest voucher program, the Indiana Choice Scholarship Program (ICSP). Partly as a result of the ICSP, total enrollment in Indiana district schools has fallen in recent years. We obtained data on enrollments and staffing in Indiana public schools through an open records request from the Indiana Department of Education, which was able to give us data from 2012 to 2016. Between those years, district schools in Indiana lost 14,452 students, but these same schools added 3,290 personnel (Figure 6.4).[23]

Thus, during the era of Indiana's voucher program, students who remained in public schools experienced a significant increase in access to public school personnel.

Conclusion

A common mantra among opponents of taxpayer-funded education choice programs is that choice harms taxpayers and that students are harmed as choice siphons money away from public schools. Yet it is simple to design choice programs to save taxpayers money, and a cautious estimate is that existing choice programs have saved state and local taxpayers at least $4.9 billion since 1998. It is also a myth that choice programs siphon money from public schools in a manner that leaves fewer resources for students who remain, as public schools retain significant funds when they lose students and appear to have increased resource levels for students who remain. Even if a district incurs a negative fiscal effect, this does not mean that the program is somehow "stealing" money from public schools. Students enter and leave districts all the time, whether to enroll in a different district's school, to access a private school, or to move out of state. Choice programs simply provide families with the option to take a fraction of public funding to the school that works best for their children. That said, these arguments from choice skeptics are very powerful in political settings.

These myths are especially misleading given the following three facts:

- On a per student basis, taxpayer funding for choice programs is only a fraction of what taxpayers spend on public school students.

- Public K–12 education is the only enterprise in our society (that we are aware of) that retains significant amounts of funding for customers it no longer serves. For example, when patients choose to leave a clinic in favor of a different provider, the clinic that loses them doesn't keep any future funds for those patients (out-of-pocket or from insurance). And when students transfer from one college to another, every dollar generated by those students (tuition, state funds, Pell Grants, GI Bill, etc.) in most states follows them.
- Twenty-six empirical studies have examined the effects of 11 private school choice programs in eight states and DC, and nearly every one of them has found that students remaining in public schools after exposure to competition from private schools experience modest gains on test scores.[24] Thus, it seems that not only are districts able to handle smaller budgets when they have fewer students, but they are able and incentivized to improve academic outcomes for students who remain.

Despite these facts, school choice skeptics seem to be most concerned that choice programs siphon money from public schools. With respect to this claim, we have a simple response: Chutzpah! The conventional public school system spends larger and larger amounts of taxpayer funds and has myriad layers of elected officials, bureaucracies, and federal, state, and local courts that make educational decisions that are imposed on students, families, and educators. Thus, it is the public education system itself that siphons the control of taxpayer funds away from families and educators.

CHAPTER SEVEN

MYTH: SCHOOL CHOICE HARMS CHILDREN LEFT BEHIND IN PUBLIC SCHOOLS

Experience shows otherwise.

Matt Ladner

In recent decades a growing list of policy innovations—open enrollment, district magnet schools, public charter schools, school vouchers, tuition tax-credit scholarships, and most recently education savings accounts—have granted families expanded opportunities to choose schools other than their assigned district institution. These policies have vocal and powerful enemies who often make the claim that choice programs harm the education of children remaining in district schools. If the education of children "left behind" were damaged by the choices of others, it would be a powerful argument against choice. Fortunately, this fear is not borne out by evidence.

The experience over the last few decades, in fact, points toward district students *benefiting* rather than suffering under a system of choice. The pages that follow note just how unusual our overall education trends have been in an era of constant efficiency and quality improvements in other areas of life. A review of the academic literature on competitive effects from choice programs follows, and an exploration of a recent case in which a state's policies and unforeseen economic circumstances combined to produce very large competitive pressures on districts, serving as a case study on the positive effects of competition.

Education Left Behind in Broad Improvements in American Life

Academic achievement, as measured by the National Assessment of Educational Progress (NAEP)—a federal assessment given to a representative sample of students—has stagnated. In the inaugural 1971 exam, 17-year-old students saw an average score of 285 on a 500-point scale in reading. In 2012, after a large increase in inflation-adjusted public school spending and staffing per pupil, the score averaged just 287. Paul Hill and Marguerite Roza summarized this unfortunate history: "Schools are highly labor intensive and getting more so, due to pressures for class size reduction and increasing use of specialist teachers. Yet on average schools are producing at best only slightly better results than at earlier times; thus, given increased costs, they are literally becoming less productive."[1]

Declining productivity of education spending stands out during an era when many goods and services have improved in quality and *declined* in price. For instance, economist Mark J. Perry of the American Enterprise Institute illustrated the normal pace of progress by demonstrating that the consumer of 2014 could purchase five home appliances (including a washer and dryer, stove, and refrigerator), and a laptop computer, a professional camera, flat screen television, and half a dozen other products all for the equivalent price of a 21-inch color television in 1964, adjusting for inflation. And the 2014 television was not only cheaper but was also superior in quality to the 1964 version.[2]

Rather than adjusting for inflation, this improvement can also be illustrated by calculating the number of hours of work needed to afford various products. In 1959, a color television cost $267, and the average wage was $2.09 per hour, so the average wage earner had to work 127.8 hours to buy a color television set. In 2013, you could buy a color television for $400, and the average hourly wage was $19.30, meaning that the average wage earner needed to work 20.7 hours to earn enough to buy a color television.[3]

We see precisely the opposite trend in American K–12 education: increases in inflation-adjusted spending per pupil and staffing with at best modest improvements in academic outcomes. This is consistent with economists having long urged caution in the provision of education by public entities. John Stuart Mill, for instance, argued against direct state provision of schooling entirely and held that public assistance should be given only to low-income children: "If the government would make up its mind to require for every child a good education, it might save itself the trouble of providing one. It might leave to parents to obtain the education where and how they pleased, and content itself with helping to pay the school fees of the poorer classes of children, and defraying the entire school expenses of those who have no one else to pay for them."[4]

Mill warned that state education would result in a "despotism of the mind" that would enforce a uniformity suiting various elites but serving society poorly. He wrote, "An education established and controlled by the State should only exist, if it exist at all, as one among many competing experiments . . . carried on for the purpose of example and stimulus, to keep the others up to a certain standard of excellence."[5]

The founders of the American public school system ignored Mill's warnings. Ironically, Albert Shanker, the founding president of the American Federation of Teachers, the nation's second-largest teacher union, essentially conceded in the pages of the *New York Times* in 1989 that Mill's warning had come to pass: "It's time to admit that public education operates like a planned economy, a bureaucratic system in which everybody's role is spelled out in advance and there are few incentives for innovation and productivity. It's no surprise that our school system doesn't improve: It more resembles the communist economy than our own market economy."[6]

Politics, as opposed to voluntary exchange, dominates the current American K–12 landscape, with local government provision of schooling, ZIP code assignment of students, and district governance structures highly susceptible to regulatory capture by strongly motivated special interest groups (primarily employee unions and district contractors).

Elections for school district governing boards tend to be low-turnout affairs, with voting rates often in the single digits. School board elections are also typically nonpartisan in nature, which further tends to minimize the information available to participating voters. The American system is also unusually vulnerable to regulatory capture by organized employee interests, in comparison to most foreign systems, due to the combination of low visibility, low turnout, and powerful incentives for political participation on the part of organized employee and contractor interests.

The Academic Research on Competitive Effects

The research literature on the impacts of choice programs on district academics shows clear academic benefits, all while choice programs use similar or fewer dollars than public schooling. These benefits should be understood in proper context: *limited* choice programs produce *limited* positive competitive effects.

Scholars have analyzed academic outcome data carefully and appropriately in order to isolate statistically significant impacts of choice programs while controlling for multiple other factors in order to establish whether these positive effects exist. Broadly speaking, students in district schools facing higher levels of competition show higher scores than those facing less competition. These competitive effects, within the limits of our current generation of programs, are positive and measurable but not revolutionary.

EdChoice found 26 empirical studies addressing how private school choice programs affect academic outcomes in public schools (Table 7.1). Of those, 24 found choice associated with statistically significant improvements in academic outcomes at public schools. One of the remaining studies found that choice had no visible impact on public schools, and one found a negative and statistically significant impact.[7] Anna Egalite conducted an independent review on competitive effect research studies and again found the evidence consistently positive in favor of choice.[8] A review of the impact of charter school competition on district achievement trends reached a similar conclusion. Finding 11 studies addressing the impact of charter competition, the review notes, "The literature provides some support for the 'healthy competition'

Table 7.1

Impact of choice programs on district student scores

Author(s)	Program	Location	Program type	Year published	Positive finding	Neutral finding	Negative finding
Egalite and Mills	Louisiana Scholarship Program	Louisiana	V	2019	✓		
Figlio and Karbownik	Educational Choice Scholarship Program	Ohio	V	2016	✓		
Gray, Merrifield, and Adzima	CEO Horizon Scholarship Program	San Antonio, TX	PV	2016	✓		
Bowen and Trivitt	Opportunity Scholarship Program	Florida	V	2014			✓
Figlio and Hart	Florida Tax Credit Scholarship Program	Florida	TCS	2014	✓		
Jacob and Dougherty	Choice Scholarship Program	Indiana	V	2014	✓		
Chakrabarti	Opportunity Scholarship Program	Florida	V	2013	✓		
Rouse et al.	Florida Tax Credit Scholarship Program	Florida	TCS	2013	✓		
Carr	Educational Choice Scholarship Program	Ohio	V	2011	✓		
Winters and Greene	John M. McKay Scholarships for Students with Disabilities Program	Florida	V	2011	✓		
Mader	Milwaukee Parental Choice Program	Milwaukee, WI	V	2010	✓		
Greene and Marsh	Milwaukee Parental Choice Program	Milwaukee, WI	V	2009	✓		
Chakrabarti	Milwaukee Parental Choice Program	Milwaukee, WI	V	2008	✓		
Forster	Educational Choice Scholarship Program	Ohio	V	2008	✓		
Forster	Opportunity Scholarship Program	Florida	V	2008	✓		
Carnoy et al.	Milwaukee Parental Choice Program	Milwaukee, WI	V	2007	✓		

(Continued)

Table 7.1

Impact of choice programs on district student scores *(continued)*

Author(s)	Program	Location	Program type	Year published	Positive finding	Neutral finding	Negative finding
Greene and Winters	Opportunity Scholarship Program	Washington, DC	V	2007		✓	
Figlio and Rouse	Opportunity Scholarship Program	Florida	V	2006	✓		
West and Peterson	Opportunity Scholarship Program	Florida	V	2006	✓		
Greene and Winters	Opportunity Scholarship Program	Florida	V	2004	✓		
Greene and Forster	Milwaukee Parental Choice Program	Milwaukee, WI	V	2002	✓		
Greene and Forster	CEO Horizon Scholarship Program	San Antonio, TX	PV	2002	✓		
Hammons	Town Tuitioning Program	Maine	V	2002	✓		
Hammons	Town Tuitioning Program	Vermont	V	2002	✓		
Hoxby	Milwaukee Parental Choice Program	Milwaukee, WI	V	2002	✓		
Greene	Opportunity Scholarship Program	Florida	V	2001	✓		

Note: V = voucher, PV = private voucher, TCS = tax-credit scholarship

Source: "The 123s of School Choice: What the Research Says about Private School Choice Programs in America," EdChoice, 2019, pp. 32–37. Egalite and Mills is updated from the version in "123s of School Choice." The 2019 version is "Competitive Impacts of Means-Tested Vouchers on Public School Performance: Evidence from Louisiana," *Education Finance and Policy*, March 11, 2019.

hypothesis and almost none for the hypothesis that students in district schools are harmed by the growth of charters. Six studies found some evidence of positive effects, four found no effects, and one found negative effects."[9]

An examination of international student-level data from 39 countries found that the share of students attending privately managed institutions had a positive and statistically significant impact on achievement. The study found that students in countries with larger shares of their enrollment in privately managed schools scored significantly higher in both math and science. The study found that "if the share of enrollment in privately managed schools was 10 percentage points higher, students scored 6 points better in math, 5 in science" after controlling for a variety of other factors.[10] A separate analysis of international student test scores in 52 countries found that a 1 percentage point increase in the private share of total primary schooling enrollment would lead to moderate increases in student math, reading, and science achievement within nations after controlling for a variety of factors.[11]

A related analysis of international achievement found that larger private school shares lead to higher levels of achievement in public schools:

> Importantly, much of the positive effect of private school shares accrues to students in public schools, suggesting that the overall effect is not simply due to privately operated schools being more effective, but rather it reflects benefits of competition. Indeed, a key advantage of international evidence is that it makes it possible to examine such general-equilibrium effects of private competition, which will not necessarily arise in situations when new programmes introduce additional school choice only on a small scale.[12]

Arizona, K–12 Opportunity, and the Great Recession

The domestic studies on competitive effects like those summarized above carefully examine school-level data to measure the impact of choice programs. The state of Arizona, however, experienced an unusually strong dose of competitive pressure during the Great Recession.

Between 1990 and 2014, national K–12 enrollment increased by 22 percent. In Arizona, the increase was 74 percent, a fact that left Arizona lawmakers, who were struggling to keep up with enrollment growth, relatively amenable to private school choice options. Lawmakers also passed a statewide open-enrollment law and one of the nation's strongest charter school laws in the 1990s. The Great Recession, meanwhile, stalled district enrollment growth while simultaneously making potential charter school facilities more affordable. The sudden slowdown in enrollment coupled with an increase in competition for students created a natural experiment in competitive effects on a larger scale than previously experienced.

Arizona has the highest percentage of children attending charter schools of any state. Not coincidentally, open-enrollment transfers are very common within and between school districts. Finally, Arizona lawmakers pioneered the use of scholarship tax credits in 1997 and education savings accounts in 2011. In terms of scale, the rank order of choice activity in Arizona is open-enrollment students outnumbering charter students approximately three to one, and charter students outnumbering private choice students by approximately the same ratio. Given the open-enrollment numbers, most parental choice is being done *by* districts rather than *to* districts in the state.

During the Great Recession, Arizona not only experienced relatively large reductions in funding, but the state's student body continued to trend further into majority-minority status, and the percentage of students eligible for a free or reduced-price lunch under federal family income guidelines increased from 45 percent in 2010–2011 to 50 percent for the 2015–2016 school year.[13]

The National Assessment of Educational Progress gave fourth- and eighth-grade mathematics and reading exams to representative samples of students in all 50 states during the Great Recession era. We can calculate a cohort gain for an age cohort of students by comparing their NAEP scores as eighth graders to those as fourth graders four years earlier. For example, the age cohort that were fourth graders in 2009 moved on to become eighth graders in 2013. We calculate the cohort gain by subtracting the 2009 fourth-grade scores from the 2013 eighth-grade scores.[14] We can track two cohorts of students by state through this period—2009 fourth graders to 2013 eighth graders for both math and reading, and then 2011 fourth graders to 2015 eighth graders for both math and reading. Between 2009 and 2013 Arizona students demonstrated the largest overall mathematics gains, and the seventh largest gains in reading between fourth- and eighth-grade. Between 2011 and 2015 Arizona again demonstrated the largest overall mathematics gains, and the third-largest reading gains among the 50 states. Arizona's scores may have been higher still without the cuts, but academic progress proved greater in Arizona than among many states with higher spending and smaller cuts.[15]

For a little deeper historical context, Arizona experienced decades of strong enrollment growth in the decades following the Second World War, usually ranking only behind neighboring Nevada in its growth rate. High rates of net migration and large average family sizes created a continuous need for additional school space.

Financing new school construction is difficult for a state with an unusual age demographic profile owing to the state's dual identity as a retirement destination and a border state. Because of its unusually high concentrations of both elderly and young people, Arizona has a relatively small working-age population to finance education for the young, as well as health care and other services for the elderly. Moreover, the earliest state-level NAEP data demonstrated that Arizona's academic results stood well below national averages. Arizona, in short, faced severe financial strains simply to provide school seats of any sort to a burgeoning student population.

Arizona thus proved to be an enthusiastic adopter of choice programs. Today it has the largest percentage of students attending charter schools, at 16 percent. A 2016 study by the Brookings Institution also found that by a wide margin Arizona had the highest percentage of students with one or more charter schools operating in their ZIP code: 84 percent. Utah ranked second with 69 percent of students having one or more charters operating in their ZIP code; Alaska and Colorado tied for third at 59 percent, with New Mexico and Florida being the only other two states to reach 50 percent or higher.[16] The Brookings measure may underestimate the impact of charters in Arizona, as many ZIP codes in the state have more than one charter school.

In 1997, Arizona lawmakers created assistance for families wishing to send their children to private schools by passing the nation's first tax-credit scholarship law. A subsequent vote of the public in a 2001 initiative, and further actions by the legislature, expanded Arizona's tax-credit scholarship system, including through the creation of separate corporate scholarship credits for students with disabilities and for middle- and low-income public school students.

In 2011, Governor Jan Brewer signed the nation's first education savings account (ESA) program into law. ESA programs—which now also operate in Florida, Mississippi, North Carolina, and Tennessee—create funded accounts with state oversight that allow parents to choose not just among *schools* but also among a variety of education *methods*. Allowable uses for funds include private school tuition, certified tutors and therapists, online education programs, university and college coursework, testing fees, and more. While an important and growing segment of the Arizona education landscape, the total size of the private space is considerably smaller than both open-enrollment and charter schools.

Before the Great Recession, Arizona school district interests would complain about charter schools and private choice, but spending per pupil had been going up, and enrollment had been growing continuously. The state was able to spend hundreds of millions of dollars annually in district construction in an effort to keep up with enrollment growth even with charters and private choice. Effectively, there were more than enough students to go around. Circumstances, however, abruptly and dramatically changed with the recession.

The Great Recession hit Arizona early and hard. The state's general fund revenue dropped 20 percent in 2009. Federal stimulus money and a temporary sales tax increase held K–12 spending reductions at bay for a time, but eventually there were real declines in funding per pupil. Despite a series of increases in funding that accompanied economic recovery, the reduction in spending helped to motivate teachers to strike in 2018.

Arizona went through the mother of all competitive effects during the Great Recession. The foreclosure crisis reduced population growth, and prices for potential charter school facilities declined dramatically. Enrollment growth in school districts came to an abrupt halt, with charters gaining market share. In the end, Arizona students would stand among the nation's leaders in NAEP gains during the 2009–2017 period.

What basically happened was that while funding per pupil decreased, competition for students increased. The decline in property prices created an opportunity for high-demand charter organizations to expand. Statewide charter school enrollment stood at 84,613 in 2006 but had expanded to 185,900 by 2017. Arizona had the highest statewide percentage of students attending charter schools in 2017, at 17 percent.

While the growth in charter schools and private choice in Arizona has been incremental, it has nevertheless triggered a robust choice environment by incentivizing open enrollment. The *inclusivity* of Arizona's choice programs created vigorous open-enrollment practices within and between school districts.

Arizona's choice policies include everyone and have created a virtuous cycle where even suburban districts participate in open enrollment. The Scottsdale Unified School District, for instance, has the capacity for 38,000 students and educates 25,000. Of that number, 4,000 transferred into a Scottsdale Unified school through open enrollment from outside the district. Having 4,000 transfer students would rank Scottsdale Unified as the ninth-largest charter management organization in Arizona, and nearly all of Arizona's 217 school districts participate in open enrollment.

Scottsdale Unified is not required by state law to participate in open enrollment, only to have an open-enrollment policy. That policy could be "Buy or rent property within our attendance boundary or go somewhere else," as is typically the case around the country. An enrollment study conducted by the district, however, revealed that 9,000 kids living within their boundaries were attending charter and private schools with the assistance of private choice programs.

The existence of these options creates a powerful incentive for districts to participate in open enrollment. Scottsdale Unified takes in 4,000 students from outside its boundaries. When Arizona districts instituted open enrollment, the incentive for other districts to follow suit increased.

The availability of open-enrollment seats leads to a crucible for new charter schools in Arizona in which parents quickly shut many down because they have other options. Funding cuts hit Arizona charter schools as well as districts, but both Arizona district and (especially) charter schools flourished academically during this period of relative austerity.

A nationwide list of charter school closures between 2000 and 2013 compiled by the Center for Media and Democracy included 290 Arizona charter schools. Also supplied were the year of each school's closing, enrollment at the school in its final year of operation, and, for

150 Arizona schools, the year the school opened. For those 150 schools, the average length of operation was four years. The average enrollment for all 290 closed schools in the final year of operation was 62 students. By law the state of Arizona grants 15-year charters, but parents have effectively been closing many long before they reach the stage of seeking a renewal.[17] Different forms of choice, in other words, interact with each other, and the availability of open enrollment and private choice has created a robust level of competition for Arizona charter schools, which seem stronger for the experience.

In short, Arizona's academic improvement during an era of austerity represents a productivity increase of the sort that you see in private industry on an ongoing basis. Arizona schools became less expensive and more effective. It is, however, at complete and utter variance with the state's earlier history of ever-growing budgets and enrollment along with relatively stagnant scores. Competition seemed to work well for students and taxpayers in the Grand Canyon State.

Looking to the Future of Competition: ESAs and Microschools

Choice under existing mechanisms improves district performance but does not, of course, ensure that district performance will be either laudable or even adequate. Schooling decisions tend to be sticky for a variety of reasons, and most of the choice programs continue to have the districts as the default. Private choice programs, for instance, tend to require public school attendance before participation can begin in the private choice program. Having districts as the default necessarily lowers the ceiling regarding competitive effects, but more powerful policy interventions may be on the horizon.

Competition produced by choice programs could be made considerably more robust if a state put all subsidies into an ESA program. Such programs are still modest in scope, with all, other than Arizona's, focusing on students with disabilities who have previously attended public school. Arizona lawmakers have also included a number of additional disadvantaged populations.

ESAs provide a far greater level of flexibility to parents than a voucher. Parents use vouchers to choose among schools, whereas ESAs give parents choices not just among schools but also among methods of education. Parents can choose to enroll their children in a school full-time, but they could also hire private tutors and therapists, pay for online education programs, and even purchase individual classes at public schools or community colleges.

Critically, the ESA model also allows parents to save a portion of funds for future higher education expenses, creating the incentive to select among providers based not only upon perceived quality but also cost. Providers thereby face the incentive to provide high-quality services at affordable prices—the opposite of the trend seen in the district system, in which spending has surged and outcomes have largely stagnated.

Small private schools—sometimes referred to as "microschools"—represent another fascinating and growing trend. All 50 states have made homeschooling legal, and the advent of homeschool co-ops made the practice more accessible to a broader group of families. Such co-ops are essentially groups of families who meet and work cooperatively to achieve common goals. Co-ops can be organized around academics, social time, arts, activities, crafts, service work, projects, and other purposes.[18] In recent years the line between a homeschool co-op and a small private school has begun to blur. In the process, many parents have begun to adopt multivendor education of the sort envisioned by ESAs but with their own money.

Wired magazine documented the rising popularity of homeschooling in Silicon Valley in a 2015 article that in part featured the family of a systems engineer dad and a feminist blogger mom who created a network of "hackerspaces" for kids. "The world is changing. It's looking for people who are creative and entrepreneurial, and that's not going to happen in a system that tells kids what to do all day," Samantha Cook, a homeschool mom, told *Wired*. "So how do you do that? Well if the system won't allow it, as the saying goes: If you want something done right, do it yourself."[19]

"The one-room schoolhouse, that symbol of rural American education that dates back to the earliest days of the Colonial era, might be on the verge of making a comeback," *Education Week* wrote in a 2016 profile of the growing trend of microschools, which it defined as "150 students in grades K–12; multiple ages learn together in a single classroom; teachers act more as guides than lecturers; there's a heavy emphasis on digital and project-based learning; and small class sizes, combined with those other factors, make for a highly personalized education."[20] Writing on the microschooling trend, Justin Cohen noted,

> Education futurists have predicted the disintegration of the 19th-century model of American schooling for many years, but the barriers to that transformation have been limited by both the intransigence of the current system and a lack of imagination about what might replace it. Micro-schooling and its teacher-led, entrepreneurial spirit might solve both of these problems, by evading the old habits, sclerotic bureaucracies, cultural biases against experimentation, antiquated labor arrangements, and low tolerance for risk that prevail in traditional schools.[21]

"Doing it yourself" has a great deal of appeal, representing a form of spontaneous order where families do not wait for the cumbersome process of policy change and instead take matters into their own hands. Microschools often are less expensive than traditional private schooling, depending upon the approach, but private tutors and microschools do cost money, which raises the question of inclusion for low-income and disadvantaged students. Some vendors have begun to utilize private choice programs such as scholarship tax credits, vouchers, and ESAs to create intentionally diverse microschools. The blog RedefinED, for instance, profiled a microschool in Florida with 50 students, 16 of whom utilized private choice programs as part of a purposeful effort to include students of various demographics and disabilities.[22]

The opportunity for educators in the microschooling movement may be even more exciting than for families. A 30-year decline in job satisfaction, fewer college students pursuing traditional teacher certification, and the ongoing retirement of the baby boom generation point to a troubled path ahead for the teaching profession. The ability of educators to start their own private enterprise to pursue their own vision of an excellent education free of bureaucracy is enormously attractive. The power to leverage choice programs to ensure that these schools are inclusive and diverse rather than islands of privilege holds an even greater appeal.

Opportunity for Families Is Accountability for Schools

In 2012, *The Economist* reviewed decades of research on the impact of charter schools and concluded,

> In rich countries, this generation of adults is not doing well by its children. They will have to pay off huge public-sector debts. They will be expected to foot colossal bills for their parents' pension and health costs. They will compete for jobs with people from emerging countries, many of whom have better education systems despite their lower incomes. The least this generation can do for its children is to try its best to improve its state schools. Giving them more independence can do that at no extra cost. Let there be more of it.[23]

Geographic monopolies run by government entities, with low amounts of information regarding school board candidates, low voter turnout, and highly organized and active employee interests will rarely provide effective, innovative, and efficient K–12 education services. This form of public education has grown increasingly outdated in a world of quickly increasing complexity and diversity.

Looking at the immediate future indicates that while public education funding is enshrined in state constitutions, the competition for public funds is likely to grow intense. The ongoing retirement of the baby boom generation, the first members of which drew a Social Security check in 2007, will place an increasing strain on state Medicaid budgets and pension systems and will serve as a drag on the rate of economic growth. The next 20 years of public education look far more challenging than the last 50, and it is not difficult to imagine a scenario in which the district system largely retains its flaws but loses a sizeable portion of its funding. Austerity does not guarantee declines in academic performance, but most states lack the policy mix that allowed Arizona to lead the nation in academic gains despite relatively severe fiscal austerity.

State lawmakers should become bolder in granting families choice, and families should be far more willing to exercise self-reliance. The good news is that both of these trends are underway, and the available evidence demonstrates that they are positive not just for those who use them, but for the performance of district schools.

CHAPTER EIGHT

MYTH: SCHOOL CHOICE ONLY HELPS THE RICH GET RICHER

Actually, the least advantaged need choice more than anyone. And they are more likely to exercise it.

Albert A. Cheng

Our post-Enlightenment egalitarian tendencies have probably made us more sensitive to a variety of social gaps. Perhaps more than anything, we are concerned about the growth of income gaps between rich and poor. Talk of achievement, graduation, and opportunity gaps are similarly ubiquitous and motivate almost every discussion about education policy.

We even obsess over gaps in more trivial matters like sports. Consider the criticism that arose when the Golden State Warriors added superstar Kevin Durant in 2016 after having two consecutive extremely successful seasons—a move that prompted a *Forbes* article titled "The Rich Get Richer."[1]

It is probably morally right to be worried about a variety of social gaps, some more than others. And given their salience, it is no surprise that the issue of gaps pops up prominently in discourse about school choice policy.

School choice only makes the rich richer, some people say. In this chapter, I am going to explain why this claim is, ultimately, false. But for now, allow me to point out that there is some truth to this myth, depending on what one means by "school choice."

Because defining terms will be important, I begin the next section by articulating and clarifying what the myth claims. I then explain how some forms of school choice actually do make the rich richer. And this phenomenon is precisely why we need more school choice, understood in a different sense entirely, especially for families from less advantaged backgrounds. Afterward, I bring some empirical evidence to bear, arguing that expanding choice benefits the poor. In the penultimate section, I address some potential rebuttals to my arguments, and I conclude with some thoughts about the ways school choice can promote social equity.

Clarifying the Myth

When critics of school choice say that choice makes the rich richer, they are expressing their concern that policies such as vouchers, tax-credit scholarships, or education savings accounts (ESAs) that provide subsidies to families to use for private school tuition or other educational services worsen social inequality. School choice in this situation more precisely refers to "private school choice."

The argument that private school choice exacerbates income inequality comprises two parts. Critics begin by pointing out that tuition rates at private schools are so high that children from low-income families will still be unable to attend because the subsidies fall short of making those options affordable. Second, and as a result, only the relatively affluent will be able to make use of those subsidies, making them even richer while leaving the poor further behind.

A back-of-the envelope calculation easily illustrates this issue. Consider the Opportunity Scholarship Program, a voucher program in Washington, DC. According to Serving Our Children, the organization that administers the program, the average voucher value for the 2019–2020 school year was $13,534 for high school and $9,022 for middle and elementary school.[2] Suppose a family wants to send a child to Sidwell Friends, the school attended by the children of Presidents Obama, Clinton, Nixon, and Theodore Roosevelt. They would need to come up with another $30,000 to cover the roughly $40,000 in tuition and additional fees.

This scenario has led some commentators to draw conclusions such as in the following 2017 *Huffington Post* opinion piece:

> For the majority of impoverished students attending public schools, vouchers don't help. Parents still have to find more money somewhere to make this happen. Poor folks just can't afford it. But rich folks can so let's reduce their bill!? They thank you for letting them buy another Ferrari with money that should have gone to give poor and middle-class kids get[*sic*] an education.[3]

The author of the piece ultimately called school choice "a scam to make private schools cheaper for rich people," one that is underwritten by corporate billionaires and their ilk.[4]

This argument is not new. Author and educator Jonathan Kozol has been making it since the 1990s:

> A $1,000 voucher, or even a $2,500 voucher, what will that buy a person? Can you buy tuition to Andover or Exeter or any other good prep school for that? Of course not. What can you do with that money? Well, if you're affluent, you could use that money to subsidize Andover tuition. If you're marginal middle class, that might just tip the balance and give you enough to pull off the tuition of a middle-grade private or parochial school. But if you're the poorest of the poor, you can't buy anything with $1,000. It's a sham to pretend to offer something to the poor when you're really offering a means for the middle class to rescue their children from the taint of the poor. The way I've heard it described is "save the best, and warehouse the rest."[5]

Does this two-part reasoning hold water? I'm going to argue that it does not.

How One Form of School Choice Helps the Rich Get Richer

This rich-get-richer scenario is theoretically possible, but empirically it is not characteristic of existing choice programs in the United States, and there are easy fixes to address these concerns. Before discussing that, however, it is worth underscoring how another form of school choice does help the rich get richer. That form of choice is the traditional, residentially assigned public school system.

When pundits debate school choice, they usually mean charters, vouchers, tuition tax-credit scholarships, or ESAs. What they often leave aside is that school choice *already exists*. When children are residentially assigned to schools, families choose schools by choosing where they live. Yet in this choice-by-mortgage arrangement, not everyone gets to exercise school choice. It is only exercised by those with (1) the means to purchase what is usually an expensive home in a high-quality public school's catchment zone, (2) the know-how and connections to navigate a complex network of bureaucrats and municipal authorities to transfer their child to their preferred traditional public school,[6] or (3) the ability to afford private school tuition without any external financial assistance.

Take my hometown of Fremont, California, as a case in point. The city is now a booming suburb in the San Francisco Bay area, and it boasts a handful of extremely high-quality district-run schools. Children will likely be in very good shape if they have the opportunity to attend, for example, Mission San Jose High School and its feeder schools such as Weibel Elementary School or Hopkins Junior High.

Incidentally, I did not attend those schools, nor have I lived in Fremont for many years. Yet Mission San Jose High has not changed much since I was last there. According to the most recent data published by the California Department of Education, 92 percent of its students are Asian, and 6 percent are white. Less than 4 percent of its students are eligible for the free and reduced-price meals, and its students score in the 95th percentile of the ACT and the SAT.[7]

Mission San Jose is a public school run by the Fremont Unified School District, but families who send their children there only have the means to exercise that choice by paying private-school-like tuition in the form of home mortgages in the school's catchment zone. At the time of this writing, the median sale price for a home is listed at about $1.5 million on Trulia.com. Median monthly rent is $3,500.

Nor is there a large-scale intra-district transfer system that enables the poorer residents of other neighborhoods to select schools outside their catchment zone. The only alternative is to pay private school tuition out of pocket, which is still not an option for many families. Under this form of choice, a select group of affluent families benefit, while families from lower socioeconomic backgrounds are excluded.

People are restricted by income when it comes to choosing where to live, and because schools are linked to place of residence it should come as no surprise that segregation by income among schools and among districts has increased over the past two decades.[8] Moreover, families who are able to send their children to high-income schools benefit not only from a high capacity to support their schools financially but also from the social and cultural capital that comes from belonging to those communities. So school choice *does* make the rich richer, but only if we are talking about the ways most families exercise (or are unable to exercise) choice in the traditional public school system.

What is the potential for other kinds of policies, particularly *private* school choice, to empower families to access better opportunities? Are private school choice programs that provide subsidies to lower-income families actually powerless to help them, as the myth claims? And to what extent do the rich benefit at public expense under these alternative policies?

Considering Some Empirical Evidence: Who Participates in Private School Choice?

General Trends in Private School Enrollment

During the fall of 2018, Richard Murnane and his colleagues from Harvard and Stanford released a study at *Education Next* documenting trends in private school enrollment from the past 50 years by household income.[9] The researchers began by pointing out a general decline in enrollment rates in private elementary schools. From its peak rate at 15 percent in 1958, only 9 percent of school-aged children attend private elementary schools today. Enrollment rates at private high schools have similarly declined over the same period, from 10 percent to under 8 percent.

Analyzing the data by household income unveils even more patterns. Enrollment rates at private elementary schools have remained steady for high-income families, hovering between 16 to 18 percent for the past half-century. In contrast, analogous enrollment rates among middle-income families have dropped sharply from 12 percent to 7 percent. Interestingly, the private school enrollment rate among the low-income families has held constant at about 5 percent.

There are a variety of speculative reasons for these trends, including the closure of Catholic schools, increasing tuition, and changes in the quality of traditional public schools. Some commentators have additionally posited that private school enrollment rates among low-income families have held steady while rates among middle-income families have declined because private school choice programs are predominantly available for the poor.

The extent to which school choice programs have sustained private school enrollment rates among the poor is up for debate, but the sustained private school enrollment rate among high-income families is almost certainly not attributable to private school choice programs. That's because these families are simply not eligible to participate in those programs and can afford tuition on their own. A brief survey of choice programs in the United States easily undermines the rich-get-richer myth. Private school choice programs are overwhelmingly used not by the rich, but by those with less. Let's take a closer look.

A Survey of Participants of School Choice Programs

As of 2019, 64 school choice programs have been established in 28 states and Washington, DC, and nearly all are geared toward assisting children from low-income families or with special needs. Almost all have eligibility requirements that generally preclude participation from families who belong to the wealthiest segments of the U.S. population.

As shown in Figure 8.1, only 10 of 64 school choice programs (16 percent of all programs) include provisions for universal eligibility. Six of these 10 programs are individual tax credits and deductions that allow families relief from state income taxes for some educational expenses, such as tuition, tutors, and supplies. The other four programs are tax-credit scholarship programs in Arizona, Georgia, and Montana that do not impose restrictions by student need or income, though the

Figure 8.1

Eligibility requirements for school choice programs

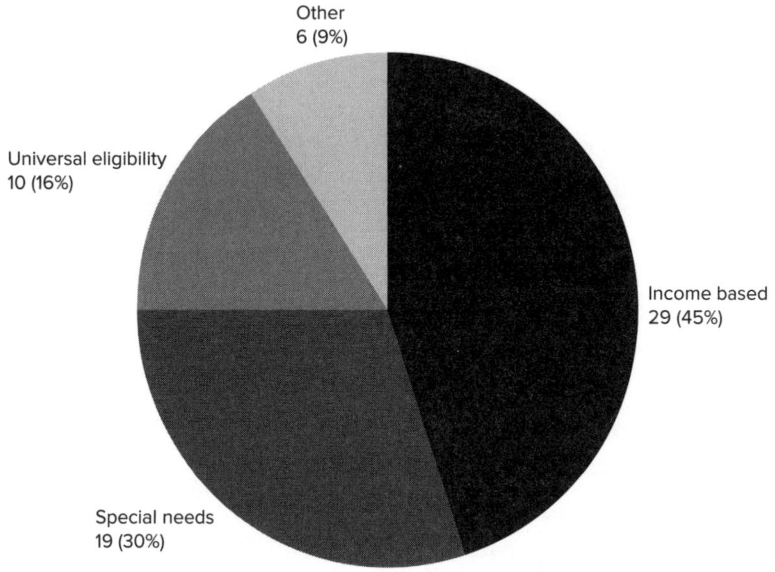

Source: "The ABCs of School Choice," EdChoice, January 16, 2019.

scholarship-granting organizations that steward these funds are charged to prioritize awards based on need. Of the remaining programs, about one-third are restricted to students with special needs, and nearly half are restricted to those who are below an established threshold. This income threshold typically ranges from the federal poverty line—about $26,000 for a family of four in 2018—to three times that. In many of these programs as well as some others, families are only eligible if they currently attend a low-performing public school, a requirement that further excludes most upper-income families.[10]

Whether the income eligibility threshold for programs targeted to lower-income families is set too high is an open question, as is whether there should be income limits for programs designed to support families with special-needs children. But the targeted nature of the vast majority of programs means that the archetypal one-percenter cannot benefit from most of these programs. In other words, claims that school choice subsidizes rich families at the expense of poorer families are simply false.

Are Subsidies Too Small to Be of Practical Value to Poor Families?

Even with programs intended to serve socioeconomically challenged families, critics still charge that private school tuition remains too high even after the subsidies. Never mind that not every private school is as expensive as Exeter or Andover. Although average tuition for nonsectarian elementary private schools was over $23,000 in 2011, rates were much lower for Catholic and non-Catholic religious elementary schools, at about $6,000 and $9,000, respectively.[11] Never mind that many private schools, especially faith-based ones, have an intrinsic social mission to serve the poor and already try to provide financial aid to families who struggle to pay full cost.[12] And never mind that some school choice programs, such as the Louisiana Scholarship Program, sometimes provide families with a subsidy equal to the full cost of tuition. Never mind, too, that policies to increase the value of the typical subsidy to better aid participating families can be proposed; after all, they are well below the typical per pupil allotment that district-run public schools receive from the state. Even with all those things aside, it is rather presumptuous and insulting to assume that families of low socioeconomic background cannot figure out how to find an affordable and suitable private school when provided with some financial aid.

Our questions can partially be answered empirically. The data on this issue suggest that very few families fail to participate in school choice programs because the subsidy is too small to be useful. In a survey of Indiana families, Evan Rhinesmith of St. Louis University and Drew Catt of EdChoice asked parents who did not make use of Indiana's school choice programs why they did not. Nearly 40 percent of parents who sent their children to district-run or charter schools indicated that they were unaware of the programs, and a slightly smaller proportion of parents said that they were happy with the current school their child attends. These were the two most popular reasons for not participating in school choice programs; about one-fifth did not meet eligibility requirements. There were indeed some parents who did not participate because they would remain unable to afford private school tuition even with the subsidy, but critics' concerns about the unaffordability of tuition are overstated. According to the data in Indiana, this issue was relevant for only about one-tenth of parents and was not any higher among low-income parents than any other income group.[13]

In my own survey work of Arizona parents, I found similar numbers. The two most popular reasons for not participating in the ESA or tax-credit scholarship programs were the same as they were in Indiana. Half of the parents were happy with the school their child currently attends, and just over one-third were unaware of these programs. How prevalent was the inability of families to afford private school tuition even after receiving public subsidies? The answer is a mere 4 percent of parents, whether we looked at the entire sample or just low-income parents.[14]

These surveys have some limitations, the most important being that they are not necessarily representative of all parents in their respective states. But until better polling is done, there are no other data to inform this issue. Strictly based on the best available empirical estimates, the concern that school choice programs are too skimpy to put private school tuition within reach for many families appears overstated. In fact, much of the evidence suggests that even among eligible families, the families participating in school choice programs are relatively less socioeconomically advantaged than families who do not participate.[15]

Still, the high cost of tuition for some private schools does preclude some families from benefiting from school choice. These cases will always exist, but they are hardly grounds for resorting to a wholesale rejection of all school choice programs. Let's not let the perfect be the enemy of the good.

Refuting Two Rebuttals

So far, I have made two empirical claims about school choice programs that undermine the claim that school choice makes the rich richer. First, almost all programs in operation today are unavailable to the very rich. Programs usually have income eligibility requirements, are only available to families who have children with special needs, and are restricted to families attending low-performing public schools. Second, the unaffordability of tuition is not a commonly reported reason for why families do not participate in school choice. These two claims run counter to the contention that school choice operates like a regressive tax by which private schools remain inaccessible to the poor but assist the rich in widening socioeconomic gaps. If anything, as other chapters in this volume suggest, the generally positive effects of school choice programs for the poor on student achievement and attainment eliminate a variety of social gaps.

Even if all this is true, critics can still raise two important rebuttals. First, they can aver that although school choice can help the relatively poor, it remains unable to help the very poor. In effect, the poorest among the poor will be left behind even if school choice programs provide some benefit to the less poor. How salient the issue of gaps should be among the poor is an open question, but critics usually take this point as a reason to have no school choice. Essentially, because school choice doesn't help everyone, then no one should have it.

Another rebuttal is that just because school choice programs primarily serve families from relatively lower socioeconomic backgrounds, there is nothing to stop policymakers from expanding them so that an increasing number of wealthier families become eligible. Indeed, some school choice advocacy organizations push for universal school choice programs. In a possible future populated by universal programs, critics worry that their nightmare situation of widening socioeconomic gaps will be realized.

Let's address both assertions.

Even Programs That Have Eligibility Requirements Won't Help the Very Poor

Proponents of school choice programs need to be candid about the possibilities that these programs may be unable to help the very poor. Indeed, some of my own research on New York City's School Choice Scholarships Foundation (SCSF) program suggests as much.

In 1997, SCSF offered scholarships for private school tuition worth up to $2,340 to more than 1,000 families with first- through fifth-grade children who qualified for the federal free lunch program.[16] Lotteries were used to determine which of the 25,000 students who applied for a voucher received one. Because the program targeted low-income families, nearly half of participating families had household incomes of less than $13,000.

Using these lotteries to conduct random-assignment studies, my colleagues and I found that the program improved four-year degree completion rates among African Americans students by 5 percentage points. Given that only 10 percent of African Americans and students from non-immigrant families who applied for but did not receive a voucher earned a four-year degree, this effect is quite large.

However, when we dug further to consider how socioeconomic status interacted with these effects, we found that the benefits of SCSF were concentrated among the moderately poor but not the extremely poor. Among families with household incomes less than $13,000, the offer of a voucher had no discernable effect. It is only among families with incomes greater than $13,000 where we found effects of 6 percentage points.[17] These effects are still meaningfully large, but they raise the question of how effective school choice programs can be for the extremely disadvantaged.

Proponents of school choice may do well to not overpromise what their proposals can accomplish. At the same time, educational programs of all types that deliver significant benefits to the neediest families from the lowest socioeconomic backgrounds remain elusive. The inability of school choice to be a panacea is not reason enough to jettison the idea. Requiring perfection will leave us with nothing, because perfect programs and institutions do not exist.

Still, this logic is constantly invoked as a reason not to support school choice. Between 2009 and 2012, the Obama administration proposed downsizing and eventually ending the school voucher program in Washington, DC. One of the arguments that then–Secretary of Education Arne Duncan offered was that the program only served a fraction of low-income students who lived in the nation's capital. He said, "We remain convinced that our time and resources are best spent on reforming the public school system to benefit *all* students."[18] Basically, if some students cannot benefit from vouchers, then no students should.

There is at least some merit to wanting to benefit more students rather than a select few, but Secretary Duncan effectively told parents who wanted to exit DC public schools to please wait, be patient, and give him more time to fix things. Just how much more time, exactly, was he looking for? It seems unconscionable that policymakers feel they can keep a parent from pursuing a solution now while touting the ever-elusive panacea. Michelle Rhee, former chancellor of DC Public Schools, once likened this reasoning to someone walking to a lake and finding hundreds of children drowning. This person doesn't have much time and has only 10 life jackets, so he concludes, "I can't save every kid with only 10 life jackets, so I'll tell all the kids to hang on while I build a yacht to save them all."[19]

I do not want to malign Secretary Duncan, because I understand that he was constrained by numerous political forces and priorities. Yet the logic of denying choice to everyone simply because it can only help a few seems absurd. Otto von Bismarck famously characterized politics as the "art of the possible." He wanted to convey the wisdom of pragmatism and of not letting a need for ideological purity interfere when deciding the best course of action to take. In efforts to improve educational institutions or, more broadly, to seek the common good, one does not need to always make sure that the most idealistic solution gets implemented. Instead of always going for the home run, perhaps a few base hits and even some sacrifice bunts or flies might be enough to win the game. School choice may be just that for low-income students who need it the most—an imperfect solution, but one that makes them better off.

If We Keep Supporting Choice, It Will Eventually Be Expanded to Include the Rich

Even if choice programs are beneficial to the poor now, they may evolve into something else. Although most programs are currently targeted to less socioeconomically advantaged families, there is nothing to suggest that most programs in the future will not include provisions for universal eligibility. In fact, some advocacy groups often push for universal programs rather than merely means-tested ones. So even if existing programs do not exacerbate socioeconomic inequality, we may eventually live in a future where some do.

Some concern about this possible future is reasonable, and proponents of school choice should at least take this claim seriously and be vigilant. However, concerns about a hypothetical scenario in the future are not a compelling reason to oppose existing programs today or efforts to establish new ones. There are opportunities for course corrections, and there is the possibility that the hypothetical scenario might just never occur. If no risks are taken, however, nothing will happen.

On the other hand, let's entertain the possibility that expanding eligibility may actually be essential to benefiting the socioeconomically disadvantaged. The problem with programs that are targeted for the poor is that they exist largely on political thin ice. Though programs specifically aimed at improving the lot of the poor jibe with our egalitarian and empathetic intuitions, they lack the political constituency that would keep them from getting easily nixed.

If the goal is to provide the poor with something, it would behoove policymakers to provide it to the rich. This is political economy 101. Despite frequent apocalyptic projections of the insolvency of other welfare programs like Social Security or Medicare, politicians are never going to commit political suicide by proposing to eliminate them. Why? Because a wide coalition of voters—rich and poor alike—will revolt at seeing their benefits taken away. In contrast, proposals to cut programs like food stamps and Medicaid are more politically feasible because the poor lack the resources to be as significant a political bloc as the rich, who have the resources to lobby.

Being a political realist can be disheartening, but a dose of realism is necessary to shape the world into a better place. This political reality, in fact, is true in matters of education policy. I lived in Cambridge, Massachusetts, during the fall of 2016 and had the opportunity to cast a vote on Question 2, a measure that, if passed, would have increased the number of charter schools in the state. At the time, several charter schools in urban areas such as Boston, Lawrence, and Chelsea that served students from low socioeconomic backgrounds were poised to expand but could not because of enrollment caps. Waitlists for these charter schools were long and unsurprising given that random-assignment research demonstrates that they annually close about one-third and one-fifth of the achievement gaps in math and English, respectively.[20] These effects are exceptional in educational research. Despite the cogent appeals to pass Question 2 based on the research evidence as well as the principle of equity,[21] the measure was easily defeated by a 2-to-1 margin.

Why did suburban and rural voters cast a vote in favor of traditional public schools instead of charters? The answer is simple. They like their public schools, and they have the political coalition to protect their preferences.

This is not to say that families from low socioeconomic backgrounds cannot be politically mobilized. School choice programs, in fact, increase feelings of self-efficacy among participating families.[22] When the Obama administration terminated the District of Columbia's Opportunity Scholarship Program in 2009, families using the voucher demonstrated. The administration responded by reviving the program and agreeing to fund it for participating students until they graduated. The program now sits more secure because of the legislation introduced in 2011 by Speaker John Boehner (R-OH) and Senator Joe Lieberman (I-CT). Time will tell how long this program will remain politically viable, and one must wonder if it would be more secure if a wider coalition, including wealthier families, had the opportunity to participate in it.

The important point is that there may be a trade-off to consider. Yes, there may be legitimate reasons to worry about whether expanding eligibility for private school choice programs will contribute to rising income inequality. But policymakers may need to entertain this course of action if they want to benefit the poor.

Conclusion

Does school choice make the rich richer? Yes and no. If one is talking about the predominant form of school choice today—choice by mortgage, where students are assigned by place of residence to district-run schools—then the answer is yes. If one is talking about private school choice programs like vouchers, tax-credit scholarships, and ESAs, the answer is no. The reason that the rich are not getting richer from these kinds of school choice programs is that they are primarily only available to lower-income families; even among the eligible population of families, there is little evidence that it is only the relatively advantaged who use these opportunities. Moreover, the contention that the poor do not benefit from these programs because private school tuition remains unaffordable is overstated. This problem is not common among families who participate in school choice programs.

The world without school choice is one in which the rich get richer because they have the financial, social, and political capital to support their own schools instead of the schools poorer families must attend. School choice breaks this institutional arrangement and empowers poorer families to better provide for their children's educational needs.

In the 2018 *Education Next* poll, my colleagues and I found that a plurality of the American public who had an opinion about universal school vouchers or tax credits supported these ideas by large majorities (64 to 36 percent and 69 to 31 percent, respectively). The public is split on vouchers targeted to lower-income families, although support for all three of these programs is higher among blacks and Hispanics than among whites. Support is also higher among low-income families than among higher-income families.[23]

It is quite telling that support for school choice is higher among families from traditionally underserved backgrounds. More advantaged families seem to be behaving self-interestedly at the expense of the poor by not supporting school choice programs. On the other hand, higher support for these programs among families from lower socioeconomic backgrounds likely demonstrates that they recognize the benefit that such programs provide, even if they are no panacea. After all, the research consistently shows higher satisfaction rates among participating families.[24] School choice programs empower families and can act as a social equalizer. Isn't that a good thing?

CHAPTER NINE

MYTH: SCHOOL CHOICE NEEDS REGULATION TO ENSURE ACCESS AND QUALITY

Accountability to parents beats accountability to bureaucrats.

Lindsey M. Burke and Jason Bedrick

The debate over school choice is often portrayed as being between those who support market-based reforms—vouchers, tax-credit scholarships, education savings accounts—and those who oppose them. The reality, however, is much more complicated. School choice supporters are ideologically diverse, including both libertarians, who embrace a free market in education, and equalitarians, who believe that guaranteeing access to a quality education requires substantial government intervention.[1]

Policies might expand choice and competition, so the equalitarian argument goes, but a market in education would not help—and might even hurt—low-income families without certain regulations. "Even if a free market for schooling were efficient, it's hard to argue it would be fair," claims Douglas Harris of Tulane University in New Orleans. "In the average free market, wealthier people get higher quality items while low-income families get the lowest. That might be tolerated when we are talking about buying breakfast cereal at the grocery store—but not when we are talking about schools."[2]

To hedge against perceived inequalities created through systems of choice, equalitarians argue that four specific regulations—at a minimum—are needed to govern school choice programs.

First, the government must intervene to ensure that private schools enroll disadvantaged children. The freedom to choose is meaningless if there are no options from which to choose. As Louisiana Superintendent of Education John White has argued, "Especially among elites, markets alone have proven unlikely to stimulate a systemic interest in serving large numbers of students with disabilities, English language needs, and the direst manifestations of multigenerational poverty."[3] Due to the concern that high-performing schools might exclude disadvantaged children, equalitarians support requiring private schools that accept vouchers (or similar benefits) to adopt open-enrollment policies, often with a lottery in the event of oversubscription.

Second, they argue that even if a child is guaranteed admission to a school, choice is meaningless without the ability to pay for it. Because the monetary value of vouchers and similar benefits is usually significantly less than the level of per pupil funding at government-run schools, the voucher amounts often do not cover the full cost of tuition. Equalitarians therefore support prohibiting private schools that accept vouchers from charging families more than the value of the voucher.[4]

Third, even if a child is guaranteed a fully subsidized seat at a school, choice lacks value if the available options are of low quality. To ensure a minimum of quality, equalitarians generally insist upon private schools obtaining accreditation before receiving students using vouchers.

Finally, because accreditation alone is insufficient to guarantee quality, equalitarians support requiring standardized testing. "To ensure high-quality choices for students and families," argues Harris, "there must also be a mechanism to weed out consistently low-performing schools." The favored mechanism among equalitarians is mandating administration of a single standardized test (rather than allowing schools to choose from a menu of testing options) and, often, tying it to ineligibility for the voucher program if the school's test scores are persistently below a certain level.

The equalitarians' proposed policies are seductive. They seek to harness the benefits of market forces while using targeted regulations to address real issues concerning equity, fairness, and academic quality. As White argues, "Elite institutions tend to set a high bar for admissions and a low bar for measurement when left to their own devices."[5] If the equalitarian policies achieved their desired ends, they would produce an education system that is more equitable and of higher quality than the one we have now.

Unfortunately, good intentions do not necessarily lead to good outcomes. What if these regulations fail to achieve their stated ends? What if they actually have the opposite effects? And can equalitarian ends be achieved without recourse to technocratic equalitarian means?

Case Studies: Florida and Louisiana

To investigate the effectiveness of the equalitarian policies, it is useful to consider the experiences of two states with school choice programs for low-income students that have very different regulatory regimes: Louisiana and Florida.

Louisiana's voucher program has all of the equalitarians' recommended regulations: an open-admissions requirement, price controls, accreditation, and a mandate to administer the state test with consequences tied to performance. By contrast, Florida's tax-credit scholarship program eschews all these regulations, though it does require schools to administer their choice of a number of nationally norm-referenced tests and publicize the results. Holding all else equal, if equalitarians are correct, low-income students in Louisiana should have greater access to higher-quality private schools than low-income students in Florida.

Of course, not all else *is* equal. States differ significantly in their demographics and countless other observable and unobservable factors. Without use of randomized controlled trials, it is difficult to demonstrate conclusively that any given state's policies outperform another state's. But it is unfeasible, legally and constitutionally, to randomly assign one policy to some states and another policy to others.

Still, if a state's school choice program were to achieve widespread access for low-income families to higher-quality schools than their assigned district schools *without* equalitarian regulations, it would demonstrate that those regulations are not *necessary* to achieve equalitarian ends. Likewise, if a school choice program *with* equalitarian regulations provided only limited access to a market in education, and high-quality research found persistently poor results relative to the district school system, then it would demonstrate that those regulations are not *sufficient* to achieve equalitarian ends. That is, in fact, what the respective experiences of Florida and Louisiana show.

The Florida Tax-Credit Scholarship Program

In 2001, Florida became the third state to enact a tax-credit scholarship program. Under the program, corporate donors receive dollar-for-dollar credits for contributions to approved scholarship funding organizations (SFOs).[6] The SFOs provide scholarships to students from low-income families to attend private schools. During the 2017–2018 academic year, 107,095 Florida students received scholarships worth an average of $6,011 to attend 1,801 private schools.[7] That's about 4 percent of the 2.9 million students attending Florida public schools, which spend about $10,000 per pupil annually, on average.[8]

The program does not mandate open-enrollment policies, impose price controls, or require that private schools be accredited to receive scholarship students. The program does mandate that schools administer a standardized test to scholarship students in grades 3–10, but it does not mandate a single test.[9] Instead, schools may choose from among a list of nationally norm-referenced tests.

The scholarships aid some of the most disadvantaged children in the state in terms of income and racial or ethnic background, and as measured by test scores. To be eligible, families can earn up to 260 percent of the federal poverty line ($65,260 annually for a family of four in 2018–2019), with priority given to families earning less than 185 percent of the poverty line ($46,435 for a family of four in 2018–2019).[10] Families earning up to 200 percent of the poverty line ($50,200 for a family of four in 2018–2019) receive full scholarships worth between $6,519 and $7,111 depending on their grade level. Until 2019, families earning more than that received partial scholarships reduced by 12 percent to 50 percent as income increased.[11] According to Step Up for Students, the SFO that provides more than 99 percent of the tax-credit scholarships, the average household income of actual recipients in 2017–2018 was just $25,731, and more than seven in 10 students were Hispanic, black, or multiracial.[12]

According to a series of state-mandated annual reports, scholarship students score lower on standardized exams than eligible nonparticipants *before* entering the program. In their 2016–2017 report, researchers from Florida State University found that "compared to eligible non-participant students, new [tax-credit scholarship] students had poorer test performance both in English Language Arts and math before entering the [scholarship] program and they tended to come from lower-performing public schools."[13] Despite their socioeconomic disadvantages and previous low performance, after entering the program, scholarship students performed at about the national average on standardized tests, outscoring their demographic peers.

The scholarship program also has a positive effect on college enrollment. According to a 2017 Urban Institute study, participation in the scholarship program "increased college enrollment rates by 6 percentage points, or about 15 percent, for students who participated in the [scholarship] program at some point during their education."[14] The positive effects were larger the longer a student participated in the program. Among students who had used scholarships for four or more years, the enrollment rates were as much as 17 percentage points (or about 46 percent) higher than for nonparticipating students.

In summary, Florida's tax-credit scholarship program provides a large number of disadvantaged, low-income students with access to an education that is superior, on average, to that provided by their assigned school. Moreover, it does so without having adopted any of the equalitarians' recommended policies.

The Louisiana Scholarship Program

Enacted in 2008 and expanded in 2012, the Louisiana Scholarship Program (LSP) provides vouchers to low-income families earning up to 250 percent of the federal poverty line ($62,760 for a family of four in 2018–2019) whose children were either switching out of a low-performing public school (rated C, D, or F by the state's accountability system) or a public school in the Recovery School District (an entity established to oversee turnarounds of low-performing schools), or entering kindergarten.[15] During the 2016–2017 academic year, the LSP provided vouchers worth an average of $5,869 to 6,995 students attending 120 private schools.[16] That's about 1 percent of the 725,000 students attending Louisiana public schools, which spend about $12,500 per pupil annually, on average.[17] More than 80 percent of voucher recipients are black, and about 5 percent are Hispanic.[18]

The LSP imposes all of the equalitarian regulations discussed above. To accept LSP students, private schools must be approved by the state board of education, use an open-admissions process, and accept the voucher as the "full payment of all educational costs" (including tuition and all fees, such as for meals, field trips, or before- or after-school care).[19] Private schools must also administer the state test to all scholarship students.[20] Participating private schools may be cut off from scholarship students if their test scores are deemed to be too low.[21]

In January 2016, the LSP shocked the education policy world when two separate teams of researchers conducting randomized controlled trials (RCTs) concluded that the LSP had a large negative effect on the math and reading test scores of students participating in the first two years after its expansion (2012–2013 and 2013–2014).[22] All previous RCTs on school voucher programs had found neutral-to-positive effects on participating students.[23]

The negative effects of the LSP appeared to shrink over time, getting smaller in the second year, and by the third year the differences could no longer confidently be said to exist.[24] However, the null results were at least partially due to some voucher students returning to the district school system, and the most recent assessment again found statistically significant negative results.[25]

The causes of the negative effects are a matter of some dispute.[26] Part of the disparity is almost certainly related to the nature of the tests. Private schools had been accustomed to administering nationally norm-referenced tests, but participating in the LSP required administering the state test. District schools had already aligned their curriculum to the state test, but many private schools had not, creating a district school advantage. (Private schools becoming accustomed to the new test may explain some of the improved performance in the second and third years of the program.) Another factor was that students had to switch out of a public school to be eligible to receive a voucher, and students tend to have temporary performance dips after switching schools, with low-income and minority students experiencing larger negative effects.[27]

Another substantial factor is likely the regulatory environment. During the first two years after the expansion, only about one-third of Louisiana private schools accepted vouchers—a considerably lower rate than in most other states' private school choice programs.[28] According to a study by the American Enterprise Institute, the primary reasons that the leaders of nonparticipating schools opted not to participate were related to regulations.[29] In particular, school leaders were afraid of the effect that open admissions might have on student preparedness for their school's academic rigor, as well as how it would affect their school's "independence, character, or identity." School leaders also expressed concerns about administering the state accountability test and the pressure it would exert to adopt the state's curriculum standards.

These concerns appear to have dissuaded many higher-performing schools from accepting LSP students, rendering participating schools of lower quality, on average. One of the initial LSP studies contained some suggestive evidence of regulation-induced quality reduction.[30] In the decade before the LSP was expanded statewide, the nonparticipating schools experienced modest enrollment growth (about 3 percent, on average). By contrast, over the same period, the participating schools experienced a significant *decline* in enrollment (about 13 percent, on average). In other words, private schools that had been able to attract students before the LSP expansion tended to reject the vouchers, while voucher-accepting schools tended to be those where enrollment had been falling.

In 2017, researchers found even more substantial evidence that equalitarian regulations were partly responsible for higher-performing schools eschewing vouchers. Using Great Schools scores as a proxy for quality, the study found "a consistent negative relationship" between school quality and the likelihood that it would participate in the LSP, though the correlation was not statistically significant, meaning it may have been a function of random chance.[31] However, the study found a significant link between prior enrollment trends and willingness to participate: "A 100 student increase in enrollment was associated with a 28-percent decrease in the likelihood of participation in the LSP."[32]

The best that can be said regarding the LSP's dismal performance is that equalitarian regulations failed to guarantee access to high-quality schools. More realistically, the regulations likely had a deleterious effect, especially when operating in concert.

Equalitarian Regulations: Intent versus Effects

Mandatory Open Admissions

Equalitarians argue that school choice programs should require participating schools to enroll all students who apply (barring capacity issues) in order to ensure that students have broad access to private schools. Otherwise, they argue, it is the schools that are doing the choosing, not disadvantaged families. Open-admissions mandates prevent schools from limiting admissions based on select criteria, such as academic performance, religion, or gender. Public funding, they argue, should flow only to schools that are open to the entire public.

The argument has intuitive appeal, but the ironic effect is to limit the options available to families using vouchers. Open-admissions mandates prevent families from using vouchers at schools with certain missions or that are oriented around voluntary communities. They also discourage participation by schools designed to serve certain types of students, such as the academically gifted or students with special needs. College voucher programs, such as Pell Grants, are publicly funded *without* imposing open-admissions requirements out of recognition that the purpose of the funding is to expand opportunities to enroll in the learning environments that are the right fit for individual students. That requires diverse options.

Private schools are intentional communities often built upon specific belief systems or codes of conduct. Families select into private schools, and unlike with the public system, no children are assigned to a private school that operates under beliefs with which they disagree. Many schools specialize. There are single-sex schools, schools that serve children with specific special needs, religious schools, and schools that teach according to a certain pedagogical style, such as Montessori. Private schools are clear with parents about their mission and the terms of their relationship. In turn, families voluntarily decide whether to enter that relationship. But if private schools must choose between operating according to their beliefs or accepting students using vouchers, families using vouchers cease to have access to a meaningfully diverse set of options.

In the aforementioned American Enterprise Institute survey, three out of four Louisiana private school leaders who opted not to have their school accept voucher students cited concerns about open admissions.[33] Likewise, the first experimental evaluation of the effects of various regulations on anticipated private school participation in voucher programs found that regulations preventing selective admissions significantly reduced the likelihood that private schools would participate in a hypothetical voucher program in Florida. Specifically, requiring open admissions decreased the likelihood that a private school principal would be "certain to participate" by 17 to 21 percentage points, or 70 to 84 percent.[34] A follow-up study of private school principals in New York and California similarly found that open-admissions requirements would reduce the likelihood of private school participation in a hypothetical school voucher program by 19 percentage points, or 60 percent.[35] Although well intentioned, open-admissions requirements can limit the quantity and quality of available options by depressing overall private school participation.

Price Controls

Practically speaking, families cannot access a school they cannot afford. Equalitarians therefore propose prohibiting voucher-accepting schools from charging families more in tuition and fees than the value of the voucher. However, rather than expand access to quality schooling options, such price controls may have the opposite effect.

The problems associated with price controls are well documented.[36] First and foremost, price ceilings disrupt supply and demand, leading to shortages when the price is below the marginal cost to educate a child. Price controls may also impede the ability of market forces to induce systemic improvement. Markets improve quality over time by encouraging the growth of superior firms relative to inferior firms. When prices are allowed to fluctuate with supply and demand, they convey information. Price controls distort that market signal. When schools cannot charge more than the value of the voucher—especially where that value is significantly less than the average cost to educate a child—participating schools lack an incentive to do more than fill empty seats. That may benefit the relatively few students fortunate enough to get access to vouchers, but it impedes both systemic improvement and the ability to achieve scale.

Price ceilings can induce some private schools to eschew accepting vouchers entirely. A recent Cato Institute study of programs in Ohio and Milwaukee, Wisconsin, both of which impose price controls, found that schools with higher tuition were less likely to participate in the voucher programs.[37] In addition, Corey DeAngelis, Lindsey Burke, and Patrick Wolf found that schools with higher tuition "are more likely to be deterred by the regulation that mandates that all schools take the voucher amount as full payment."[38]

It's true that low-income families cannot access schools that they cannot afford, but price controls can have the net effect of reducing options for low-income families by excluding schools that they *could* afford with the assistance of a voucher. A low-income family might not be able to afford $7,000 in tuition but might be able to afford $2,000 with a $5,000 voucher, especially with additional financial assistance from other sources. But if a school does not accept vouchers due to price controls, then the regulation has not achieved its intended purpose of expanding access.

Accreditation

Accreditation is an innocuous-sounding requirement intended to establish a bare-minimum level of quality, and it is often a prerequisite for schools to participate in a choice program. Without accreditation, the theory goes, parents, students, and taxpayers would have little accountability for how education funding is spent, and dollars could flow to low-quality schools. As a result, accreditation requirements permeate

American education policy, both at the K–12 and higher-education levels. And at all levels, accreditation tends to increase bureaucratic compliance burdens and barriers to program entry, rather than to establish and maintain high levels of academic excellence.

Among the 40 states whose departments of education responded to a survey conducted by *Education Next,* 20 required all public schools in the state to be accredited.[39] In some states that do not require schools be accredited, there can nonetheless be an extensive documentation process that can take more than a year to complete.

Such procedures are not confined to public schools. Take the District of Columbia's Opportunity Scholarship Program (DCOSP), the nation's only federally funded and congressionally approved school voucher program. The DCOSP has been in operation since 2004, and Congress has passed several reauthorizations since its inception. The 2017 reauthorization required that each participating school supply a certificate of accreditation to the administering entity *upon program entry,* demonstrating that the school is fully accredited before it is allowed to participate.

Discussions with school leaders who participate in the DC voucher program and with those considering participating make clear the burden such requirements impose. Accreditation, a roughly 18-month process, involves a range of tasks school leaders must complete or comply with, including a self-study, supplying evidence of sound school operations and curriculum, providing faculty qualifications, and more. The process can be overly inputs-based, with approval resting on school structure and facilities, such as having a physical library on the premises.

In conversations with DC school principals, some expressed serious concerns about accreditation minimizing their freedom to set their mission, standards, values-based teachings, and even board composition.[40] Such concerns can dissuade private schools from participating in a choice program, particularly those that are financially stable and contemplating participating in the program as a means of extending their services to low-income students. "The institution already has an established brand, they're already recognized, and parents are flocking to the institution, why go through this for the sake of, you know, a handful of additional students," noted the head of a nonprofit private school organization based in Washington.[41]

State Testing

Accreditation is often a precondition to accept vouchers, but equalitarian reformers argue that the quality of participating schools can only be guaranteed by mandating the state test. Equalitarians stress the importance of mandating a *single* test, rather than allowing schools to choose from a menu of nationally norm-referenced tests, because they believe it is necessary to have an "apples to apples" comparison of school performance. As White writes, "It is hard to argue that fragmenting or complicating academic measurement will aid parents" in understanding a given school's level of quality.[42] Some even go a step further, arguing that persistently low-performing schools should be subject to expulsion from the voucher program, as is the case in Louisiana.

Using a single test as a proxy for school quality, especially with corresponding rewards and punishments, is problematic. First, such test mandates tend to induce homogeneity in curricular offerings, significantly diluting the value of choice. Second, in order to avoid these negative effects, many high-quality schools will refuse to accept vouchers, further limiting the options available to voucher-paying students. Finally, it is not clear that state tests serve as effective proxies for school quality, which can mean excluding schools unnecessarily.

When schools are forced to administer a particular test and are rewarded or punished based on it, they face a strong incentive to teach to the test. That can distort a school's behavior in several ways, including diverting time and resources to tested subjects and away from others. For example, a study by the Center on Education Policy found that, in response to the testing mandates of the No Child Left Behind Act, "approximately 62% of school districts increased the amount of time spent in elementary schools on English language arts and or math, while 44% of districts cut time on science, social studies, art and music, physical education, lunch or recess."[43] The state test requirement can also distort schools' behavior within those subjects, such as inducing them to teach in a particular way that is aligned with the test, and teaching test-taking skills at the expense of real learning.[44]

School leaders who are worried that state testing mandates will drive curricula often eschew program participation as a result. Participating schools typically use a different curriculum from the public system, a feature that can be the very reason parents seek out private education. But in the context of state testing mandates, differentiated curricula can place private schools at a distinct disadvantage. Such requirements place school leaders in a difficult situation: they can either conform their curricula to better align to the state test, replicating a major aspect of the public system that they are intended to be distinct from, or they can decline participation in a school choice program.

It is no wonder that such mandates reduce the likelihood of private schools participating in choice programs. The aforementioned experimental evaluation of the effects of regulations on private school participation in voucher programs found that state standardized-test requirements significantly reduced the likelihood that private schools would participate in a hypothetical program. Specifically, requiring state tests decreased the likelihood that a private school principal would be "certain to participate" by 11 to 14 percentage points, or 46 to 55 percent.[45] In the follow-up study of school leaders in New York and California, the requirement that private schools participate in state standardized testing reduced the likelihood that school leaders were certain to participate in a voucher program by 9 percentage points, or 29 percent.[46] Likewise, in the American Enterprise Institute survey, 68 percent of Louisiana private school leaders who opted not to have their schools accept vouchers cited concerns about the state testing requirement.[47]

Underlying the heavy reliance on test scores is an assumption that they serve as reliable proxies of later life outcomes, such as getting and maintaining a job or enrolling in college. This assumption may not hold, as Jay P. Greene of the University of Arkansas has shown: "If increasing test scores is a good indicator of improving later life outcomes, we should see roughly the same direction and magnitude in changes of scores and later outcomes in most rigorously identified studies. We do not."[48] As Michael McShane, Patrick Wolf, and Colin Hitt recently documented in a meta-analysis of 39 studies on the effects of school choice on educational attainment, there is a weak relationship between student test scores and later life outcomes.[49] Their admonition that "policymakers need to be much more humble in what they believe that test scores tell them about the performance of schools of choice" is well taken. Test scores should not, they argue, "occupy a privileged place over parental demand and satisfaction as short-term measures of school choice success or failure."[50]

Given this, it is encouraging that parents place limited value on how schools perform on state tests, opting instead for a more holistic approach to education. The research literature suggests that parents choose schools for their children based on a variety of factors, such as school culture,[51] academics,[52] school name recognition or reputation,[53] safety,[54] teacher quality and demographics,[55] transportation,[56] parents' values,[57] and the peers who would be attending school alongside their children.[58] Parents tend to list performance on state tests as one of the least important factors they consider when choosing.[59] In the largest-ever survey of parents participating in a school choice program, Florida parents were asked to list the top three factors they considered when selecting a school. Most listed a religious environment/instruction (66 percent) and morals/character/values instruction (52 percent).[60] These were followed by a safe environment (36 percent), academic reputation (34 percent), and small class sizes (31 percent). The least important factor for parents was standardized test scores, which only 4 percent identified as one of their top three factors.

To the extent that parents have a strong preference for schools that inculcate good values and character, their skepticism of standardized tests is justified. A literature review by Corey DeAngelis finds a disconnect between the effects of schooling on test scores and noncognitive skills, such as character, conscientiousness, effort, and tolerance.[61] This should not be surprising. As discussed above, regulatory regimes that place a heavy emphasis on standardized tests create strong incentives for schools to focus on what is tested over what is not. Yet as parents know, some of the most important aspects of a good education are not tested nor easily testable.

The equalitarian impulse to impose a single test is understandable but misguided. Standardized tests are a tool. Like any tool, they are useful for some purposes but not others. Test scores can provide valuable information about student performance, but the benefits of an apples-to-apples comparison are outweighed by the adverse outcomes of the regulation, including the distortionary effects on curriculum and pedagogy and the corresponding decision of higher-quality schools to refrain from participating in the choice program. In contrast, when schools can select from a menu of nationally norm-referenced tests without their participation being conditioned on performance, school leaders need not fear distortionary effects on their curriculum and pedagogy. That translates into higher rates of private school participation and hence more—and more varied—options for families to choose from.

Conclusion

Despite the absence of equalitarian regulations in Florida—or perhaps even because of their absence—more than 100,000 low-income students are using tax-credit scholarships to attend schools where they outperform their demographic peers nationally and graduate from high school and enroll in college at higher rates than their Florida district school peers. Meanwhile, low-income students in equalitarian Louisiana have access only to a small proportion of the state's private schools, and those tend to be lower-performing schools than the district schools to which the students were otherwise assigned.

The different outcomes in Florida and Louisiana do not prove that a free market in education produces superior outcomes to a more heavily regulated market. They do, however, dispel the myth that equalitarian regulations are *necessary* for low-income families to have access to high-quality education providers, or even that they *guarantee* access or quality. Equalitarian regulations are neither necessary nor sufficient to achieve their stated ends, and they may well prove harmful to the pursuit of those ends.

In the absence of strong evidence that equalitarian regulations produce clearly beneficial results, policymakers should wield the regulatory pen with humility. They should refrain from interfering with private school autonomy in ways that limit the ability of families to choose from a diverse selection of learning environments, including via open-admissions mandates and price controls. Likewise, accreditation and test scores should be used to inform parents' choices, not to grant them permission to choose a particular school. Policymakers should direct their efforts toward empowering families with funding that is comparable to what students receive in the public sector, along with information to meaningfully and holistically assess school quality. Ultimately, the greatest form of accountability is schools needing to attract parents who are empowered to choose.

CHAPTER TEN

MYTH: ANY SCHOOL CHOICE IS WELCOME SCHOOL CHOICE

Embracing hamstrung forms of choice could lead to less educational freedom.

John Merrifield

It should be easy to provide additional schooling options in a way that can make some children better off without making anyone worse off, but the political process creates hazards. Restriction-laden school choice expansions can actually reduce choice. Poor policy design can create the basis for false or misleading narratives that poison the well for better-designed policies. That said, even good policy design cannot eliminate all legitimate grounds for controversy. The purpose of this chapter is to describe the trade-offs of different policy options, to explain how good design can address them, and to dismiss bogus grounds for opposition to well-designed reforms.

Perceived Trade-Offs—Some Genuine

Trade-offs may not be entirely avoidable. When they are not, careful description and, if possible, measurement are in order so that potential negatives can be weighed fairly against positives.

Fixed Costs Can Yield Budget Stress

It is widely asserted that a loss of students often does not reduce the cost of running a traditional public school (TPS) sufficiently to offset the loss of state per pupil funding. Basically, school officials say they have less money to cover nearly the same costs. Such budget stress could hurt TPS schoolchildren if the schools' effectiveness depends on funding,[1] which is intuitive but quite often not the case. Inflation-adjusted per pupil funding has tripled since the 1960s,[2] with anything but a proportional result.[3] Theoretically, budget stress based on fixed costs could force curtailment of resource use that would have yielded net benefits to TPS schoolchildren. However, that budget stress would be rare even without defensive steps available to public school system officials, such as adjustment of attendance-area boundaries. For example, suppose several schools lose three students each; that's not enough to leave a teacher vacancy unfilled. But through slight adjustments in the attendance-area boundaries, the enrollment losses can be combined into one attendance area, allowing the district to avoid hiring a teacher. Some of that is necessary to yield a cost savings in districts that are not growing.

The fixed-cost issue is a mostly bogus one for opposition to choice. When students leave a TPS, there is little potential for meaningful cost reduction only if student losses are small, widely dispersed among the TPS, and not offset by student population growth. When there is growth in the school-age population, school choice expansions allow the public school system to reduce teacher hiring and avoid or delay costly new school construction.

The best way to prevent the fixed-cost issue from possibly creating budget stress in nongrowing areas is to propose significant school choice programs likely to attract high levels of participation. It's another reason to avoid school choice expansions that are too small to address the deep, national need for transformation of entire K–12 school systems. When more children move, savings from school closures and the hiring of fewer teachers are more easily realized.

We need decentralized planning to have a major role in determining what is taught and how, where, and to whom it is taught.[4] Consumer choice, free enterprise, and market-determined prices are the key elements of decentralized planning. "Price-less" central planning, the predominant basis, globally, for determining what is taught, how, where, and to whom has not produced a high-performing school system. Little known, and even less well understood, is that the world's best-performing school systems, as defined by Programme for International Student Assessment (PISA) scores,[5] are only 10 to 15 percent better than the terrible U.S. system.[6] Price formation through consumer and entrepreneur choice has been the only successful process for signaling and motivating the best use of resources. Because central plan optimization has *never* produced a high-performing industry, we know it has a very low upside as a way to improve school systems.

Increased Regulation Risk

To genuinely expand choice, policy reform must level the financial playing field between traditional public schools and the alternatives that are eligible to receive the government payments. Unfortunately, dollars collected through taxation often arrive at private schools with strings attached, sometimes a large number. The strings can be so onerous that eligible private schools, which could include privately owned chartered public schools (CPS), become de facto traditional public schools. The effects can go beyond compromising the benefits of choice expansion. The changes that result from private sector schools accepting the legislated funding conditions can make the school system even more uniform[7] and hence less likely to yield innovations or valued instructional approaches not available in traditional public schools. Over the long term that threatens to yield stagnation, and it eliminates schooling options that some families were willing to pay tuition for on top of the taxes that finance the TPS they opted out of.[8]

These are not necessarily sufficient reasons to reject a proposed choice expansion. The newly accessible TPS alternatives are choices, and even after the strings take their toll, parents may believe that the private alternative to the assigned TPS is sufficiently better for their child to make the effort to overcome resistance to change. Gains resulting from such a bounded reform may still top the losses to the existing, self-financed private school attendees. A do-no-harm attitude could therefore eliminate potentially large gains for many to prevent possibly small losses to a few. But it is also possible that regulated school choice could make us worse off, on net, by bringing government control into otherwise autonomous private schools.

It's possible to end up with more *choices* but a lot less educational freedom at the same time.

The key drawback of choice expansion with strings attached is that the debilitating effects of the strings will lead to only modest positive effects. That would feed broad-brush, anti-school choice (and anti-free market) narratives. It's akin to testing proposed medicines at a fraction of the recommended dosage and then concluding they don't work. President Barack Obama argued against school choice expansion by noting that private school choice had not, to date, made drastic improvements in student tests scores, which does accurately describe the findings of studies of the restriction-laden existing U.S. programs, but not the potential for improvement through greatly expanded and string-free choice. Basically, Obama opposed potentially transformative amounts of choice because the tiny amounts available to date had not been transformative.

The right approach to the regulation risk is to craft school choice expansions to minimize that risk. As a means to level the financial playing field between current and potential schooling options, vouchers maximize the increased regulation risk, and nonrefundable tuition tax credits minimize it because courts typically rule that nonrefundable credits are not government funds, whereas vouchers clearly are, and tax-credit-motivated funders choose whether or not to donate.[9] Given the many potential education savings account (ESA) uses—private school tuition, tutoring, therapies, and so on—government hard-funded ESA deposits are hard to regulate.

ESAs may be the best option for expanding choice with minimal strings. Vouchers tend to be heavily regulated, and without a credit bankability feature, nonrefundable tax credits would be only a tiny fraction of tuition costs for most families. The direct personal tax liability of parents when their children are in school is only a small fraction of their tax liability, including school taxes, which they pay all of their adult lives. Bankability would allow families to bank credits for recovery, if necessary, long after their children are past school age; for example, to pay off a loan taken out to pay private school tuition. So without bankability of nonrefundable credits, the greater ability to level the playing field that we get with ESAs as the school choice expansion vehicle may be worth their slightly greater regulation risk versus nonrefundable tax credits.

The Toxic Mix Risk

I'm following the most widely cited real risk with *perhaps* the least cited, despite the significant scope of the risk. The common denominators of chartered public school legislation have created a toxic combination of a potential for private gain, a shortage-creating price control, and terribly low-performing TPSs. Because of the ban on tuition—tuition price control at zero—a lot of CPSs have a significant shortage of seats. Persistent shortages virtually eliminate producer accountability to their clients. When unhappy customers are readily replaced from waitlists, and the alternatives to a CPS seat are awful, quality suffers because it allows cost reduction without loss of revenue. The potential to reduce expenses with little or no revenue loss creates a significant temptation even for nonprofit charters, which can shift cost reductions into higher staff pay or benefits, or greater fees for management companies. Combining the potential for profit with near-zero accountability to parents creates a powerful magnet for scoundrels and charlatans, and a temptation for the once pure. And there's probably much more negative effect on quality than what rises to the level of an alleged scandal. When a school does not have to provide good service or pursue innovation to stay full, there is also the potential for parents to sour on school choice entirely.

Long waitlists buffer CPS operators from the normal negative effects of reducing the quality of their product. Accountability to customers is not restored until a waitlist falls to near zero. The term "toxic mix" is appropriate because children suffer, and the quality erosion may be seen by many people as scandalous, although all of what might eventually deserve the label scandalous is not readily apparent to parents.[10] So complaints may be well known, even clearly scandalous, but terrible TPS alternatives moderate flight from scandal-beset CPS options. Perceived scandal, being politically potent,[11] could unfairly endanger the school-choice movement. That could be true even though chartering, because of widespread long waitlists, is much more a matter of chance (via lottery) than the most common form of school choice that it is widely perceived to be. Persistent, clearly scandalous conditions at nearby TPSs (due to weak/perverse incentives and the standard reasons for central planning failure) are less significant, politically, because these schools are part of an entrenched status quo and because TPS operators cannot gain personally from deliberately cutting quality to lower costs.

As an aside, note that loss of TPS market share is the most cited risk, but it does not pose any risk to schoolchildren. Our state governments have been acting like it's a real risk, doing backflips and spending billions to continue using a process—an evolved, implicit business plan for deciding what should be taught, where, how, and to whom—with a terrible track record. We have every reason to believe that our "nation at risk" low-performing school system is a predictable outcome of the political process,[12] and that the system and political process, not the people employed to run it, are responsible for that dismal track record.

Few people, if any, have clearly identified the toxic combination of profit potential, shortage, and awful TPSs as likely responsible for many of the alleged scandals threatening the charter movement specifically and school choice expansion in general. Indeed, many CPS proponents appreciate the shortages/waitlists for being obvious evidence of unmet demand. They don't recognize that it's very costly evidence. As noted above, scandals can become an existential threat to CPSs and the school choice movement. A Google search of "charter school, scandal" yielded nearly 5.4 million hits, which furnished a long list of links to stories about CPS-related, allegedly scandalous behavior.[13] Those alleged scandals need to be investigated thoroughly before they become the basis of a devastating anti-choice talking point.

Engaged, empowered parents are in a much better position than charter authorizers to detect and penalize quality reduction. The way to empower them is with price decontrol, alongside low barriers to new CPS formation. That, plus profit potential, is a virtuous mix, because then school operators become motivated to innovate, enhance quality cost-effectively, and invest where new or better schooling options are in greatest demand. Price decontrol would mean letting market forces set CPS tuition levels. When the demand for CPS slots exceeds the supply available with public and donor funding, then that CPS can levy a tuition copayment, payable by families or third-party copayment assistance sources, and still fill the school. A copayment level that yields profit attracts competition, which brings the copayment amount down to the level needed by efficient CPS operators to earn a normal rate of return on their investments. That level may be zero. A tuition price of zero that results from competition does not yield the quality erosion, and potential scandal, that results from mandating zero tuition.

The potential to achieve increased school funding by elevating quality, or through innovative instructional approaches, to allow charging a market-determined tuition copayment has the added benefit of eliminating CPS dependence on donor funding, which we can clearly see has not been nearly sufficient for CPS supply to meet CPS demand at the shortage-creating price point of zero. The donor money can do much more good by indirectly helping charters through copayment assistance for low-income families. However, since charters are public-private hybrids, it may be that such price-signal-driven transformation may be politically infeasible. If that proves to be the case, we'll have to achieve school choice expansion, and school system reform, through private school choice.

The price decontrol challenge represents another case where potential gain creates potential loss. Price decontrol means that some charters will no longer be free, which will clash with every state's law that says that for equity/access reasons, schooling needs to be free. Even though the existence of free schooling is a costly illusion,[14] the political demand for zero tuition means that price decontrol creates a major equity issue.

To grasp that the *equity* problem is smaller than widely perceived, we need to ask who might be made worse off by allowing charters (or any school) to charge a market-determined copayment. Only the waitlisted charters, and others that cannot fund their instructional approaches without a copayment, are likely to sustain, against competition, a nontrivial tuition copayment. The children made worse off by price decontrol would be those who failed to secure donor-funded copayment assistance that would have otherwise won a lottery to get into a CPS able to fund their instructional approach, at the same quality level, without the ability to levy a copayment. My reaction is that even without the donor-funded copayment assistance, price decontrol would not harm very many children. There is a huge upside to taking the actual, much-smaller-than-assumed risk that the copayment would force some children to accept an assigned TPS. Price decontrol would yield a huge increase in CPS availability and eliminate the conditions primed for scandal that pose an existential threat to school choice expansion of any kind.

The Increased Stratification Risk

There is room for plenty of confusion here. Even with the element of choice, some school choice expansion opponents exhibit a near knee-jerk reaction in the form of an oft-expressed fear of more segregation. Confusion may arise by implying that choice can yield forced sorting. Additional confusion may arise from the fact that it would be hard to create more stratification than we have in the current assigned public school system—decades of formal, court-ordered integration efforts notwithstanding. Widespread rejection of busing to address the stratification by socioeconomic status rampant in the current system led to some school choice expansion—especially magnet schools—as the policy choice for ameliorating the kind of stratification many people believe will result from school choice expansion. Confusing, indeed.

School choice expansion can increase stratification where there is room to increase it and when available choices are very similar. That is, if the schools are uniform in terms of what they teach, student body composition can be a proxy for income, which can be a proxy for school quality. Public school choice might create that situation. Because the appearance of fairness is a political imperative, and because every TPS must appear ready to educate all but the most severe special-needs children, every TPS must aim to do the same things. Traditional public schools differ somewhat in how well they do that, though the perception of the degree of difference is much greater than the actual differences.[15] The vast majority of school effectiveness studies find that a student body's socioeconomic factors explain all or nearly all of the differences in student outcomes.[16] Many find it stunning that these studies basically say that schools are equally bad,[17] but that result is perfectly consistent with the track record of central planning approaches across every industry, and such approaches dominate school system funding and governance globally.[18] The mixed findings of studies aiming to measure the school choice–stratification connection support my contention that the devil, and God, are in the details.

Choice expansion that includes and creates choices with significant differences might yield destratification, with families from different racial or class backgrounds coming together because some in each group want Montessori education and others STEM-focused or arts-based education. In contrast, expanding choice to include only schools with similar personnel and pedagogies could worsen stratification by rendering "effectiveness" at delivering a uniform instructional approach the only seemingly substantive grounds on which families could choose. When there is widespread agreement on which schools are the best—when they only differ in terms of how well they do the same things—higher income families will secure slots in the best schools, and it can appear that class or race were the grounds for making school choices.[19]

Policies that increase stratification can poison the well for all school-choice expansion proposals. If that risk is significant, it is yet another reason to avoid the restriction-laden policies that would only create movement among existing choices. That would include public school choice and charter laws that preclude significant TPS-CPS differences.

The Risk of Relying on Incrementalism

The issue here is whether it is worth supporting small programs. It may be logistically possible to rescue some children from adverse circumstances long before it is politically possible to provide meaningful choice beyond TPSs to most families. Yet highly limited choice will have highly limited effects and will not approach price system–orchestrated decentralized planning outcomes. Accepting what is politically possible now may not pave the way politically for the large-scale, transformational school choice expansions we need. Nonetheless, many school choice proponents have felt the need to defend all school-choice extensions and to characterize many weak ones as experiments akin to full-scale choice.

No private choice programs have progressed substantively beyond their original design. They have not been progressively re-enacted with fewer restrictions. Consider Milwaukee, the oldest of the modern voucher programs. Despite the significant 1998 expansion from its tiny 1990 beginning, Milwaukee's vouchers are still worth much less than TPS per pupil funding, copayment is mostly forbidden (a debilitating price control at the voucher amount),[20] and private schools are suffering increased regulation. Arizona's ESA expansion, passed by the legislature in 2017, might have been an exception, but that expansion did not survive a repeal referendum. Even though the expanded ESA would have fallen far short of the proper universal, near-nondiscrimination standard that would have enabled those exercising school choice to enjoy about the same level of public funding as the children enrolled in a TPS, it still might have prompted significant changes in Arizona's menu of schooling options.

Because of the widespread tendency to assert that all school-choice expansions are important experiments—even those that help just a few thousand kids—enactment of restriction-laden programs can jeopardize eventual transformational school system change that would help millions. Of course, improving the lives of "just" thousands is a laudatory lifetime accomplishment. What we need is to find ways to do that without getting stuck far short of the universal nondiscrimination standard and of having the predictably small effects of small programs poison the well for programs that would produce urgently needed transformational change.

The Means-Testing Risk

In addition to the thousands-now-versus-millions-eventually risk, proposing choice expansion limited to the children of the relatively poor reinforces the widely held misimpression that all is well for higher-income people. For one thing, some wealthier people live in low-income areas. For example, in an area of Memphis that had a median family income of only 40 percent of the metro area median in 2016, 5 percent of the families still had annual incomes over $75,000. The difference between that 5 percent in part of the Memphis metro area and the state average of about 29 percent over $75,000 shows that when higher-income families are assigned to the metro area's lowest-performing schools, many of them leave and further concentrate poverty and its terrible symptoms.[21] We could reduce the incentive to leave low-income areas by expanding choice for all residents of low-income areas. In other words, if there is irresistible political pressure for means-testing, we should limit choice expansion to low-income *places*, not low-income *people*. Universal availability of tuition vouchers to residents of San Antonio's low-income Edgewood School District spurred in-migration to gain discounted access to private schools.[22] It happened because even way above an annual family income of $75,000, a nearly $5,000 per pupil annual discount is still a big deal, and even in higher-income areas all is not well with the public schools. Incentives matter to educators and parents, as do monopolies. Grounding school system governance and funding practices on the heroic assumption that they do not matter undermines the schooling of all children.[23]

Though targeting poor places may be the only currently feasible route to development and school system improvement, it has to be recognized that greater family affluence and better school funding do not make the centrally planned instructional practices fit all of the children assigned to them. Indeed, the highly sought-after TPSs are often not as good as a lot of people think. All is not well in the suburbs any more than all is perfect in the world's top-scoring school systems. Some outstanding school outliers notwithstanding, our better schools are often still not good.[24] Enacting school choice policies that imply that our better schools are at least okay will prevent much-needed system-wide improvements.

Limiting the expansion of choice to lower-income families also reduces the potential benefits of choice, and measured gains, that are politically important. Excluding the purchasing power of higher-income families from discounted use of private schools greatly curbs competition, as well as the potential to sustain new schooling options that are expensive until experience and development of key inputs bring down costs.

A Not-So-Gold Standard

A likely reason that school choice programs have small, though mostly positive, measured effects is random assignment research, the so-called Gold Standard for assessing effects.[25] Yet random assignment to treatment or control conditions makes much more sense for assessing new drugs and medical procedures than for assessing impacts of school choice programs. The group not given a medicine being tested is much less likely to be affected by the treatment given to the experimental group than are the TPS stayers who are compared to the students who use private school choice programs. Because school choice competition benefits the control group, an evaluation of a school choice program is more like studying a vaccine for a highly contagious disease than an allergy medicine. Since the effectiveness of any treatment administered to a broadly and deeply bad school system depends on the treatment's ability to measurably improve the aggregate outcomes of the whole system, properly defined as all schools, public and private, we should be comparing school *systems* with and without the treatment. Instead, we have been comparing students who chose other schools to similar students who opted to stay in their assigned TPS, which is a valid comparison only if the school choice treatment does not affect the stayers. So, the comparison is worse than invalid for the school choice programs that positively impact the stayers, as we must hope they do, and as research indicates.[26] The more stayers benefit from school choice expansions, the more effective the program is, but because the typical measure of school choice program effectiveness is the difference between stayers' and leavers' performance, the less effective the program will appear to be. The high propensity of typical assessment practices to yield wrong and misleading findings means beware of assessments of programs that can improve TPS performance.

The high propensity to use random-assignment studies for any program where large, system-wide effects are not obvious is another source of false-narrative risk, making school choice appear less helpful than it actually is. And it is another reason to prefer school choice expansions likely to produce large effects. Had the Edgewood voucher users taken the same standardized tests as the Edgewood TPS stayers, there would probably have been a misleading gold standard study. Why misleading? Because despite any evidence of a planned district response to the loss of the voucher applicants, the outcomes of Edgewood's TPSs improved while vouchers were available. Maybe the district's improvement during the time vouchers were available was just a coincidence, but if it did not find a coincidence, a gold standard study conducted on Edgewood would have asserted much smaller voucher user gains than actually occurred.

Summary and Ways to Move Forward

Increased uniformity through regulation of participating private schools is a significant risk, but the greatest risk lies in creating and feeding the false narratives of school choice failure or irrelevance. Both risks are increased by enacting what Milton Friedman called charity vouchers, and otherwise narrowly targeted paths to choice expansion, and by enacting policies such as pricelessness that favor some schools over others and that create profit out of weak accountability to customers. Some policy combinations can yield the potential to connect "choice" and perceived scandal, which can have a high political cost. Vice President Al Gore famously asserted that scandal is much more consequential, politically, than routine failure. "Scandals are front-page news, while *routine failure* is ignored," he said.[27] Meanwhile, policies that only slightly erode the public funding advantages of traditional public schools, and narrowly targeted programs more generally, risk falling victim to President Obama's argument that choice just does not matter much. Overcoming inertia, reinforced by an electorate that is overextended and utterly underinformed about education policy, is formidable enough without policies that foster deliberate misinformation, confusion, and scandal.

Since the school choice movement is not monolithic, we cannot force a unified response to risky policy changes. Since inertia and poorly informed voters may preclude the needed transformational school system change, it may be wise to accept some of the risks described above with the aim of helping as many children as possible when such opportunities arise. The challenge is to properly characterize both new policies' potential to change school systems for the better as well as the risks they create, especially the risk of scandal. For the CPS-related scandal risk, "inoculation" studies are in order. For example, a study carefully documenting the dysfunctional-market basis for alleged CPS scandals is long overdue.

We need a high-quality school choice scorecard that skillfully condenses the vast majority of significant risk factors into a single number or two for specific school choice expansion proposals and for entire school systems, to include all of the schools, public and private, that are subject to the same governance and funding policies. The United States has 51 school systems—50 states plus the District of Columbia—and even more if territories are included in the count. For scoring school systems, the Cato Institute Education Market Index or the Education Freedom Index may suffice, or at least serve as good starting points for an appropriate index.[28] A scorecard focused on specific policies and proposals could build upon some existing indices and grading rubrics. For example, the Center for Education Reform's A–F scorecard for state laws pertaining to CPSs is a good starting point for charter school policies.[29] Preferable, though, would be a 0–100 scale, because the more limited A–F scale would assign a lot of F's to programs that, despite severe shortcomings, including political risks and other negative effects, still yield net benefits to schoolchildren.

A key benefit of a scorecard that accurately rates and contextualizes school choice expansions would be to prevent some existing indices and grading schemes from being a source of misinformation. For example, the Grover Whitehurst and Ellie Klein Education Choice and Competition Index is not nearly as comprehensive as its title implies.[30] Still, it has a lot of useful information about the largest U.S. school districts and could be quite helpful for assessing choice expansion within the public school system.

We especially need a scorecard that prevents relatively small changes from being seen as huge. For example, the Whitehurst-Klein index assigns "A" grades to places that provide only choice among public schools.

And its scoring rubric does not recognize that the competition process, including market entry/exit choices, is typically driven by price change and opportunity for profit. Genuinely competitive settings can include nonprofits but cannot exclude for-profit service providers. For example, the New Orleans system does not allow for-profit providers or market-driven price formation, but it still got the highest possible Whitehurst-Klein score. New Orleans is a far cry from a system that would level the playing field between public and private schools and thus maximize the potential for transformational change.

An example of potential for rivalry, without genuine competition, is the magnet schools that are in some Whitehurst-Klein scoring rubrics. The district officials directly involved with magnet schools, which are specialized district schools, have nothing tangible directly at stake in the enrollment level of the magnet schools, or in the schools' effectiveness at executing their specialized missions. They will not be forced to exit the district if the magnet schools do not meet expectations, and they will not share profits if they create a popular, cost-effective school. Likewise, the district officials who authorize such schools will not suffer for picking specialty areas that are less popular, or more costly, than the other specialty areas they might have chosen. Those are things the price system would reward or punish.

Other noteworthy Whitehurst-Klein blind spots are the definition of "availability" and the assumption that the presence of other schools necessarily yields competition. To Whitehurst-Klein, "present" equals "available," which is, sadly, not nearly true of magnet schools, or for choice among traditional public schools, or for charters. Public school choice can exist officially, but usually it does so with little choice in practice. Schools that must aim to serve all children cannot differ greatly, and school leaders typically have little or no reason to behave competitively. With just choice from the district's uniformly comprehensive schools, nearly all families will likely agree on which schools are the best choices, so the probability of gaining an open seat in a preferred school is very low—that is, there will be little availability. In contrast, with the menu of specialized schooling options that would very likely exist with low entry barriers for less uniform schools, price formation, and change to reward innovation and guide resources to their most valuable uses, the diversity of children would cause families to differ on which schools are the best choices for their children. They would then naturally move toward different specialized schools of choice.

The Center for Education Reform's charter law scorecard also needs some competition from a scorecard that considers more of the elements of school choice policies that supply genuine competition. The scorecard is pretty good at assessing how charters actually differ, but it overlooks whether for-profit charters are allowed. Proper contextualization would also require consideration of significant charter law similarities such as price controls (tuition copayment not allowed) and nonselective admissions. Consistent with the toxic combination discussion above, allowing for-profit chartered public schools should reduce the school choice score if not accompanied by an ability to charge prices, but profit potential should increase the school choice score in the presence of copayments and low barriers to CPS formation.

We need to make every reasonable effort to optimize school choice as a school system reform strategy, and a big part of that is fostering realistic expectations for current and potential school choice expansions. We need to do that because not every school choice policy is necessarily a good one, and many of them are anything but riskless. Such risks include major political risk to the feasibility of productive school system reform.

Chartering, which is only barely school choice, is the basis for the greatest risks. It creates alleged scandal and eliminates some private schooling options.[31] But it is entrenched, and through price decontrol it would yield the much-needed decentralized planning of what is taught, and where, how, and to whom. There is no point to saying not to do chartering in its current, price-controlled form. We have to inoculate school system reform against its considerable risks and assertively explore the opportunities presented by the chartering starting point.

Small, narrowly targeted private school choice expansions can qualify as too risky when they impose a lot of restrictions and when many private schools accept them. That is, the risk is especially noteworthy when the restrictions are terrible but not terrible enough to cause many existing and potential private schools to avoid joining the expansion.

So we especially need to identify actual and potential restrictions that might act as a wolf in sheep's clothing. Until we've done that, we won't know all of what is dangerous enough to merit opposition.

Open enrollment among TPSs can also qualify as too risky. It delivers choice among schools that differ only in how they define and produce comprehensive learning sites that must strive to do all the same things for everyone in order to satisfy the appearance of the fairness imperative. As with some popular charter schools, those schools offering the best versions of comprehensive schooling will quickly fill up, converting minimal choice into a de facto lottery system at the best district-run schools. And we'll achieve some choice-based movement within the system only if the principals and superintendents do not band together and agree to not take each other's kids. While this arrangement creates some perception, politically, that there is meaningful choice, in reality there is virtually none.

That said, it is very difficult to cite political risks as enough justification to oppose something that would immediately deliver some children from possibly awful circumstances. Lost time cannot be recovered. Some damage is permanent. But because the political risks are large and very real, it is up to us to prioritize efforts to minimize them. This is why I argue that at least one prominent organization needs to create an effective risk identification and reduction program.

CHAPTER ELEVEN

MYTH: STUDENTS WITH SPECIAL NEEDS LOSE WITH SCHOOL CHOICE

The power to choose beats the promises of politicians.

Inez Feltscher Stepman

It might seem axiomatic that students with special needs are among those who most need individualized attention. But the public school system, despite federal guarantees enforced by the bureaucratic might of education officials at all levels of government, has often failed to provide students with the customized services they need to succeed. Federal statutes theoretically guarantee students with disabilities access to free and appropriate public education, yet thousands of families still find themselves fighting the system tooth and nail to get their children the education they deserve.

Our generally one-size-fits-all education system often doesn't really fit anyone particularly well, but it is an especially poor setup for those students who vary the most in terms of the services, environment, teaching styles, and curriculum that will help them reach their full potential. This mismatch is more than a superficial problem that can be fixed with additional regulation, court decisions, and oversight. Instead, it's a deep misalignment between a class of students who are in desperate need of flexibility, multiple options, and personal evaluation, and a system that is set up to provide none of those things.

In contrast, a system of educational freedom, one that provides choices to parents, who know the learning needs of their children best, is a much better fit for students with special needs. That's why instead of continuing to fight bruising uphill legal battles to enforce the federal government's parchment guarantees, many parents are turning to education choice options in the states. Through programs such as vouchers, tax-credit scholarships, or education savings accounts (ESAs)—the last of which is particularly well suited to the diverse learning requirements of children with special needs—parents can ensure that their children get the best educational experiences possible.

Family Profile: Kate and John McCustion (Mississippi)

Kate and John McCustion are the parents of a child with dyslexia in Mississippi, a state with an ESA program specifically for students with dyslexia. When the McCustions' experiences with their child's individualized education program (IEP) meetings—and the services the public school could provide—failed to improve outcomes for their son, they decided to seek solutions outside the public system, a system where they believed incentives were fundamentally misaligned. As they write:

> The lack of training and lack of knowledge [our son's] teachers and school as a whole have in how to teach a dyslexic child is of no fault of their own. Which is precisely why a choice for us as his parents needs to be made available. We love his school and his teachers; I know they want him to succeed, but they are ill-equipped to provide him the instruction he needs. We are faced now with possible litigation in fighting for our district to provide for our child. Without an educational choice program, that is our only course of action.
>
> We have sat through numerous Individualized Education Plan (IEP) meetings and nothing has changed in terms of outcomes for our child. The latest tests performed by the school shows he is more than 1,000 points below proficient, and he has been that way within their Special Education Department for the last three years. In meetings with our administration, I have been left not just feeling, but knowing, that his success does not benefit them financially; therefore, it is okay for him to continue to slip through the cracks. That is not okay for any child, and certainly not mine.[1]

Special Needs and the Public System

It seems that every week brings another heartbreaking story about a child whose special needs were not met—to say the least—by the public school system. In October 2018, the *New Yorker* published an investigation into the treatment of Seth Murrell in Donalsonville, Georgia.[2] Seth, who has various developmental delays and has been diagnosed with autism, was placed into a special education program known as the Georgia Network for Educational and Therapeutic Support, in a school named Pathways, where his teachers were rarely equipped or experienced in dealing with his special needs. But things got worse.

In what was the latest of a string of violent incidents in the school over the years, six-year-old Seth was beaten by his teacher for trying to take off his shoes repeatedly, something many autistic children do because they find them uncomfortable. The whole experience was caught on camera, and the teacher went to jail for simple battery.[3]

There are supposed to be federal laws in place to protect students like Seth.

The Individuals with Disabilities Education Act (IDEA), initially authorized in 1975 as the Education for All Handicapped Children Act, promises all students a "free and appropriate public education" in the "least restrictive environment," as defined by courts, not families. To carry out the act's promises, a team of professionals from the district and parents are supposed to meet annually to hammer out a student's IEP, which is supposed to include assessment, accommodations, and any special services offered, as well as placement in appropriate programs, classes, and even schools.[4] Parents are supposed to be equal partners with districts in creating their children's IEPs, although many feel that their input is undervalued and that districts are more interested in checking boxes than creating a plan that really works for each student. And access to special education and an IEP are themselves contested matters, with parents' wishes often falling by the wayside whether they want their child to be officially classified with an IEP or not. Another law, Section 504 of the 1973 Rehabilitation Act, affords some federal guarantees to some students who do not quite fall into the restrictive classifications necessary for an IEP.

If this all sounds bureaucratic and difficult to navigate and enforce, that's because it is. Many parents of children with special needs have struggled to get the public schools to turn the IDEA's nice words into tangible gains for their kids. In March 2017, the Supreme Court ruled that IDEA's guarantees meant that school districts were on the hook for more than de minimis educational benefits. Chief Justice John Roberts wrote in the *Endrew F. v. Douglas County School District* majority opinion, "When all is said and done, a student offered an educational program providing 'merely more than de minimis' progress from year to year can hardly be said to have been offered an education at all."[5]

While special-needs advocates cheered the decision, little has changed in the contentious world of IDEA lawsuits against districts that fail to live up to the law's lofty rights claims. In fact, an *Education Week* investigative piece found that "school districts are not losing cases because of the *Endrew F.* standard," and that most of the cases citing the new *Endrew* standard still ended with victories for school districts.[6] Perhaps that is why one writer in *The Atlantic* characterized attending her child's IEP meeting as "hell,"[7] and the popular blog Scary Mommy has a list of "don'ts" for new IEP parents, which includes a warning not to go into that first meeting with the "horror stories" they've heard and read.[8]

Arguably, IDEA was always a flimsy guarantee that substituted bureaucratic oversight for the real accountability provided by parents and families. The intimate knowledge families have about their children's special needs is even more important in a context where traditional assessments, such as standardized testing, provide even less information than usual about how well a child is doing.

If IDEA was ever a useful framework for ensuring that children with special needs get the quality education they deserve, that framework is outdated now. IDEA was last reauthorized in 2004, but the law has not been radically overhauled since it was first written in 1975. In the ensuing decades, both the landscape of special education and our understanding of the underlying conditions themselves have changed dramatically. For example, while decades ago the number of children diagnosed with autism was one in 5,000, today it is one in 68, and the half-million students with the diagnosis make up almost 8 percent of the children enrolled in special education.[9]

Applied behavior analysis, a type of behavior intervention, is recognized today by the medical field as a successful, empirically based treatment for autism. This treatment has profound implications for how children on the autism spectrum learn, but because it was developed in the medical context instead of the educational, the IDEA system has been slow to recognize it as necessary, even though it's covered by health insurance providers and even Medicaid.[10]

Parents of children on the spectrum do not care whether the federal government classifies the activities that help them as medical treatments or special education; they just want the services that best benefit their children. The IDEA system, which is slow moving and inflexible, has shown itself ill-equipped to handle the changes in knowledge and practice surrounding just one of the many categories of special-needs learners, forcing parent advocates to retroactively launch a difficult and sustained lobbying effort to get the system to recognize their preferred services.

Why would anyone assume that the same system will do better with advances that may help the next group of learners?

School Profile: The Julie Billiart Schools (Ohio)

The Julie Billiart Schools are a network of Catholic private schools that exclusively serve students with special needs in Ohio. For 64 years, they have provided individualized instruction modeled around the needs of each child who comes through their doors. Their work would be financially impossible without Ohio's two school choice programs for students with special needs: the EdChoice Scholarship and the Jon Peterson Scholarship. The latter is the legal mechanism by which parents struggling with the services provided in the public schools give up their claim in exchange for a scholarship to a certified provider. For many families in Ohio, a Julie Billiart School has been that provider.

The schools' president and CEO, Lannie Davis Frecker, spoke with Mike McShane of EdChoice about the education her schools provide for their students and how that experience differs from that on offer in the public schools:

> I had already fallen in love with the mission and fallen in love with the kids, and our model, and what we can do, and how different it is from the public schools. I've had experience in the public schools, as well. I believe in all types of education, but what we can do at Julie Billiart Schools is very different. We can set up individualized curriculum for that child to meet their needs and our environment truly does meet the child's needs. We fit the child instead of the child having to really fit into us.[11]

The Advantages of Choice

Often choice programs can offer parents exactly what they struggle to acquire in the traditional public system: the power to demand what works for their child and the flexibility to implement successful strategies and treatments that result in real learning and growth.

While many programs are still too new to be studied extensively, there is ample evidence to suggest that choice programs improve the lives of students with special needs and their families. In addition to the evidence collected on students who are officially labeled as in need of special services by traditional public school standards, there are likely many more whose needs are met in choice environments without the label. In fact, multiple studies have confirmed that students are less likely to be labeled as special needs in schools of choice, possibly because the complicated incentives to tag a student (or not) as special needs warps public school decisionmaking about who qualifies.[12]

In Arizona, while students with special needs are not the only group currently eligible for ESAs, they were the only ones eligible in early 2013, meaning that all of the parents surveyed at that time about their experiences with the program were parents of students with special needs. When asked about their previous public school experiences, almost half reported that they were dissatisfied, but every single respondent said they were satisfied with the ESA. Additionally, the vast majority of parents, 71 percent, said they were "very satisfied."[13]

On the other side of the country, parents in Florida's McKay voucher program, which limits eligibility to students with special needs, report higher success rates in their new chosen schools than in the traditional system. Fewer than one-third of participants indicated that, prior to receiving the voucher, their children were getting all the services they were entitled to under federal laws like IDEA and the Americans with Disabilities Act from their assigned public schools. But in the schools their children attended with the voucher, 86 percent of parents reported getting all the services they were promised upon enrollment.[14]

The evaluation of the McKay program noted other differences between the recipients' former public schools and their chosen schools. For example, average class size dropped from 25.1 in the public schools to 12.8 in the chosen schools. Behavioral problems were also reduced in the chosen schools, with over 40 percent of participants reporting that their children had behavioral issues in the public schools, but less than half of those parents reported that those problems continued in chosen schools. Perhaps it is unsurprising that 93 percent of McKay parents reported being satisfied with the program, compared to just a third who were satisfied with their child's former public school.[15]

Academic performance for students with special needs is hard to measure, as many students have wildly varying challenges that can affect how well standardized testing represents their progress. However, there is some evidence that using a school choice program, like Florida's McKay vouchers, results in improved reading and math performance, particularly for students with milder disabilities. In addition, the same study found positive effects from the special-needs scholarship program on the performance of geographically adjacent public schools, suggesting that, contrary to claims of opponents, public schools may actually see academic improvement as the result of a special-needs scholarship program.[16]

Perhaps more important, but often overlooked, are the cultural factors that separate a student's experience in one educational environment from another. School choice has made a big difference for many families of students with special needs when it comes to the environment and peers their children are surrounded by. While bullying and bad experiences with other students are hardly confined to the special-needs community, many children in that community are singled out because of differences from the general population of students. In the McKay voucher family survey, almost half reported that their child had been "bothered often" by other students, and a full quarter had been physically assaulted in public schools because of their disabilities. In their schools of choice, only 5 percent reported being bothered often, and just 6 percent reported being assaulted.[17] Certainly any assault on a child in school is one too many, but that sharp decrease represents a huge burden lifted off many families.

The School Choice Landscape

School choice for students with special needs is not theoretical. More than 100,000 students across the country are already participating in the

Table 11.1

Choice programs for special-needs students

State	Program name	Program type	Number of participating students
Arizona	Empowerment Scholarship Accounts	ESA	6,422
Arizona	Lexie's Law for Disabled and Displaced Students	Tax-credit scholarship	1,103
Arkansas	Succeed Scholarship Program for Students with Disabilities	Voucher	260
Florida	Gardiner Scholarship Program	ESA	11,917
Florida	John M. McKay Scholarships for Students with Disabilities Program	Voucher	30,066
Georgia	Georgia Special Needs Scholarship Program	Voucher	4,664
Indiana	Choice Scholarship Program	Voucher	36,290
Louisiana	School Choice Program for Certain Students with Exceptionalities	Voucher	394
Mississippi	Equal Opportunity for Students with Special Needs Program	ESA	356
Mississippi	Mississippi Dyslexia Therapy Scholarship for Students with Dyslexia	Voucher	252
Mississippi	Nate Rogers Scholarship for Students with Disabilities Program	Voucher	1
North Carolina	Personal Education Savings Accounts Program	ESA	277
North Carolina	Special Education Scholarship Grants for Children with Disabilities	Voucher	1,546
Ohio	Jon Peterson Special Needs Scholarship Program	Voucher	5,621
Ohio	Autism Scholarship Program	Voucher	3,668
Oklahoma	Lindsey Nicole Henry Scholarships for Students with Disabilities	Voucher	827
South Carolina	Refundable Educational Credit for Exceptional Needs Children*	Individual tax credit	322
South Carolina	Educational Credit for Exceptional Needs Children	Tax-credit scholarship	1,951
Tennessee	Individualized Education Account Program	ESA	137
Utah	Carson Smith Special Needs Scholarship Program	Voucher	978
Wisconsin	Special Needs Scholarship Program	Voucher	692

Source: EdChoice, "School Choice FAQs: Can School Choice Help Students with Special Needs?"

Note: *This program is an individual tax credit, which some advocates consider a school choice program and others do not.

21 programs designed with them specifically in mind, and that number does not include the potentially thousands more who participate in programs with broader general eligibility (Table 11.1).[18]

ESAs hold particular promise for students with special needs. Because these programs give full control over a percentage of the dollars allocated for a child's education to the family, parents have been using the programs in Arizona, Florida, Mississippi, North Carolina, and Tennessee not only to enroll their children in private schools specifically geared toward particular learning challenges, but also to completely customize their children's educations.

ESAs can be used on any government-approved educational service, which includes various therapies, one-on-one instruction or tutoring, and supplies for home instruction. This full flexibility can be a godsend to parents of students who, because of their disabilities, do not do well in a classroom setting educationally or socially.

Because most school choice programs peg the amount of money a child's family receives to the per pupil amount sent to the district, and most funding formulas award higher dollar amounts to districts for educating children with special needs, the scholarship sums can be quite high. In programs exclusively for students with special needs, the median sum awarded to families is $6,520.50, but five programs average scholarships around or in excess of $10,000, and in one—the Autism Scholarship Program in Ohio—in excess of $20,000. The median award in Arizona, for example, is $14,000 for the upcoming school year. That can be a life-changing amount of money for parents struggling to provide their child with the services that can allow him or her to achieve in a way impossible in the one-size-fits-all public system.

Student Profile: Chloe Hood (Oklahoma)

Chloe's parents, David and Tara Hood, first noticed something was wrong when their daughter was about three years old. "She wasn't really speaking. . . . She started throwing horrible fits." After Chloe was diagnosed with autism, David and Tara found out about the state's Lindsey Nicole Henry Scholarship program from an autism group they reached out to for help. With the help of the scholarship, the Hoods now send Chloe to Good Shepherd Catholic School, which specializes in educating children like Chloe.

"Every child there . . . is special in their own way and they all have their own challenges," David says. "They don't just teach them academics ABCs and that sort of thing, they teach them life functioning skills," Tara adds. The Hoods "don't know what [they] would do without the school." Her parents now call Chloe a "chatterbox," when before she was not speaking. "She's done a 180."[19]

Objections to Choice

Many of the objections to choice for students with special needs are familiar to proponents of school choice in general, such as that choice programs "drain" money from the system and that the options chosen by parents lack "accountability" to education experts and bureaucrats. More specific to special education, some disability rights advocates worry that because the federal protections provided in IDEA and Section 504 do not apply to private education providers in most states, students with special needs will be shortchanged in school choice programs.

In states such as Louisiana and Tennessee, school choice recipients retain some or all of their IDEA and Section 504 rights when they utilize a program. In others, such as Arizona and Georgia, parents agree to forego their federal rights in exchange for access to the choice program. In still other states, such as Nevada and Utah, state law is silent on the issue.[20]

But even strong proponents of the IDEA system have to acknowledge that parents are often happy to sign away "rights" that have not served their children in the public system, in exchange for the flexibility and power that choice programs provide.[21] It is paternalistic to second-guess these families' choices and consign them to a public system because, in theory, that public system guarantees their children certain rights, while outside of it private options are offering the real experiences their children need.

Some proponents of the IDEA "guarantees" suggest that the solution is for private providers to be held to the same standards and federal mandates as public schools. This view is shortsighted. Often parents are utilizing education choice programs exactly because they are fleeing a public system that has failed to live up to those federal promises. Stacking the same failed bureaucratic restrictions on top of private providers will produce the same frustrating result as it has in the public system parents are escaping.

The way private education providers serve students with special needs will be different from the public system, and that is a difference families strongly value. While it is obviously important that parents always understand what they are giving up when they leave the public school system, calls to apply IDEA and Section 504 mandates to private schools are ultimately misguided. Parents should have the right to choose between the federally guaranteed "rights" that have produced so many adversarial meetings and litigation, and the real accountability that comes with power over the dollars spent on their child's education.

Key Policy Elements

Universal Eligibility

While there are upwards of six million students with special needs in the United States,[22] they are still a relatively small minority of the more than 56 million school-age children in the United States.[23] Programs will always be at risk, and the market of providers will always be smaller as long as choice is restricted to particular categories of students, such as those with special needs and those whose families have lower incomes. Expanding choice eligibility to all students not only will help the students who have access to the programs, but it will also help students with special needs in particular by growing the market of options and creating a broad political coalition of beneficiaries to protect programs from challenges.

Assessment Flexibility

Recent research casts doubt on the predictive power of standardized test scores on important outcomes later in life for all students.[24] However, standardized testing can be particularly unhelpful in assessing the progress of students with many kinds of disabilities. Many observers, including the American Federation of Teachers, have pointed to the unnecessary stress and anxiety standardized testing produces in some students with special needs.[25] And teachers have voiced their frustrations at a standardized regime that often does not take into account students' IEPs and other challenges that may make a test unrepresentative of a student's progress.[26]

Lay Off the Red Tape

Some may be tempted to try to enforce the lofty-sounding dictates of IDEA, as well as other state regulations intended to ensure equal treatment of students with disabilities, on choice programs. While well intentioned, these regulations ultimately may short-circuit the exact differences that make choice appealing to families and homogenize the educational landscape.

One such example is the demand that every school serve every student who comes to its doorstep, regardless of whether or not that school is equipped to serve each student's needs best. While it's important that every child has access to a great education, ultimately, trying to serve everyone equally is what has made special needs services so lackluster in the public schools: in trying to serve every student, they often end up serving few very well.

By contrast, the private school sector has been able to support schools that exclusively serve students with particular disabilities or challenges. While not every student will find a good fit in every school, overall, a diverse marketplace of options is best equipped to supply a good fit for everyone. In contrast, the failed public model, which requires every school to provide an education to every student, consequently homogenizes what every student needs, leaving many unserved. Public schools themselves often admit this reality, and in some cases fund private services for students whose needs they repeatedly fail to meet or cannot meet while balancing the learning of their other students.[27]

Another well-meaning example of regulation that has hurt students with special needs is the requirement that a child first "try out" public school before becoming eligible for a choice program. While a year of any child's learning is crucial and shouldn't be "sacrificed" to second-guessing parents' preferences, this requirement is particularly onerous for children with special needs, who sometimes must go into a classroom environment that seriously sets back their progress in order to qualify for the scholarship that supports the education their families know is best for them.[28]

Conclusion

In many ways, the difference between the traditional public system and the emerging network of choice programs for students with special needs amounts to the difference between theory and practice. The federal government, along with states, purports to offer children a guaranteed "free, appropriate public education." In reality, enforcing that promise means endless adversarial IEP meetings, constant follow-up and paperwork with administrators, and struggling against the reality that even a well-meaning teacher in a traditional classroom setup can only customize the education of one child so much. And that's in the cases that don't go to court.

By contrast, the choice system offers fewer paper guarantees. Private schools and individual providers are often not subject to the web of bureaucratic mandates in place supposedly to ensure fairness for special-needs students. But in their place, real accountability to parents and endless flexibility for how educational services are delivered provide the on-the-ground education many families in the traditional system are desperate for.

In a universal choice system, the parchment promises of traditional public schools will not disappear. Any parent who wishes to put his or her shoulder against what often feels like a brick wall may still do so. But choice programs have granted thousands of families across the country the freedom to *truly* create individualized education plans for their children with special needs. Instead of hard-won concessions in the sometimes-litigious battles between parent advocates and school districts, many parents are discovering that holding the purse strings makes all the difference.

Real accountability, as opposed to bureaucratic compliance, comes naturally with the power to hire and fire the teachers, therapists, and other educational providers who work with your child.

Students with special needs and their families require real power to hold education providers accountable for their promises, and providers need the flexibility to deliver on them. Education choice, in contrast to federal mandates, can provide both for the millions of special needs families across the nation.

CHAPTER TWELVE

MYTH: ONLY RICH PARENTS CAN MAKE GOOD CHOICES

Poor families care about their children too.

Virginia Walden Ford

"Poor parents are simply too stupid to choose the right schools for their children. Only rich parents are capable of making good educational choices for their kids."

If that sounds offensive to you, that's because it is.

It's also completely wrong. My experiences over 20 years, and mountains of research, disprove this pernicious myth.

But still the myth persists. The idea that low-income families lack the intellect, the decision-making skills, or the sheer ability to choose schools for their children is a nasty legend that simply will not go away.

Spreading the Myth

Chances are you have not heard this myth repeated as bluntly as I wrote it in my first sentence. But the myth is out there, and it is spreading. You also may not know that perpetuating this myth is a key goal of school choice opponents intent on dividing Americans rather than bringing people together.

The perpetrators of this myth are as clever as they are mendacious, usually dismissing poor parents and their rights by claiming they are just trying to protect those families' interests. They make their utter disdain sound like compassion.

Poor parents lack the "resources" to choose good schools, the "support systems" to make choices, the "time" to compare and contrast schools, and the "social networks" necessary to understand the differences between good and bad schools, they say.

The result of these parental deficiencies, opponents argue, is catastrophic for children. In the *Los Angeles Times*, a teacher wrote that parental choice was actively hurting children: "I watched thousands of students . . . receive a subpar education because policymakers oversubscribed to the free-market notion that parents will fix the schools if only you let them vote with their feet."[1] In *Forbes*, an opponent of school choice said, "Some parents and students feel loyal even to a school that is struggling. And not all parents are willing to put their own kids' interests ahead of others."[2]

Opponents of school choice try to advance these views with biased studies. The research, they say, shows that low-income parents make "flawed choices" because they don't focus enough on test scores in deciding where to send their children to school and instead prioritize other things, such as their children's safety.[3] Apparently, surviving in a tough neighborhood should take a back seat to filling out some bubbles on a Scantron sheet.

But the argument that gets the most traction is this one: because wealthier people put so much thought into picking their children's schools, poor parents don't have the brainpower to match up.

A guest columnist for *The Washington Post* doubted that a poor parent could come close to her level of school-searching skills: "I navigated the school choice maze as a university professor with good income, flexible hours, reliable transportation, and a strong parent network. Imagine the process of school choice for parents of students attending failing schools, with limited income, or relying on public transportation. Don't let school choice trick you."[4]

My Experience with Low-Income Families

For more than two decades, I have worked with low-income parents and advocated some of America's most ambitious school choice policies. Most notably, I worked with parents and various organizations to enact the District of Columbia's Opportunity Scholarship Program (DCOSP), which provides private school scholarships to low-income families. This program was enacted in 2004 after many years of legislative wrangling and community advocacy.

In gearing up to pass this legislation, we held hundreds of community meetings all throughout the District of Columbia and went door to door to meet with parents. At each and every meeting, parents asked the type of important, necessary, and pointed questions about school choice and about the private schools their children could have an opportunity to attend if they received a scholarship. One by one, these parents told me that even though they had not had the kind of education they needed or deserved, they wanted better for their children. They wanted educational environments that included more discipline, smaller class sizes, and improved student safety. Low-income parents also often identified the opportunity for a religious education in their reasons for choosing a private school, and they placed high school graduation and receiving college information at the top of their list of important priorities.

It was true that most low-income parents did not prioritize aggregate standardized test scores in choosing schools for their children. While a few parents identified test scores as the top reason for selecting a school, most did not. Interestingly, their reasoning for not placing an emphasis on test scores echoes many of the arguments frequently made by school choice supporters and opponents alike: test scores simply do not tell the whole story about a school or about how a student will perform there.

It turns out that the low-income families were wiser than many of the academics who have poured time and money into researching this topic.[5] Far from simply making choices quickly, almost every parent I met wanted as much information as possible about the schools that their children might attend. Yes, some parents faced obstacles in getting that information, but that did not prevent them from seeking and obtaining it.[6] As we continued to go out into the community to introduce parents to the DCOSP, we met many excited and motivated parents and students.

One mother's persistence comes to mind. At a parent meeting, I saw a mother walk into the door with a two-page list of questions, a list filled with issues that she wanted to address before she chose a school for her daughter. When we divided the group of 100 parents into groups, I expected this mother to be quite aggressive about asking those questions. Instead, she was very quiet, and as the others in the group got into a lively discussion about their children, I slid over in my chair to her.

I asked why she wasn't asking the questions she brought. She placed the two pages in my hand and explained to me that she could not read but that she had asked a family member to write her questions down for her. I took the papers and was delighted at the kinds of things she wanted to know about. We had a great discussion, and she was adamant that her daughter would get the education she deserved. She wanted to be part of choosing the school her daughter would attend.

This was a familiar theme in our outreach: parents who had the toughest of lives wanted—and were willing to work hard for—their children to have better opportunities.

During one meeting in our community, we observed a man who clearly had had too much to drink. Hoping to avoid a scene, I decided to escort him quietly and gently outside. I approached the disheveled and foul-smelling man and gestured toward the exit. "What are ya' doin'?" he blurted out. "I'm here to fill out an application for my son! There is a private school near here that I want him to go to." He actually came with pamphlets and brochures about the school he wanted for his child.

This father and I worked together until the paperwork was completed except for one document that he had to obtain from a DC government office. We told him we'd pick it up the next morning, but it had to be early to ensure his son qualified for this round of scholarships. The next morning, as we pulled up early, not confident that he'd be there, we saw him sitting in front of the building, document in hand. He had been there for several hours, waiting for us. His son ultimately received a scholarship to attend second grade at the private school of his parents' choice.

Exactly one year later, we were hard at work when one of my assistants told me that an unfamiliar man had asked to see me. I walked outside and saw a clean-cut gentleman dressed in khakis and a button-down shirt. For a moment, I had no clue who he was, but as he began to speak, I recognized him. It was the father I had helped.

"I want to thank you for helping me," he said. "When I saw my son succeed in school, it made me want to do better too." He informed me of his progress in an employment training program and his work toward a GED. He had joined a substance abuse rehabilitation program and had finally reconnected with a second son whom he had neglected. He was a changed man.

Another time, I met with a mother of two boys at her apartment. When I arrived for our meeting, I was told that one of her sons had been assaulted by some other boys in the community the night prior for no reason except that his mother did not let him hang outside. He was hurt badly, so I offered to come back another evening. She said there was absolutely no way she would postpone. She was determined to hold this meeting for her family and for her friends who lived in her community to make sure they had all the information needed to qualify for a scholarship.

To that mother, receiving a scholarship was her children's way out of a troubled community. There were several neighbors there with similar stories. I spent a long evening helping them fill out applications for their children to get scholarships to attend better schools.

Another of the families we worked with had six children, two sets of twins and two singles. The mother and father wanted what was best for all these children and were among the first families to sign up for the DCOSP during one of our events. As we got to know this family, we found that the father was very ill but was determined to do all he could to help his family while he was able. He and his wife attended every sign-up event not only to sign their children up but to help their neighbors. All six of their children received scholarships and enrolled in a school that their parents felt would nurture them as the father became sicker. Before he died, he told me that he was happy he would be leaving his wife and children in a good educational place.

Through my time working with these families, I saw every myth about low-income parents shatter before my very eyes, including the cruel tale that poor families refuse to take the "time" to get their children a good education.

One mother with three children visited schools all over DC and found what she strongly believed would be a good school for her family.

The only problem was that it was across town from where she lived and would require taking three buses and the subway to get there. She was determined that she could make this trek every day with her young children, and to the delight of all, she did—every day until they finished at the school.

The Results: Happier Students and Stronger Families

We did not just talk with parents. Some of the greatest joy came from talking with low-income students themselves.

I remember an eight-year-old third-grader who happily told us that she wanted to be a translator at the United Nations. Thanks to a scholarship, she had a head start on that dream by taking Arabic and Spanish at the private school she was attending.

I remember a 15-year-old 10th-grader who was finally able to refine her talent for art when she transferred to a private school with a strong art program. Upon graduation she attended college and studied Japanese and art. She is now a translator for a Japanese company *in Japan* and has exhibited in art galleries around the city where she lives and works.

I met a young 13-year-old girl and her grandmother at an information event about the DCOSP. I asked the girl why she was there, and she told me that she needed a scholarship to be "the hope of the family." She continued to share with me that her cousin had been their "hope." He was a senior, doing well, when one night coming home from the library he had been shot and killed when two gangs were shooting across the street at each other and hit his bus. It was devastating to their family, but this girl decided that she would be the one to do well and make her family proud. Her grandmother was her biggest supporter and asked me to please help her. The girl received a scholarship, attended a private school, and graduated at the top of her class. She went on to an Ivy League college, where she graduated with honors, and then headed to graduate school to receive her PhD. Two weeks after the girl graduated with her PhD, her grandmother passed away.

One night at the end of an application event, a volunteer mentioned to me that a 13-year-old boy had been standing around the entire time we were there. I introduced myself and told him that if he was interested in a scholarship, he should bring his parents to sign up for the program the next day. He explained that he lived with his grandmother who was not able to get around, but he really did want to sign up and receive a scholarship. He lived nearby, so we gathered the application and went to his house. He and his grandmother were delighted to have this opportunity to apply. We got all his information and went back for further documentation the next day. They had all they needed, and he received a scholarship. I can still remember the smiles on their faces.

In so many of these situations, these students inspired their parents—and everyone in the family became an advocate of school choice.

I vividly recall one young woman whose mother was disabled. This mother was desperate for her daughter to do well in school, and the daughter herself was very excited about the possibility of attending a Catholic high school that she and her mother had often observed while driving around their community. She received a scholarship and excelled at that school. Even with her disability, her mother became an outstanding advocate for the DCOSP and a champion for her daughter. Her daughter graduated from college in 2019.

Some of my proudest moments come when I get to listen to our scholarship "kids" give graduation or keynote addresses and talk about their experiences. Their accomplishments are not just personal; they reflect positively on their entire families. I sat with one mother at an event where her daughter was giving a speech. The mother whispered to me, "I know we would not be here if I hadn't had the opportunity to receive a scholarship and choose a school that worked for my daughter."

She was, indeed, referring to their entire family.

The truth is that hundreds of lives are changed for the better because of school choice programs. As more and more low-income and working-class families are participating in school-choice programs, we are seeing parental involvement soar. Parents know that their kids are going to succeed if the world is opened up to them, and they want to be part of that. Parents who have never before been part of their children's educational experience are working in partnership with the schools to ensure that their children receive the best education possible.

The evidence is not just anecdotal but based in research. As captured in the summary for *The School Choice Journey: School Vouchers and the Empowerment of Urban Families* by researchers Thomas Stewart and Patrick Wolf, "Washington, DC's Opportunity Scholarship Program provides a realistic look at how urban families experience the process of using school choice vouchers and [are] transform[ed] from government clients to consumers of education and active citizens."[7] Evan Rhinesmith's review of the evidence also finds that every single study on the topic indicates that families are satisfied with private school choice programs in the United States.[8]

Common Sense

The myth that poor parents are simply too stupid, or badly informed, to choose the right schools for their children is just that—a myth. And it is a cruel myth at that. But even if you do not agree with the research, or if you doubt my experiences, I invite you to view this issue through the lens of what we ourselves expect from our families, friends, neighbors, and strangers in everyday life. We expect people to make choices. We expect people to understand right from wrong and good from bad. We expect people to be able to make choices when it comes to their work, their food, and their housing. We expect people to be able to make hundreds of choices every single day.

This is one of the tenets—one of the pillars—of civil society. People need to be able to make choices, and we must trust people to make choices that—most of the time—will at least be in their own self-interest. We hope that they will make choices driven by wisdom, research, guidance, and a sense of morality. When people choose to stray from this path of making good and sensible choices, society regularly ridicules those bad choices and embarrasses those who make them.

I mention this because if you believe education experts who say that poor parents cannot or will not make good choices for their children's education, you need to also believe that the free will and self-determination that undergirds all of society must be faulty too. After all, education—and choosing schools—cannot possibly be the only thing that people cannot do on their own. And if it is, isn't that strange? Isn't it strange that people make hundreds of personal choices every day, and millions of choices in their lifetimes, but apparently no poor person is qualified to choose the right education for their own children?

In the 20 years that I've been involved in advocating a better education for all children, I can say that, yes, sometimes people make bad choices in life—in all aspects of their lives. But the overwhelming majority of the time, low-income families see school choice as a lifeline to a better life and more opportunities for their children, and they reach for that brass ring. They make good choices.

How to Truly Help Low-Income Families

Supporters and opponents of school choice stand at a crossroads. If school choice opponents truly want to do what is right for families, they cannot continue to regard poor people as too stupid to make good decisions. Depriving all families of choices is not a workable solution either. If skeptics truly want low-income parents to have more resources, time, and networks to choose schools, then I invite them to help in efforts to provide the information and support that parents desperately want and need about school choice.

Supporters of school choice should also provide families the support and help they need. The more information, empowerment, and support that families receive, the better.

Here is what we can all do to help low-income families make the best choices for their children's education.

1. **Sponsor information sessions.** Parents want the best for their children, but they have questions. In-person meetings and community events are perfect times to provide parents with more information about the options available to them.
2. **Go door to door, and create social networks online.** Reaching out to parents to give them information about schools that they could choose for their children is key. Some low-income families do not have any information

about the schools, and helping them gather that information helps them make better decisions.

3. **Reach people where they are.** Even though large gatherings help in some respect to inform parents, I found that going to their homes, community centers, churches, and elsewhere in the community is a far better way to get parents to open up about their desires for their children.
4. **Hold school fairs.** Partnering with schools that can give parents information and talk to them about their schools is a very successful way to get parents engaged and involved in the process of looking for the right school for their children.
5. **Demand that all schools be more responsive to parents.** It is so important for supporters and advocates to encourage schools to work closely with low-income and working-class parents, remembering that this may be a first-time experience for them. Remind parents that they can and should be involved in their children's educational experience, and guide them along the way.

Conclusion

In my more than 20 years of working with low-income and working-class families, I have learned as much from the parents and students as they have from me and other supporters. I have watched parents spend countless hours visiting schools, watched them attend events with long lists of questions to ask supporters and educators, watched them agonize over whether they were making the absolute best decision for their children, and watched the joy they felt when their children did well in the school they chose. It's been an amazing experience, and all of us have learned that no matter what their income is, nothing is more important to families than finding the right educational environment for their children.

NOTES

Chapter One

1. See David Brooks, "People Like Us: We All Pay Lip Service to the Melting Pot, but We Really Prefer the Congealing Pot," *The Atlantic*, September 2003; Robert H. Wiebe, *The Segmented Society: An Introduction to the Meaning of America* (New York: Oxford University Press, 1979).

2. National Center for Education Statistics, "Digest of Education Statistics: 2018," Table 105.30, https://nces.ed.gov/programs/digest/d18/tables/dt18_105.30.asp?current=yes.

3. National Center for Education Statistics, "Digest of Education Statistics: 2018," Table 104.10, https://nces.ed.gov/programs/digest/d18/tables/dt18_104.10.asp?current=yes.

4. Charles Murray, *Coming Apart: The State of White America, 1960–2010* (New York: Crown Forum, 2012), p. 12.

5. Jon Teaford, "The Transformation of Massachusetts Education: 1670–1780," in *The Social History of American Education*, ed. B. Edward McClellan and William J. Reese (Urbana: University of Illinois Press, 1988), p. 30.

6. See Bernard Bailyn, *Education in the Forming of American Society* (New York: W. W. Norton and Co., 1960), pp. 15–21; N. Ray Hiner, "The Cry of Sodom Enquired Into: Educational Analysis in Seventeenth-Century New England," in *The Social History of American Education*, ed. B. Edward McClellan and William J. Reese (Urbana: University of Illinois Press, 1988), p. 9; Lawrence A. Cremin, *American Education: The Colonial Experience, 1607–1783* (New York: Harper Torchbooks, 1970), pp. 123–24.

7. Bernard Bailyn, *Education in the Forming of American Society* (New York: W. W. Norton and Co., 1960), pp. 22–23.

8. Albert Fishlow, "Levels of Nineteenth-Century American Investment in Education," *Journal of Economic History* 26, no. 4 (December 1966): 418.

9. David B. Tyack, *The One Best System: A History of American Urban Education* (Cambridge, MA: Harvard University Press, 1974), p. 66.

10. Many Founders, including George Washington and Noah Webster, feared disunity, with Benjamin Rush calling for common schooling: "By producing one general and uniform system of education, [common schooling] will render the mass of the people more homogeneous and thereby fit them more easily for uniform and peaceable government." "Thoughts upon the Mode of Education Proper in a Republic," in *Essays on Education in the Early Republic*, ed. Frederick Rudolph (Cambridge, MA: Belknap Press of Harvard University Press, 1965), p. 9.

11. Horace Mann, "Report for 1845," in *Life and Works of Horace Mann*, ed. Mary Mann (Boston: Horace B. Fuller, 1868), p. 422.

12. For a good discussion, see Charles Lesley Glenn Jr., *The Myth of the Common School* (Amherst, MA: University of Massachusetts Press, 1987).

13. Lewis Joseph Sherrill, *Presbyterian Parochial Schools: 1846–1870* (New Haven, CT: Yale University Press, 1932), p. 49.

14. Vincent P. Lannie and Bernard C. Diethorn, "For the Honor and the Glory of God: The Philadelphia Bible Riots of 1840," *History of Education Quarterly* 8, no. 1 (Spring 1968). The date was corrected to "1844" in the subsequent issue.

15. Sherrill, *Presbyterian Parochial Schools*, p. 12.

16. 1937–38 district data from "120 Years of American Education: A Statistical Portrait," U.S. Department of Education, Table 20; 1937–38 population data from "Historical National Population Estimates: July 1, 1900 to July 1, 1999," U.S. Census Bureau; 2015–16 district data from "Digest of Education Statistics: 2017," U.S. Department of Education, Table 214.10; 2015 population data from "American FactFinder," U.S. Census Bureau.

17. For instance, see Benjamin Justice, *The War That Wasn't: Religious Conflict and Compromise in the Common Schools of New York State, 1865–1900* (Albany: State University of New York Press, 2005).

18. John J. Convey, *Catholic Schools Make a Difference: Twenty-Five Years of Research* (Washington: National Catholic Educational Association), p. 19; enrollment as a percentage of total elementary and secondary enrollment calculated using *Statistical Abstract of the United States: 1994,* U.S. Bureau of the Census, Table 240.

19. Leon F. Litwack, *North of Slavery: The Negro in the United States 1790–1860* (Chicago: University of Chicago Press, 1961), pp. 113–17.

20. *Keyes v. School District No. 1,* Denver, 413 U.S. 189 (1973).

21. *Milliken v. Bradley*, 418 U.S. 717 (1974).

22. Erica Frankenberg et al., "Southern Schools: More Than a Half-Century after the Civil Rights Revolution," the Civil Rights Project and the Center for Education and Civil Rights, May 2017.

23. Gary Orfield, John Kucsera, and Genevieve Siegel-Hawley, "E Pluribus . . . Separation: Deepening Double Segregation for More Students," The Civil Rights Project, September 2012, p. 34.

24. James S. Coleman, Sara D. Kelly, and John A. Moore, "Trends in School Segregation, 1968–73," Urban Institute, 1975, p. 27.

25. Typical black exposure to whites is from Gary Orfield et al., "E Pluribus . . . Separation," p. 36. Typical white exposure to blacks was calculated using National Center for Education Statistics, Common Core of Data, https://nces.ed.gov/ccd/, October 15, 2018. National racial share by age is from National Center for Education Statistics, "Digest of Education Statistics: 2018," Table 101.20, https://nces.ed.gov/programs/digest/d18/tables/dt18_101.20.asp?current=yes.

26. For instance, "Race and Ethnicity in a New Era of Public Funding of Private Schools: Private School Enrollment in the South and the Nation," Southern Education Foundation, March 2016; Chris Ford, Stephanie Johnson, and Lisette Partelow, "The Racist Origins of Private School Vouchers," Center for American Progress, July 12, 2017.

27. "Private School Enrollment, Tuition, and Enrollment Trends: October 1979," Bureau of the Census, U.S. Department of Commerce, p. 6.

28. Share calculated using National Center for Educational Statistics, "Digest of Education Statistics: 2016," Table 105.30, https://nces.ed.gov/programs/digest/d16/tables/dt16_105.30.asp.

29. Reynolds Farley, Toni Richards, and Clarence Wurdock, "School Desegregation and White Flight: An Investigation of Competing Models and Their Discrepant Findings," *Sociology of Education* 53, no. 3 (July 1980): 123–39.

30. Christine H. Rossell and David J. Armor, "The Effectiveness of School Desegregation Plans, 1968–1991," *American Politics Quarterly* 24, no. 3 (July 1996): 289.

31. Farley et al., "School Desegregation and White Flight."

32. Howard Schuman, Charlotte Steeh, Lawrence D. Bobo, and Maria Krysan, *Racial Attitudes in America: Trends and Interpretations*, rev. ed. (Cambridge, MA: Harvard University Press, 1997). White results on pp. 123–24, black results on pp. 248–49.

33. Schuman et al., *Racial Attitudes in America*, p. 126.

34. Erica Frankenberg, and Rebecca Jacobson, "The Polls—Trends: School Integration Polls," *Public Opinion Quarterly* 75, no. 4 (Winter 2011): 789–801.

35. T. Keung Hui and David Raynor, "Wake County Busing Fewer Students for Diversity," *News and Observer*, August 15, 2015; T. Keung Hui, "Thousands of

Wake Students Will Change Schools Next Year. Is Your Child Affected?," *News and Observer*, November 20, 2018.

36. *Milliken v. Bradley*, 418 U.S. 717 (1974).

37. See Nancy H. St. John, "De Facto Segregation and Interracial Association in High School," *Sociology of Education* 37, no. 4 (Summer 1964): 326–44; Janet W. Schofield, "The Impact of Positively Structured Contact on Intergroup Behavior: Does It Last under Adverse Conditions?," *Social Psychology Quarterly* 42, no. 3 (September 1979): 280–84; Roslyn A. Mickelson, "Subverting Swann: First- and Second-Generation Segregation in the Charlotte-Mecklenburg Schools," *American Educational Research Journal* 38, no. 2 (Summer 2001): 215–52; James Moody, "Race, School Integration, and Friendship Segregation in America," *American Journal of Sociology* 107, no. 3 (November 2001): 679–716; Elizabeth Stearns, "Interracial Friendliness and the Social Organization of Schools," *Youth and Society* 35, no. 4 (July 2004): 395–419; Pat António Goldsmith, "Schools' Role in Shaping Race Relations: Evidence on Friendliness and Conflict," *Social Problems* 51, no. 4 (November 2004): 587–612.

38. Mickelson, "Subverting Swann."

39. John B. McConahay, "The Effects of School Integration upon Students' Racial Attitudes and Behavior: A Critical Review of the Literature and a Prolegomenon to Future Research," *Law and Contemporary Problems* 42, no. 3 (Summer 1978): 100–101.

40. McConahay, "Effects of School Integration," 77–101; Daniel S. Sheehan, "A Study of Attitude Change in Desegregated Intermediate Schools," *Sociology of Education* 53, no. 1 (January 1980): 51–59; Lee Sigelman et al., "Making Contact? Black-White Social Interaction in an Urban Setting," *American Journal of Sociology* 101, no. 5 (March 1996). See also Amy Stuart Wells et al., "How Desegregation Changed Us: The Effects of Racially Mixed Schools on Students and Society," in *In Search of Brown*, ed. Daniel Cardwell (Cambridge, MA: Harvard University Press, 2005).

41. Moody, "Race, School Integration, and Friendship Segregation."

42. Brent Berry, "Friends for Better or for Worse: Interracial Friendship in the United States as Seen through Wedding Party Photos," *Demography* 43, no. 3 (August 2006): 491–510.

43. Gordon W. Allport, *The Nature of Prejudice* (Boston: Beacon Press, 1954).

44. Allport, *Nature of Prejudice*, p. 281 [italics added].

45. Elizabeth A. Harris, and Winnie Hu, "Asian Groups See Bias in Plan to Diversify New York's Elite Schools," *New York Times*, June 5, 2018.

46. *Parents Involved in Community Schools v. Seattle School District No. 1*, 551 U.S. 701 (2007).

47. Mariano Narodowski, "The Chile Experiment: Comparing Chile's Free School Choice Model with Quasi-Monopoly Educational Systems in Latin America on Academic Outcomes and Segregation," EdChoice, May 2018, p. 13.

48. Chang-Tai Hsieh and Miguel Urquiola, "The Effects of Generalized School Choice on Achievement and Stratification: Evidence from Chile's Voucher Program," *Journal of Public Economics* 90 (2006): 1477–1503.

49. Gregory Elacqua, Mark Schneider, and Jack Buckley, "School Choice in Chile: Is It Class or the Classroom?," *Journal of Policy Analysis and Management* 25, no. 3 (2006): 577–601.

50. Claudio Sapelli, "The Chilean Voucher System: Some New Results and Research Challenges," *Cuadranos de Economia* 40, no. 121 (February 2003): 530–38.

51. Gregory Elacqua, "The Impact of School Choice and Public Policy on Segregation: Evidence from Chile," *International Journal of Educational Development* 32, no. 3 (May 2012): 444–53.

52. Mariano Narodowski, "The Chile Experiment: Comparing Chile's Free School Choice Model with Quasi-Monopoly Educational Systems in Latin America on Academic Outcomes and Segregation," EdChoice, May 2018.

53. Anders Bohlmark, Helena Holmlund, and Mikael Lindahl, "School Choice and Segregation: Evidence from Sweden," Institute for Evaluation of Labour Market and Education Policy working paper, 2015.

54. See Jay P. Greene, "The Racial, Economic, and Religious Context of Parental Choice in Cleveland," presentation at Association for Public Policy Analysis and Management meeting, November 5, 1999; Howard L. Fuller and George A. Mitchell, "The Impact of School Choice on Integration in Milwaukee Private Schools," *Current Education Issues*, no. 2000–02 (June 2000); Jay P. Greene and Marcus A. Winters, "An Evaluation of the Effect of D.C.'s Voucher Program on Public School Achievement and Racial Integration after One Year," Manhattan Institute, 2006; Greg Forster, "Segregation Levels in Milwaukee Public Schools and the Milwaukee Voucher Program," Friedman Foundation, 2006; Greg Forster, "Segregation Levels in Cleveland Public Schools and the Cleveland Voucher Program," EdChoice, 2006.

55. Paul E. Peterson and David E. Campbell, "An Evaluation of the Children's Scholarship Fund," Program on Education Policy and Governance, Harvard University, 2001; Jay P. Greene, Jonathan N. Mills, and Stuart Buck, "The Milwaukee Parental Choice Program's Effect on School Integration," School Choice Demonstration Project, 2010; Christine H. Rossell, "A Report on the Effect of the 2012–13 Scholarship Program on Racial Imbalance in Louisiana School Districts under a Desegregation Court Order as of 2012–13," for *Brumfield v. Dodd, Civ.* A. No. 71-1316 (2013).

56. Anna J. Egalite, Jonathan N. Mills, and Patrick J. Wolf, "The Impact of the Louisiana Scholarship Program on Racial Segregation in Louisiana Schools," Education Research Alliance/School Choice Demonstration Project, 2016.

57. Jay P. Greene, "Civic Values in Public and Private Schools," in *Learning from School Choice*, ed. Paul E. Peterson and Bryan C. Hassel (Washington: Brookings

Institution Press, 1998), pp. 83–106; Jay P. Greene and Nicole Mellow, "Integration Where It Counts: A Study of Racial Integration in Public and Private School Lunchrooms," paper presented at the Annual Meeting of the American Political Science Association, August 1998.

58. William Jeynes, *Religion, Education, and Academic Success* (Greenwich, CT: Information Age Publishing, 2003).

59. Valerie E. Lee, Robert G. Croninger, and Julia B. Smith, "Equity and Choice in Detroit," in *Who Chooses? Who Loses? Culture, Institutions, and the Unequal Effects of School Choice*, ed. Bruce Fuller and Richard F. Ellmore (New York: Teachers College Press, 1996), pp. 70–91.

60. Ke Wang, Amy Rathbun, and Lauren Musu, "School Choice in the United States: 2019," National Center for Education Statistics, September 2019, https://nces.ed.gov/pubs2019/2019106.pdf.

61. Burleigh B. Gardner, Benjamin D. Wright, and Rita Dee, "The Effect of Busing Ghetto Children into White Suburban Schools," Chicago Catholic School Board, 1970.

62. Paul E. Peterson and David E. Campbell, "An Evaluation of the Children's Scholarship Fund," Program on Education Policy and Governance, Harvard University, 2001.

63. Gautam Rao, "Familiarity Does Not Breed Contempt: Generosity, Discrimination, and Diversity in Delhi Schools," *American Economic Review* 109, no. 3 (2014): 774–809.

64. M. Danish Shakeel and Corey A. DeAngelis, "Can Private Schools Improve School Climate? Evidence from a Nationally Representative Sample," *Journal of School Choice* 12, no. 3, (2018): 426–45; DeAngelis and Martin F. Lueken, "Are Choice Schools Safe Schools?," EdChoice Working Paper 2019-2, April 3, 2019.

65. Thomas F. Pettigrew and Linda R. Tropp, "The Meta-Analytic Test of Intergroup Contact Theory," *Journal of Personality and Social Psychology* 90, no. 5 (2006): 751–83.

Chapter Two

1. Chris Ford, Stephenie Johnson, and Lisette Partelow, "The Racist Origins of Private School Vouchers," Center for American Progress, July 12, 2017.

2. For a summary of this literature, see Elise Swanson, "Can We Have It All? A Review of the Impacts of School Choice on Racial Integration," *Journal of School Choice* 11, no. 4 (2017): 507–26.

3. Randi Weingarten, "School Choice: Past and Present," *Huffington Post*, July 23, 2017.

4. Urusula Hackett and Desmond King, "The Reinvention of Vouchers for a Color-Blind Era: A Racial Orders Account," *Studies in American Political Development* 33, no. 2 (2018): 234–257.

5. Eleni Schirmer and Michael W. Apple, "(Un)Chaining Democracy," *Education Review // Reseñas Educativas* 25 (2018): 1–13; Leo Casey, "When Privatization Means Segregation: Setting the Record Straight on School Vouchers," *Dissent Magazine*, August 9, 2017.

6. For antecedents, see Adam Smith, *An Inquiry into the Nature and Causes of the Wealth of Nations*, ed. William B. Todd, Glasgow Edition of the Works of Adam Smith (Oxford: Oxford University Press, 1976), Book 5, Chapter 1, Part 3, Article 2; John Stuart Mill, *On Liberty* (London: John W. Parker and Son, 1859), Chapter 3.

7. Milton Friedman, "The Role of Government in Education," in *Economics and the Public Interest*, ed. R. Solo (New Brunswick, NJ: Rutgers University Press, 1955), pp. 5-6, footnote 2. Friedman's personal papers, including correspondence with Solo, further evince his direct attention to the concerns posed by segregation.

8. Casey, "When Privatization Means Segregation."

9. Milton Friedman, "Lecture on Education and the State," Institute for Humane Studies Miscellaneous Records, June 23, 1955.

10. Gary S. Becker, *The Economics of Discrimination* (Chicago: University of Chicago Press, 1957); Jean-Baptiste Fleury, "Wandering through the Borderlands of the Social Sciences: Gary Becker's Economics of Discrimination," *History of Political Economy* 44, no. 1 (2012): 1–40.

11. Becker, *Economics of Discrimination*, Chapter 8.

12. Milton Friedman, *Capitalism and Freedom* (Chicago: University of Chicago Press, 1962): pp. 99–100.

13. Friedman, *Capitalism and Freedom*, pp. 100, 91.

14. Friedman, *Capitalism and Freedom*, p. 100.

15. Milton Friedman, "Education and the State," Milton Friedman Papers, Hoover Institution, June 23, 1955.

16. Milton Friedman to Warren Nutter, Milton Friedman Papers, Hoover Institution, March 2, 1959; Warren Nutter and James M. Buchanan, "The Economics of Universal Education," Thomas Jefferson Center for Political Economy, University of Virginia, 1959.

17. "Free Choice in Schools to Be Topic," *Charlottesville (VA) Daily Progress*, April 23, 1960; Milton Friedman, "The Market and Discrimination," Milton Friedman Papers, Hoover Institution, 1960; Milton Friedman to Leland Yeager, Milton Friedman Papers, Hoover Institution, February 1, 1961.

18. Phillip W. Magness, Art Carden, and Vincent Geloso, "James M. Buchanan and the Political Economy of Desegregation," *Southern Economic Journal* 85, no. 3 (January 2019). Leon Dure, the primary architect of the 1959 version of Virginia's

tuition grant system, explicitly intended his policy to impede the closure of the Prince Edward schools. See Leon Dure, "A Plan of Action," *Richmond Times-Dispatch*, January 20, 1958.

19. *Allen v. County School Board of Prince Edward County, Virginia*, 198 F. Supp. 497 (1961).

20. Milton Friedman, "The Voucher Idea," *New York Times*, September 23, 1973.

21. Albert O. Hirschman, *Exit, Voice, and Loyalty* (Cambridge, MA: Harvard University Press, 1970).

22. For more on Dure, see James H. Hershman, "The Opponents of Virginia's Massive Resistance," doctoral diss., University of Virginia, 1978.

23. Allie E. S. Stephens to Leon Dure, Leon Dure Papers, box 3, University of Virginia, April 3, 1963.

24. From Leon Dure Papers, box 3: Oliver Hill to Leon Dure, January 15, 1959; Leon Dure to Oliver Hill, March 12, 1959; E. B. Henderson to Leon Dure, January 14, 1959; Leon Dure to E. B. Henderson, July 20, 1959.

25. School desegregation plan submitted by John S. Battle Jr., Records of the Charlottesville School Board, box 3, University of Virginia, February 18, 1959.

26. Hardy C. Dillard, "Desegregation and the Future," Hardy Cross Dillard Papers, University of Virginia, January 26, 1959.

27. John S. Battle Jr., speech to Venable Elementary PTA, John S. Battle Jr. Papers, University of Virginia, March 23, 1959; "Battle Cautions against Move to Private Schools," *Charlottesville (VA) Daily Progress*, March 23, 1959.

28. Hardy C. Dillard to Robert Whitehead, Robert Whitehead Papers, box 23, University of Virginia, May 11, 1959.

29. "Private Schools Are Linked to Engulfment by Negroes," *Richmond News-Leader*, March 24, 1959; "News Briefs," *Hattiesburg (MS) American*, March 24, 1959, p. 8.

30. Ted McKown, "Forum Argues 'Free Choice' Plan," *Charlottesville (VA) Daily Progress*, March 27, 1959.

31. CPE memorandum, Charlottesville School Board Records, box 23, folder 22, University of Virginia, March 1959.

32. John S. Battle Jr., "Scholarship Program May Result in Even More Integration," *Lynchburg (VA) News*, April 29, 1959.

33. Battle, "Scholarship Program May Result in Even More Integration."

34. Lon K. Savage, "Tuition Plan Purpose Still Argued," *Richmond Times-Dispatch*, September 2, 1962.

35. "School Board in Arlington Rests Case," *Washington Evening Star*, September 3, 1958; Allan Jones, "Pupil Criteria Are Attacked in School Suit," *Richmond Times-Dispatch*, September 4, 1958; *Thompson v. County School Board of Arlington County*, 166 F. Supp. 529 (E.D. Va. 1958).

36. John Barron, "Joy and Reeves Duel in Court on Pupil Suit," *Washington Evening Star*, July 22, 1960; "Bonds for Drew Addition Asked," Desegregation of Arlington County Public Schools Records File #1291, Arlington Public Library, September 22, 1961.

37. Robert F. Williams, "Memorandum to Division Superintendents," Charlottesville School Board Records, box 4, folder 15, University of Virginia, April 28, 1959.

38. Robert M. Andrews, "Tightened Restrictions on Tuition Grants Asked," *Richmond Times-Dispatch,* November 2, 1960.

39. Robert F. Williams, "Hardly a Surprise," *Virginia Journal of Education*, November 1964.

40. *Griffin v. State Board of Education*, 296 F. Supp. 1178 (E.D. Va. 1969).

41. "Report on the Virginia Plan for Universal Education," Thomas Jefferson Center for Political Economy, Occasional Paper No. 2, 1965.

42. *Griffin v. School Board*, 377 U.S. 218 (1964); *Griffin v. State Board of Education*, 239 F. Supp. 560 (E.D. Va. 1965).

43. Brief of Citizens for Education Freedom, Amicus Curiae, filed February 14, 1964, Supreme Court of the United States, *Griffin et al. v. County School Board of Prince Edward County.*

Chapter Three

1. "When It Comes to American History Knowledge, Woodrow Wilson Foundation Finds Only One State Can Pass U.S. Citizenship Exam," Woodrow Wilson Foundation, February 15, 2019.

2. Jonah Edelman and Randi Weingarten, "Op-Ed: School Vouchers Don't Just Undermine Public Schools, They Undermine Our Democracy," *Los Angeles Times*, May 31, 2017.

3. Sarah M. Stitzlein, "Public Schooling and Democracy in the United States," in *Oxford Research Encyclopedia of Education*, ed. George W. Noblit (Oxford: Oxford University Press, 2017).

4. S. G. Tallentyre, *The Friends of Voltaire* (London: Smith, Elder & Co., 1906), p. 199.

5. The first use of this clever approach was in John L. Sullivan, James Piereson, and George E. Marcus, *Political Tolerance and American Democracy* (Chicago: University of Chicago Press, 1982).

6. Tejvan Pettinger, "Definition of Public Good," Economics Help, July 2018, https://www.economicshelp.org/micro-economic-essays/marketfailure/public-goods/.

7. Paul A. Samuelson, "The Pure Theory of Public Expenditure," *Review of Economics and Statistics* 36, no. 4 (1954): 387–89.

8. Mark Walker, "Public Goods: Examples," University of Arizona, undated, http://www.u.arizona.edu/~mwalker/11_PublicGoods/Public%20Goods%20 Examples.pdf.

9. For example, see Andrea Canning and Leezel Tangloa, "Ohio Mom Kelley Williams-Bolar Jailed for Sending Kids to Better School District," ABC News, January 26, 2011.

10. For an empirically grounded analysis of how K–12 education fails to meet the definition of a public good, see Corey A. DeAngelis, "Is Public Schooling a Public Good? An Analysis of Schooling Externalities," Cato Institute Policy Analysis no. 842, May 9, 2018.

11. Foundational works include Arthur Maass, *Muddy Waters: The Army Engineers and the Nation's Rivers* (Cambridge, MA: Harvard University Press, 1951); Samuel Huntington, "The Marasmus of the ICC: The Commission, the Railroads, and the Public Interest," *Yale Law Journal* 61, no. 4 (1952): 467–509; M. Marver Bernstein, *Regulating Business by Independent Commission* (Princeton: Princeton University Press, 1955); George Stigler, "The Theory of Economic Regulation," *Bell Journal of Economics and Management Science* 2 (1971): 3–21; Theodore J. Lowi, *The End of Liberalism: The Second Republic of the United States*, 2nd ed. (New York: W. W. Norton & Co., 1979); Jean-Jacques Laffont and Jean Tirole, "The Politics of Government Decision-Making: A Theory of Regulatory Capture," *Quarterly Journal of Economics* 106, no. 4 (1991): 1089–127.

12. Mark Chenoweth and Peggy Little, "Secret Laws for the Powerful," *Wall Street Journal*, July 24, 2019, p. A17.

13. Terry M. Moe, *Special Interest: Teachers Unions and America's Public Schools* (Washington: Brookings Institution, 2011); Robert Maranto, "Lessons from a Charter Lottery Loser: To Compete with Charter Schools, Reach Out to Outsiders," *American School Board Journal* 205, no. 5 (2018): 41–43.

14. For example, see Julie R. Trivitt and Patrick J. Wolf, "School Choice and the Branding of Catholic Schools," *Education Finance and Policy* 6, no. 2 (2011): 202–45; Albert Cheng, Julie R. Trivitt, and Patrick J. Wolf, "School Choice and the Branding of Milwaukee Private Schools," *Social Science Quarterly* 97, no. 2 (2016): 362–75; Elizabeth Tuten, "What Do Parents Want in Schools?," *Communities in Schools* blog, October 4, 2017.

15. *What Parents Want from Education: The Case for Real Choice*, Artemis Strategy Group, pp. 8–9.

16. Ruth Joy, *The American Covenant, Catholic Anthropology and Educating for American Citizenship: The Importance of the Catholic School Ethos, or, Four Men in a Bateau*, Kent State University, diss., August 2018; Margaret F. Brinig and Nicole Stelle Garnett, *Lost Classroom, Lost Community: Catholic Schools' Importance in Urban America* (Chicago: University of Chicago Press, 2014); Anthony S. Bryk, Valerie E. Lee, and

Peter B. Holland, *Catholic Schools and the Common Good* (Cambridge, MA: Harvard University Press, 1993).

17. About Us," National School Board Association, October 21, 2019, https://www.nsba.org/About.

18. For example, see Diane Ravitch, *Reign of Error: The Hoax of the Privatization Movement and the Danger to America's Public Schools* (New York: Vintage, 2014); Samuel E. Abrams, *Education and the Commercial Mindset* (Cambridge, MA: Harvard University Press, 2016).

19. For example, see Michael B. Berkman and Eric Plutzer, *Ten Thousand Democracies: Politics and Public Opinion in America's School Districts* (Washington: Georgetown University Press, 2005); William G. Howell, *Besieged: School Boards and the Future of Education Politics* (Washington: Brookings Institution, 2005); Christopher R. Berry and William G. Howell, "Accountability Lost: Student Learning Is Seldom a Factor in School Board Elections," *Education Next* 8, no. 1 (2008): 66–72.

20. Peter Meyer, "A Board's Eye View: Lessons from Life in Public Office," *Education Next* 4, no. 2 (2004): 30–37.

21. Andrew D. Catt, *Public Rules on Private Schools: Measuring the Regulatory Impact of State Statutes and School Choice Programs* (Indianapolis: Friedman Foundation for Educational Choice, 2014).

22. For example, see John Dewey, *Democracy in Education* (New York: Macmillan, 1916); Lawrence Cremin, *American Education: The National Experience* (New York: HarperCollins, 1980).

23. Harry Brighouse, *School Choice and Social Justice* (Oxford: Oxford University Press, 2000).

24. Charles Leslie Glenn Jr., *The Myth of the Common School* (Amherst: University of Massachusetts Press, 1987).

25. "Public Schooling Battle Map," Cato Institute, October 21, 2019.

26. Scott Franklin Abernathy, *School Choice and the Future of American Democracy* (Ann Arbor: University of Michigan Press, 2005), p. 14.

27. Albert O. Hirschman, *Exit, Voice, and Loyalty: Responses to Decline in Firms, Organizations, and States* (Cambridge, MA: Harvard University Press, 1970).

28. For example, see Brian Barry, "Review Article: 'Exit, Voice, and Loyalty,'" *British Journal of Political Science* 4, no. 1 (1974): 79–107.

29. Albert O. Hirschman, *Rival Views of Market Society and Other Recent Essays* (New York: Viking Penguin, 1986), 89.

30. For an example of this phenomenon in action, see Thomas Stewart and Patrick J. Wolf, *The School Choice Journey: School Vouchers and the Empowerment of Urban Families* (New York: Palgrave Macmillan, 2014).

31. Jay P. Greene, *Education Myths: What Special Interest Groups Want You to Believe about Our Schools—and Why It Isn't So* (Lanham, MD: Rowman & Littlefield, 2005).

32. Greene, *Education Myths.*

33. Corey A. DeAngelis, "Do Self-Interested Schooling Selections Improve Society? A Review of the Evidence," *Journal of School Choice* 11, no. 4 (2017): 546–58.

34. Andrew D. Catt et al., *The 123s of School Choice: What the Research Says about Private School Choice Programs in America* (Indianapolis: EdChoice, 2019).

35. Patrick J. Wolf, "Civics Exam: Schools of Choice Boost Civic Values," *Education Next* 7, no. 3 (2007): 66–72.

Chapter Four

1. Clint Bolick, *Voucher Wars: Waging the Legal Battle over School Choice* (Washington: Cato Institute, 2003), 15–43.

2. *Davis v. Grover*, 480 N.W.2d 460, 465 (Wis. 1992).

3. *Jackson v. Benson*, 578 N.W.2d 602 (Wis. 1998).

4. Bolick, *Voucher Wars*, 67–88.

5. *Espinoza v. Montana Department of Revenue*, 591 U.S. ___ (2020); *Zelman v. Simmons-Harris*, 536 U.S. 639 (2002); *Gaddy v. Georgia Department of Revenue*, 802 S.E.2d 225 (Ga. 2017); *Schwartz v. Lopez*, 382 P.3d 886 (Nev. 2016); *Oliver v. Hofmeister*, 368 P.3d 1270 (Okla. 2016); *Magee v. Boyd*, 175 So. 3d 79 (Ala. 2015); *Hart v. State*, 774 S.E.2d 281 (N.C. 2015); *Meredith v. Pence*, 984 N.E.2d 1213 (Ind. 2013); *Kotterman v. Killian*, 972 P.2d 606 (Ariz. 1999); *Simmons-Harris v. Goff*, 711 N.E.2d 203 (Ohio 1999); *Jackson v. Benson*, 578 N.W.2d 602 (Wis. 1998); *Griffith v. Bower*, 747 N.E.2d 423 (Ill. App. Ct. 2001); *Toney v. Bower*, 744 N.E.2d 351 (Ill. App. Ct. 2001); *Asociación de Maestros de Puerto Rico v. Secretario del Departamento de Educación*, No. CT-2018-6, 2018 TSPR 150, 2018 PR Sup. LEXIS 137 (Aug. 9, 2018).

6. *Arizona Christian School Tuition Organization v. Winn*, 563 U.S. 125 (2011); *Gaddy v. Georgia Department of Revenue*, 802 S.E.2d 225 (Ga. 2017); *Duncan v. New Hampshire*, 102 A.3d 913 (N.H. 2014); *McCall v. Scott*, 199 So. 3d 359 (Fla. Dist. Ct. App. 2016).

7. Arizona offers a pertinent example. After the Arizona Supreme Court struck down two voucher programs as unconstitutional, *Cain v. Horne*, 202 P.3d 1178 (Ariz. 2009), while distinguishing its prior decision in *Kotterman*, supra n.5, upholding a scholarship program incentivized by tax credits, the Supreme Court let an appellate court decision stand upholding a publicly funded education savings account program from constitutional attack. *Niehaus v. Huppenthal*, 310 P.3d 983 (Ariz. Ct. App. 2013).

8. "The ABCs of School Choice," EdChoice, 2019.

9. *Zelman v. Simmons-Harris*, 536 U.S. 639 (2002).

10. The federal Establishment Clause, which applies to the states through the Fourteenth Amendment, provides that "Congress"—and, by judicial extension, the states—"shall make no law respecting an establishment of religion."

11. *Zelman v. Simmons-Harris* at 647, 649.

12. *Zelman* at 652, 653 [emphasis omitted].

13. *Espinoza v. Montana Department of Revenue*, 591 U.S. ___ (2020).

14. *Espinoza*, slip op. at 20.

15. *Espinoza*, slip op. at 20. School choice opponents will likely point to the fact that *Espinoza* turned "expressly on religious status and not religious use," *id.* at 10, to argue that the decision will have only a narrow impact. Indeed, one choice opponent was quick to say, "Roberts' opinion simply finds that because the benefits of the tax credit vouchers were being withheld solely because of the religious character of the school, it violated the free exercise clause of the First Amendment. [Roberts] didn't reach into whether those monies were used to inculcate students." Mary Ellen Klas, "Court Ruling Giving Religious Schools Access to State Aid has Limited Impact on Florida" *Miami Herald*, June 30, 2020. Of course, not addressing "religious uses" is not the same as endorsing discrimination against religious uses. Indeed, the Court in *Espinoza* declared that just because the case turned on status discrimination does not mean "that some lesser degree of scrutiny applies to discrimination against religious uses of government aid." *Id.* at 12.

16. George A. Clowes. "Voucher Wars Will Continue," Heartland Institute, July 1, 2003.

17. See Richard D. Komer, "School Choice and State Constitutions' Religion Clauses," *Journal of School Choice* 3, no. 4 (2009): 331-352.

18. See Richard D. Komer and Olivia Grady, *School Choice and State Constitutions: A Guide to Designing School Choice Programs*, 2nd ed., Institute for Justice and American Legislative Exchange Council, March 2017.

19. "Blaine Amendments," Institute for Justice, October 21, 2019, https://ij.org/issues/school-choice/blaine-amendments/.

20. For a comprehensive biography on Blaine and his political career, see Neil Rolde, *The Continental Liar from the State of Maine: James G. Blaine* (Thomaston, ME: Tilbury House, 2006).

21. Rolde, *Continental Liar*, 164–66.

22. *Mitchell v. Helms*, 530 U.S. 793, 828 (2000) (plurality opinion.): "Consideration of the [Blaine] amendment arose at a time of pervasive hostility to the Catholic Church and to Catholics in general, and it was an open secret that 'sectarian' was code for 'Catholic'"; *Zelman*, 536 U.S. at 721 (Justice Breyer dissenting), (recognizing that anti-Catholic sentiment "played a significant role" in state Blaine provisions and that references to "'sectarian' schools . . . in practical terms meant Catholic").

23. Lloyd P. Jorgenson, *The State and the Non-Public School: 1825–1925* (Columbia, MO: University of Missouri, 1987), 69–72.

24. Jorgenson, *State and the Non-Public School,* 60.

25. Jorgenson, 83–85.

26. Joseph P. Viteritti, "Blaine's Wake: School Choice, the First Amendment, and State Constitutional Law," *Harvard Journal of Law and Public Policy* 21, no. 3, (Summer 1998): 657-671.

27. See, e.g., *Oliver*, 368 P.3d at 1276; *Meredith*, 984 N.E.2d at 1228–29 ("The direct beneficiaries under the voucher program are the families of eligible students and not the schools selected by the parents for their children to attend"); *Goff*, 711 N.E.2d at 211 ("The primary beneficiaries of the School Voucher Program are children, not sectarian schools"); *Jackson*, 578 N.W.2d at 626–27 (describing vouchers as "life preservers" that have "been thrown" to students participating in the program). The two outliers are *Taxpayers for Public Education v. Douglas County School District*, 351 P.3d 461 (Colo. 2015) and *Cain*, 202 P.3d 1178. But the Colorado decision was vacated by the U.S. Supreme Court after *Trinity Lutheran Church of Columbia, Inc. v. Comer*, 582 U.S. ___ (2017), and the case became moot after Douglas County repealed the challenged program. The continuing vitality of *Cain* is in serious question after the Arizona Supreme Court let stand a decision of the Arizona Court of Appeals upholding Arizona's Empowerment Scholarship Account program. See *Niehaus*, 310 P.3d 983.

28. *Winn*, 563 U.S. at 144; *Gaddy*, 802 S.E.2d at 230; *Magee*, 175 So. 3d at 136; *Kotterman*, 972 P.2d at 618; *McCall*, 199 So. 3d at 370–71; *Toney*, 744 N.E.2d at 357, appeal denied, 754 N.E.2d 1293 (Ill. 2001); *Griffith*, 747 N.E.2d at 426 (same), appeal denied, 755 N.E.2d 477 (Ill. 2001). But see *Espinoza v. Montana Department of Revenue*, 393 Mont. 446 (2018) (reversed on other grounds by *Espinoza v. Montana Department of Revenue*, 591 U.S. ___ (2020)).

29. See *Kotterman*, 972 P.2d at 618.

30. *Niehaus*, 310 P.3d 983; *Schwartz*, 382 P.3d 886.

31. *Cain*, 202 P.3d 1178. The Arizona Supreme Court's decision in *Cain* did not turn on a distinction between religious and nonreligious schools. Rather, it turned on a distinction between public schools and private schools, concluding that one of Arizona's Blaine amendments precluded aid to all private schools. Thus, it is not clear that the U.S. Supreme Court's decision in *Espinoza* directly impacts the outcome in *Cain*.

32. *Cain*, 1184.

33. *Cain*, 1185.

34. Archived video of the *Cain* oral argument, https://supremestateaz.granicus.com/MediaPlayer.php?view_id=11&clip_id=1177.

35. See Matthew Ladner and Nick Dranias, "Education Savings Accounts: Giving Parents Control of Their Children's Education," Goldwater Institute, January 2011.

36. *Niehaus*, 310 P.3d at 988.

37. *Chittenden Town School District v. Vermont Department of Education*, 738 A.2d 539 (Vt. 1999). Of course, the *Chittenden* decision appears to have been abrogated the U.S. Supreme Court's decision in *Espinoza* and is likely no longer good law.

38. Tim Keller, "12 Myths and Realities about Private Educational Choice Programs." Institute for Justice, December 2019.

39. *Hart*, 774 S.E.2d at 289–90; *Meredith*, 984 N.E.2d at 1223; *Goff*, 711 N.E.2d at 212 & n.2; *Jackson*, 578 N.W.2d at 628; *Davis*, 480 N.W.2d at 474. But see *Bush v. Holmes*, 919 So. 2d 392 (Fla. 2006).

40. *McCall*, 199 So. 3d at 370–71.

41. "The ABCs of School Choice," EdChoice, 2019.

42. See, e.g., Arkansas Constitution Article XIV, §2; Colorado Constitution Article IX, §3.

43. *Louisiana Federation of Teachers v. State*, 18 So. 3d 1033 (La. 2013).

44. See, e.g., Arizona Constitution Article IX, §7; Mississippi. Constitution Article IV, §66.

45. See *Kotterman*, 972 P.2d at 621.

46. See, e.g., Florida Constitution Article III, §6; Ohio Constitution Article II, §15(D).

47. *Goff*, 711 N.E.2d 203. Florida's Gardiner Scholarship Program was also challenged under a single-subject provision, but the lawsuit was thrown out because the plaintiffs were not personally injured and therefore did not have standing to file the case. *Faasse v. Scott*, No. 2014-CA-001859, 2014 WL 6634183 (Fla. Cir. Ct. Oct. 7, 2014).

48. See, e.g., Arizona Constitution Article IV, §19.

49. E.g., *Davis*, 480 N.W.2d at 469.

50. See, e.g., Colorado Constitution Article IX, §15.

51. *Owens v. Colorado Congress of Parents*, 92 P.3d 933 (Colo. 2004). There is nothing in the opinion to prevent the legislature from passing a new program and funding it from another source.

Chapter Five

1. National Center for Education Statistics, "Digest of Education Statistics: 2019," Table 236.55.

2. National Center for Education Statistics, "Digest of Education Statistics: 2019," Table 236.10.

3. Andrew Crook, "AFT's Weingarten on Closure of Chavez Schools in Washington, D.C.," American Federation of Teachers, 2019.

4. Chris Churchill, "Churchill: For Better Schools, Ditch the Standardized Tests," *Times Union* (Albany, NY), 2018.

5. Corey A. DeAngelis and Heidi H. Erickson, "What Leads to Successful School Choice Programs? A Review of the Theories and Evidence," *Cato Journal* 38, no. 1 (2018): 247–64.

6. Milton Friedman, "The Role of Government in Education," in *Economics and the Public Interest*, ed. Robert A. Solo (New Brunswick, NJ: Rutgers University Press, 1955), pp. 123–44.

7. John E. Chubb and Terry M. Moe, "Politics, Markets, and the Organization of Schools," *American Political Science Review* 82, no. 4 (1988): 1065–87; J. E. Chubb and T. M. Moe, "America's Public Schools: Choice Is a Panacea," *Brookings Review* 8, no. 3 (1990): 4–12; J. E. Chubb and T. M. Moe, *Politics, Markets, and America's Schools* (Washington: Brookings Institution Press, 1990).

8. Alexis de Tocqueville, *De la démocratie en Amérique* [Democracy in America] (Paris: Librairie de Charles Gosselin, 1835).

9. Bryan Caplan, *The Myth of the Rational Voter: Why Democracies Choose Bad Policies* (Princeton: Princeton University Press, 2011); Ilya Somin, *Democracy and Political Ignorance: Why Smaller Government Is Smarter* (Palo Alto, CA: Stanford University Press, 2016).

10. Eric A. Hanushek, "Assessing the Effects of School Resources on Student Performance: An Update," *Educational Evaluation and Policy Analysis* 19, no. 2 (1997): 141–64; Eric A. Hanushek and Alfred Lindseth, "Performance-Based Funding," *Defining Ideas: A Hoover Institution Journal* 1 (2009): 101–105.

11. Corey A. DeAngelis, "Divergences between Effects on Test Scores and Effects on Non-cognitive Skills," *Educational Review* (2019); Colin Hitt, Michael Q. McShane, and Patrick J. Wolf, "Do Impacts on Test Scores Even Matter? Lessons from Long-Run Outcomes in School Choice Research," American Enterprise Institute, 2018.

12. Eric Bettinger and Robert Slonim, "Using Experimental Economics to Measure the Effects of a Natural Educational Experiment on Altruism," *Journal of Public Economics* 90, nos. 8–9 (2006): 1625–48; Diether W. Beuermann and C. Kirabo Jackson, "Do Parents Know Best? The Short and Long-Run Effects of Attending the Schools That Parents Prefer," National Bureau of Economic Research Working Paper No. 24920, 2018; Corey A. DeAngelis and Patrick J. Wolf, "Private School Choice and Crime: Evidence from Milwaukee," *Social Science Quarterly* 100, no. 6 (2019): 2302-2315; Corey A. DeAngelis and Patrick J. Wolf, "Private School Choice and Character: More Evidence from Milwaukee, Department of Education Reform (EDRE) Working Paper No. 2019-03, University of Arkansas 2019; David. J. Deming, "Better Schools, Less Crime?," *Quarterly Journal of Economics* 126, no. 4 (2011): 2063–115; Gabriel Heller-Sahlgren, "Smart but Unhappy: Independent-School Competition and the Wellbeing-Efficiency Trade-off in Education," *Economics of Education Review* 62 (2018): 66–81.

13. John Dewey, *Democracy and Education* (New York: Macmillan, 1916); Johann G. Fichte, *Fichte: Early Philosophical Writings* (Ithaca, NY: Cornell University Press, 1993); John T. Gatto, *Dumbing Us Down: The Hidden Curriculum of Compulsory Schooling* (Vancouver, Canada: New Society Publishers, 2002); Horace Mann, *Lectures on Education* (Boston: W. B. Fowle and N. Capen, 1855); Benjamin Rush, "Thoughts upon the Mode of Education Proper in a Republic," in *Essays on Education in the Early Republic*, ed. Frederick Rudolph (Cambridge, MA: Harvard University Press, 1968).

14. Raymond E. Callahan, *Education and the Cult of Efficiency* (Chicago: University of Chicago Press, 1962); John T. Gatto, *Weapons of Mass Instruction: A Schoolteacher's Journey through the Dark World of Compulsory Schooling* (Gabriola Island, Canada: New Society Publishers, 2010); Salman Khan, *The One World Schoolhouse: Education Reimagined* (New York: Twelve, 2012).

15. Paul A. Samuelson, "The Pure Theory of Public Expenditure," *Review of Economics and Statistics* 36, no. 4 (1954): 387–89.

16. Henry M. Levin, "Education as a Public and Private Good," *Journal of Policy Analysis and Management* 6, no. 4 (1987): 628–41; Christopher Lubienski, "Whither the Common Good? A Critique of Home Schooling," *Peabody Journal of Education* 75, nos. 1–2 (2000): 207–32.

17. Richard A. Musgrave, "A Multiple Theory of Budget Determination," *FinanzArchiv // Public Finance Analysis* 17, no. 3 (1956): 333–43.

18. Ronald H. Coase, "The Problem of Social Cost," *Journal of Law and Economics* 56, no. 4 (2013): 837–77; A. Pigou, *The Economics of Welfare* (London: Macmillan, 1920).

19. Richard A. Epstein, *Free Markets under Siege: Cartels, Politics, and Social Welfare* (Stanford, CA: Hoover Institution, 2008).

20. Arthur C. Pigou, *The Economics of Welfare* (London: Macmillan, 1920).

21. Lance Lochner and Enrico Moretti, "The Effect of Education on Crime: Evidence from Prison Inmates, Arrests, and Self-Reports," *American Economic Review* 94, no. 1 (2004): 155–89; Andrés Blais et al., "Where Does Turnout Decline Come From?," *European Journal of Political Research* 43, no. 2 (2004): 221–36.

22. Musgrave, "Multiple Theory of Budget Determination."

23. Friedman, "Role of Government," pp. 123–44.

24. Corey A. DeAngelis, "Is Public Schooling a Public Good? An Analysis of Schooling Externalities," Cato Institute Policy Analysis no. 842, May 9, 2018.

25. Friedman, "Role of Government," pp. 123–44.

26. Arthur C. Pigou, *The Economics of Welfare*, 4th ed. (London: Macmillan, 1932), p. 332.

27. David Friedman, "Laissez-faire in Population: The Least Bad Solution," Population Council, 1972.

28. David Friedman, "David D. Friedman on Government Education," March 28, 2009, YouTube video, https://www.youtube.com/watch?v=stJQrVkMPH4.

29. Edwin G. West, *Education and the State: A Study in Political Economy* (London: Institute of Economic Affairs, 1965).

30. Frank Dikötter, *Mao's Great Famine: The History of China's Most Devastating Catastrophe, 1958–1962* (New York: Walter & Co., 2010); Michael Ellman, "Soviet Repression Statistics: Some Comments," *Europe-Asia Studies* 54, no. 7 (2002): 1151–72; Rudolph J. Rummel, *China's Bloody Century: Genocide and Mass Murder since 1900* (New York: Routledge, 2017).

31. West, *Education and the State.*

32. Elise Swanson, "Can We Have It All? A Review of the Impacts of School Choice on Racial Integration," *Journal of School Choice* 11, no. 4 (2017): 507–26.

33. Corey A. DeAngelis and Heidi H. Erickson, "What Leads to Successful School Choice Programs? A Review of the Theories and Evidence," *Cato Journal* 38, no. 1 (2018): 247–64.

34. See, for instance, Cassandra M. Guarino, Abigail B. Brown, and Adam E. Wyse, "Can Districts Keep Good Teachers in the Schools That Need Them Most?," *Economics of Education Review* 30, no. 5 (October 2011): 962–79; Linda Darling-Hammond, "Inequality in Teaching and Schooling: How Opportunity Is Rationed to Students of Color in America," *The Right Thing to Do, the Smart Thing to Do: Enhancing Diversity in Health Professions: Summary of the Symposium on Diversity in Health Professions in Honor of Herbert W. Nickens, M.D.* (Washington: National Academies Press, 2001); Charles T. Clotfelter, Helen F. Ladd, and Jacob L. Vigdor, "Teacher Mobility, School Segregation, and Pay-Based Policies to Level the Playing Field," *Education Finance and Policy* 6, no. 3 (Summer 2011): 399–438.

Chapter Six

1. Benjamin Scafidi, "Georgia 2020: Educational Opportunity for All Georgia Students," Georgia Public Policy Foundation, 2018.

2. The overall weighted average for the average value of vouchers per student in FY 2015 and tax-credit disbursements per student via tax-credit scholarship programs in FY 2014 was $4,453. The weighted average of K–12 public school spending in these programs' jurisdictions was $11,210. Because we're comparing costs of some programs that exclusively serve special-needs students with average public school costs, this 40 percent share is an overestimate. Authors' calculations are based on data from Martin F. Lueken, "The Fiscal Effects of Tax-Credit Scholarship Programs in the United States," *Journal of School Choice* 12, no. 2 (2018): 181–215; and Martin F. Lueken, "Fiscal Effects of School Vouchers: Examining the Savings and Costs of America's Private School Voucher Programs," EdChoice, 2018.

3. As an example, a former public high school principal who now heads a public school advocacy organization stated in the *Washington Post* that the number one negative consequence of choice was that "privatized school choice will inevitably reduce funding for your local neighborhood public schools." Valerie Strauss, "Three big problems with school 'choice' that supporters don't like to talk about," *Washington Post*, May 3, 2017.

4. Author's calculation based on data from National Center for Education Statistics, "Digest of Education Statistics: 2018," Table 208.20, https://nces.ed.gov/programs/digest/d18/tables/dt18_208.20.asp?current=yes; National Center for

Education Statistics, "Digest of Education Statistics: 2018," Table 206.10, https://nces.ed.gov/programs/digest/d17/tables/dt17_206.10.asp?current=yes.

5. "The 123s of School Choice: What the Research Says about Private School Choice Programs in America," EdChoice, 2019, pp. 32–37.

6. Robert M. Costrell, "The Fiscal Impact of the Milwaukee Parental Choice Program in Milwaukee, Wisconsin, 1993–2008," Fayetteville, AK: School Choice Demonstration Project Milwaukee Evaluation Report #2, University of Arkansas, 2008; Robert M. Costrell, "The Fiscal Impact of the Milwaukee Parental Choice Program: 2010–2011 Update and Policy Options," Fayetteville, AK: School Choice Demonstration Project Milwaukee Evaluation Report #22, University of Arkansas, 2010.

7. "123s of School Choice."

8. Julie R. Trivitt and Corey A. DeAngelis, "The Fiscal Effect of Eliminating the Louisiana Scholarship Program on State Education Expenditures," Department of Education Reform (EDRE) Working Paper no. 2016-06, University of Arkansas, June 2016.

9. Corey A. DeAngelis and Julie R. Trivitt, "Squeezing the Public School Districts: The Fiscal Effects of Eliminating the Louisiana Scholarship Program," EDRE Working Paper no. 2016-10, University of Arkansas, August 2016.

10. Robert M. Costrell, "The Fiscal Impact of the Milwaukee Parental Choice Program: 2010–2011 Update and Policy Options," School Choice Demonstration Project Milwaukee Evaluation Report #22, University of Arkansas, 2010.

11. Martin F. Lueken, "Fiscal Effects of School Vouchers: Examining the Savings and Costs of America's Private School Voucher Programs," EdChoice, 2018.

12. See Lueken, "Fiscal Effects," p. 86, n. 24, for additional details.

13. Based on the range of assumptions employed, tax-credit scholarship programs generated between $1,650 and $3,000 per student in net savings for taxpayers, or $1.7 billion to $3.4 billion between 1998 and 2014.

14. Anthony G. Girardi and Angela Gullickson, "Iowa's School Tuition Organization Tax Credit: Tax Credits Program Evaluation Study," Tax Research and Program Analysis, Iowa Department of Revenue, December 2017.

15. Jonathan N. Mills and Patrick J. Wolf, "The Effects of the Louisiana Scholarship Program on Student Achievement after Four Years," EDRE Working Paper no. 2019-10, University of Arkansas, April 2019; M. Dynarski et al., "Evaluation of the DC Opportunity Scholarship Program: Impacts Two Years after Students Applied," National Center for Education Evaluation and Regional Assistance, Washington, 2018.

16. "Florida Tax Credit Scholarship Program," Office of Program Policy Analysis and Government Accountability, March 1, 2010.

17. Patrick J. Wolf and Michael McShane, "Is the Juice Worth the Squeeze? A Benefit/Cost Analysis of the District of Columbia Opportunity Scholarship Program," *Education Finance and Policy* 8, no. 1 (2013): 74–99.

18. Stephen Q. Cornman, Lei Zhou, Malia R. Howell, and Jumaane Young, "Revenues and Expenditures for Public Elementary and Secondary Education: School Year 2015–16 (Fiscal Year 2016): First Look (NCES 2019-301)," National Center for Education Statistics, Washington, 2018.

19. The two largest federal K–12 education programs are Title I and the Individuals with Disabilities Education Act (IDEA). Title I grants are based largely on census poverty estimates and education costs in each state, and IDEA allocations are based on characteristics of the general population rather than public school enrollment; see Lueken, "Fiscal Effects."

20. Benjamin Scafidi, "The Fiscal Effects of School Choice Programs on Public School Districts," Friedman Foundation for Educational Choice, 2012; Robert Bifulco and Randall Reback, "Fiscal Impacts of Charter Schools: Lessons from New York," *Education Finance and Policy* 9, no. 1 (2014): 86–107; Martin F. Lueken, "The Tax-Credit Scholarship Audit: Do Publicly Funded Private School Choice Programs Save Money?," EdChoice, 2016; Dorfman uses an econometric approach and finds estimates of short-run variable costs significantly higher than the three prior studies. Jeffrey H. Dorfman, "The Economics of Building a Voucher or Educational Savings Account Program in Georgia," Georgia Public Policy Foundation, 2019, https://secureservercdn.net/198.71.233.138/m01.813.myftpupload.com/wp-content/uploads/2019/03/190227IASchoolchoicefinal-min.pdf.

21. Benjamin Scafidi, "Back to the Staffing Surge: The Great Teacher Salary Stagnation and the Decades-Long Employment Growth in American Public Schools," EdChoice, 2017.

22. Thomas D. Snyder and Charlene M. Hoffman, "Digest of Education Statistics: 1994," National Center for Education Statistics, 1994, p. 56, Table 42, and p. 91, Table 84; Thomas D. Snyder and Charlene M. Hoffman, "Staff and Teachers in Public Elementary and Secondary Schools, by State: Fall 1987 to Fall 1993," National Center for Education Statistics, April 1995, Table 203.45.

23. Author calculations from data files provided by the Indiana Department of Education. Charter and virtual schools are excluded.

24. "123s of School Choice."

Chapter Seven

1. Paul Hill and Marguerite Roza, "Curing Baumol's Disease: In Search of Productivity Gains in K–12 Schooling," Center on Reinventing Public Education, July 2010.

2. Mark J. Perry, "The Magic and Miracle of the Marketplace: Christmas 1964 vs. 2014—There's No Comparison," American Enterprise Institute, December 18, 2014.

3. Mark J. Perry, "Data Reveal That the Average Working American Is Better Off Today Than in the 1950s, and 'Wage Stagnation' Is a Myth," American Enterprise Institute, January 29, 2014.

4. John Stuart Mill, *On Liberty* (London: John W. Parker and Son, 1859), chap. 13.

5. Mill, *On Liberty.*

6. Albert Shanker, "A Message to the President: Put Merit in Merit Schools," *New York Times*, July 23, 1989.

7. "The 123s of School Choice: What the Research Says about Private School Choice Programs in America," EdChoice, 2019, pp. 32–37.

8. Anna J. Egalite, "Measuring Competitive Effects from School Voucher Programs: A Systematic Review." *Journal of School Choice* 7, no. 4 (2013): 443–64.

9. Brian Gill, "The Effect of Charter Schools on Students in Traditional Public Schools: A Review of the Evidence," *Education Next*, November 2, 2016.

10. Ludger Woessmann, "Why Students in Some Countries Do Better: International Evidence on the Importance of Education Policy," *Education Matters* 1, no. 2 (Summer 2001): 64-74.

11. Corey A. DeAngelis, "Does Private Schooling Affect International Test Scores? Evidence from a Natural Experiment," *School Effectiveness and School Improvement*, May 29, 2019.

12. Ludger Woessmann and Martin West, "Competition from Private Schools Boosts Performance System-Wide," *VoxEU*, December 2, 2010.

13. National Center for Education Statistics, "Digest of Education Statistics: 2018," Table 204.10, https://nces.ed.gov/programs/digest/d18/tables/dt18_204.10.asp?current=yes.

14. The NAEP Mathematics and Reading exams have been scaled and timed to allow for the calculation of cohort gains, for more details see Richard J. Cowley, *Growth in School Revisited Achievement Gains from the Fourth to the Eighth Grade. Publication of ETS* (Princeton: Educational Testing Service, 2003), https://www.ets.org/Media/Research/pdf/PICGROWTH2.pdf.

15. NAEP revised the science exams starting in 2009 and at the time of this writing provides statewide science scores for the 2009 to 2015 period. The latest available mathematics and reading scores extend to 2017.

16. Diane Whitmore Schanzenbach, Megan Mumford, and Lauren Bauer, "Who Has Access to Charter Schools?," Brookings Institution Hamilton Project, 2016, p. 4.

17. Matthew Ladner, "In Defense of Education's 'Wild West,'" *Education Next* 18, no. 2 (Spring 2018): 17-23.

18. Jeanne Faulconer, "What Is a Homeschool Co-op?," TheHomeSchoolMom, 2014.

19. Jason Tanz, "The Techies Who Are Hacking Education by Home Schooling Their Kids," *Wired*, February 4, 2015.

20. Arianna Prothero, "Micro-Schools Could Be New Competition for Private K–12," *Education Week* 35, no. 19 (January 2016): 11.

21. Justin C. Cohen, "School Disruption on the Small Scale: Can Micro-Schools Break Out of an Elite Niche?," *Education Next* 17, no. 2 (Spring 2017): 28-33.

22. Ron Matus, "Lessons from the Renaissance Micro-School," *RedefinED* (blog), 2018.

23. Will Fitzhugh, "A 20-Year Lesson: Evidence from America and Britain Shows That Independence for Schools Works," *The Economist*, July 7, 2012.

Chapter Eight

1. Allen St. John, "The Rich Get Richer: Former NBA MVP Kevin Durant Signs 2-Year Deal with Golden State Warriors," *Forbes*, July 4, 2016.

2. Serving Our Children, "How It Works," https://servingourchildrendc.org/our-program/how-it-works/.

3. Steven Singer, "Top 10 Reasons School Choice Is No Choice," *Huffington Post*, February 19, 2017.

4. Singer, "Top 10 Reasons."

5. Marge Scherer, "On Savage Inequalities: A Conversation with Jonathan Kozol," *Educational Leadership* 50, no. 4 (December 1992/January 1993): 4–9.

6. An increasing number of localities are offering what is called public school choice. Cities such as New York, Denver, and New Orleans have enrollment systems that allow families to apply for admission in a variety of traditional district-operated schools or charter schools outside conventional assignment zones. Other localities have voluntary busing programs that enable families to attend schools in districts outside their assigned school district. Boston's Metropolitan Council for Educational Opportunity (METCO) program is an existing example of such a program. These kinds of programs, however, remain relatively uncommon.

7. Education Data Partnership, "Mission San Jose High," Ed-Data, http://www.ed-data.org/school/Alameda/Fremont-Unified/Mission-San-Jose-High, September 22, 2018.

8. Ann Owens, Sean F. Reardon, and Christopher Jencks, "Income Segregation between Schools and School Districts," *American Education Research Journal* 53 (2016): 1159–97.

9. Richard J. Murnane, Sean F. Reardon, Preeya P. Mbekeani, and Anne Lamb, "Who Goes to Private School?," *Education Next* 18 (Fall 2018): 58–66.

10. "The ABCs of School Choice," EdChoice, 2019.

11. Murnane et al., "Who Goes to Private School?"

12. Albert Cheng and Patrick J. Wolf, "Religious School Brands as a School Choice Communication Tool," in *Family Involvement in Faith-Based Schools*, ed. Diana Hiatt-Michael (Charlotte, NC: Information Age Publishing Inc., 2017), 15–32.

13. Andrew D. Catt and Evan Rhinesmith, "Why Indiana Parents Choose: A Cross-Sector Survey of Parents' Views in a Robust School Choice Environment," EdChoice, 2019.

14. Andrew D. Catt and Albert Cheng, "Families' Experiences on the New Frontier of Educational Choice," EdChoice, 2019.

15. Corey DeAngelis, "Vouchers Tend to Serve the Less Advantaged," *Education Next*, March 8, 2018.

16. Numbers reported for SCSF are in 2018 dollars.

17. Albert Cheng, Matthew M. Chingos, and Paul E. Peterson, "Experimentally Estimated Impacts of School Voucher on Educational Attainments of Moderately and Severely Disadvantaged Students," Program on Education Policy and Governance, Harvard University, 2019.

18. Greg Rosalsky, "Obama Administration Softens Position on D.C. Voucher Program," *Huffington Post*, June 18, 2012 [emphasis added].

19. Michelle Rhee, personal communication, October 26, 2017.

20. Albert Cheng, Collin Hitt, Brian Kisida, and Jonathan N. Mills, "'No Excuses' Charter Schools: A Meta-Analysis of the Experimental Evidence on Student Achievement," *Journal of School Choice* 11 (2017): 209–38; Sarah Cohodes, "Charter Schools and the Achievement Gap," *Future of Children* (Winter 2018): 1–16.

21. Sarah Cohodes and Susan M. Dynarski, "Massachusetts Charter Cap Holds Back Disadvantaged Students," Brookings Institution Evidence Speaks Reports, September 15, 2016; Thomas J. Kane, "The Cost of the Charter Cap: Evidence Shows Low-Income, Urban Students Pay the Price," *CommonWealth*, October 5, 2016.

22. Daniel Hamlin and Albert Cheng, "Parental Empowerment, Involvement, and Satisfaction: A Comparison of Choosers of Charter, Catholic, Christian, and District-Run Public Schools," *Education Administration Quarterly* (forthcoming).

23. Albert Cheng, Michael B. Henderson, David Houston, Paul E. Peterson, and Martin R. West, "Public Support Climbs for Teacher Pay, School Expenditures, Charter Schools, and Universal Vouchers," *Education Next* 19, no. 1 (2019): 8–26.

24. Samuel Barrows, Albert Cheng, Paul E. Peterson, and Martin R. West, "Do Charters Pose a Threat to Private Schools? Evidence from Nationally Representative Surveys of U.S. Parents," *Journal of School Choice* 13 (2019): 10–32; Evan Rhinesmith, "A Review of the Research on Parent Satisfaction in Private School Choice Programs," *Journal of School Choice* 11 (2017): 585–603.

Chapter Nine

1. As Terry Moe wrote in *Schools, Vouchers, and the American Public* (Washington: Brookings Institution, 1990), 35, equalitarians are "less impressed with the free market" and believe school choice policies "are not just about choice, competition, and performance incentives," nor are school vouchers "necessarily for all children," but rather such policies are "about bringing equal opportunity to the children in greatest need." For a lengthier discussion of the differences between the libertarian and equalitarian visions for school choice policies, see Myron Lieberman, *The Educational Morass* (Lanham, MD: Rowman & Littlefield Education, 2007), 195–219. Lieberman writes,

> The supporters of school choice differ on the extent of government regulations they will accept. The libertarian wing wants to restrict government regulation of private schools . . . ; they prefer as little regulation as possible, but it is inaccurate to portray them as insistent upon the complete absence of regulations or upon limiting regulation to health and safety issues. Their main concern is that state education bureaucracies hostile to vouchers will try to regulate them out of existence. . . .
>
> The equalitarians propose a variety of measures intended to bring about equity. These measures include the prohibition of add-ons [i.e., paying tuition out of pocket beyond the value of the voucher], the requirement that private schools that admit voucher-bearing students reserve a certain percentage of admissions for children from poor families, and the use of lotteries when there are more applications than vacancies. These and other measures favored by equalitarians weaken competition. (pp. 208–09)

2. Douglas N. Harris, "Two Views: Why School Vouchers Won't Work—an Economist's Perspective," *Statesman*, March 27, 2017.

3. John White, "America's Most Disadvantaged Students Need Real Accountability, Not Ideology," *Flypaper*, January 12, 2016.

4. It should be noted that equalitarians, libertarians, and others have expressed concerns that schools will raise tuition to capture the full value of the voucher in addition to what parents are willing to pay. Our focus in this chapter is on the specifically equalitarian concern.

5. White, "America's Most Disadvantaged Students."

6. "Florida Tax Credit Scholarship Program," EdChoice, https://www.edchoice.org/school-choice/programs/florida-tax-credit-scholarship-program/, April 20, 2020.

7. "Florida Tax Credit Scholarship Program."

8. National Center for Education Statistics, "Digest of Education Statistics: 2017," Table 203.20, https://nces.ed.gov/programs/digest/d17/tables/dt17_203.20.asp;

National Center for Education Statistics, "Digest of Education Statistics: 2017," Table 236.75, https://nces.ed.gov/programs/digest/d17/tables/dt17_236.75.asp.

9. "K-20 Education Code," 2018 Florida Statutes, 2018.

10. "Florida Tax Credit Scholarship Program."

11. "Florida Tax Credit Scholarship Program."

12. "Step Up for Students Office of Policy and Public Affairs," Florida Tax Credit Scholarship 2017–18 Fact Sheet, March 2018.

13. Zahid Kisa, Melissa Dyehouse, Toby Park, Brian Andrews-Larson, and Carolyn Herrington, "Evaluation of the Florida Tax Credit Scholarship Program: Participation, Compliance, and Test Scores," Learning Systems Institute, 2018, pp. v–vi.

14. Matthew Chingos and Daniel Kuehn, "The Effects of Statewide Private School Choice on College Enrollment and Graduation," Urban Institute, September 27, 2017.

15. "Louisiana Scholarship Program," EdChoice, https://www.edchoice.org/school-choice/programs/louisiana-scholarship-program/, April 20, 2020.

16. "Louisiana Scholarship Program."

17. "Enrollment in Public Elementary and Secondary Schools, by Region, State, and Jurisdiction: Selected Years, Fall 1990 through Fall 2027," National Center for Education Statistics, 2018; "Total and Current Expenditures per Pupil in Fall Enrollment in Public Elementary and Secondary Schools, by Function and State or Jurisdiction: 2014–15," National Center for Education Statistics, 2017.

18. Anna J. Egalite and Jonathan N. Mills, "The Louisiana Scholarship Program," *Education Next* 14, no. 1 (2014).

19. "RS 17:4021," Louisiana State Legislature; "RS 17:4022," Louisiana State Legislature.

20. "RS 17:4023," Louisiana State Legislature.

21. Participating private schools with an average of at least 10 LSP students per grade or at least 40 participating students enrolled in tested grades must meet a certain threshold on the LSP's "Scholarship Cohort Index" (the equivalent of a "D" grade in the public school accountability system).

22. Jonathan N. Mills and Patrick J. Wolf, "The Effects of the Louisiana Scholarship Program on Student Achievement after Two Years, Education Research Alliance for New Orleans, 2016, https://scdp.uark.edu/the-effects-of-the-louisiana-scholarship-program-on-student-achievement-after-four-years; Atila Abdulkadiroğlu, Parag A. Pathak, and Christopher R. Walters, "Free to Choose: Can School Choice Reduce Student Achievement?," National Bureau of Economic Research, 2015.

23. "Empirical Research Literature on the Effects of School Choice," EdChoice, https://www.edchoice.org/school-choice/empirical-research-literature-on-the-effects-of-school-choice/, April 20, 2020.

24. Mills and Wolf, "Effects of the Louisiana Scholarship Program."

25. Mills and Wolf, "Effects of the Louisiana Scholarship Program."

26. Jason Bedrick, "The Folly of Overregulating School Choice," *Education Next*, January 5, 2016; Douglas Harris, "The First Negative Effects of Vouchers and the Predictable Misinterpretation," *Education Week*, January 6, 2016; White, "America's Most Disadvantaged Students"; Jason Bedrick, "On Regulating School Choice: A Response to Critics," *Education Next*, January 14, 2016.

27. "School Choice Regulation: Friend or Foe?," Cato Institute, March 4, 2016, https://www.cato.org/events/school-choice-regulation-friend-or-foe; Eric Hanushek, John Kain, and Steven Rivkin, "Disruption versus Tiebout Improvement: The Costs and Benefits of Switching Schools," *Journal of Public Economics* 88, no. 9 (August 2004): 1722–1746.

28. Jonathan N. Mills and Patrick J. Wolf, "Vouchers in the Bayou: The Effects of the Louisiana Scholarship Program on Student Achievement after Two Years," *Educational Evaluation and Policy Analysis* 39, no. 3 (2017): 464–84; Atila Abdulkadiroğlu, Parag A. Pathak, and Christopher R. Walters, "Free to Choose: Can School Choice Reduce Student Achievement?," *American Economic Journal: Applied Economics* 10, no. 1 (2018): 175–206; Yujie Sude, Corey A. DeAngelis, and Patrick J. Wolf, "Supplying Choice: An Analysis of School Participation Decisions in Voucher Programs in Washington, DC, Indiana, and Louisiana." *Journal of School Choice* 12, no. 1 (2018): 8–33.

29. Brian Kisida, Patrick J. Wolf, and Evan Rhinesmith, "Views from Private Schools: Attitudes about School Choice Programs across the States," American Enterprise Institute, 2015.

30. Abdulkadiroğlu et al., "Free to Choose."

31. Yujie Sude et al., "Supplying Choice."

32. Corey A. DeAngelis, "Unintended Impacts of Regulations on the Quality of Schooling Options," *Education Next*, September 19, 2017.

33. Kisida et al., "Views from Private Schools."

34. Corey A. DeAngelis, Lindsey M. Burke, and Patrick J. Wolf, "The Effects of Regulations on Private School Choice Program Participation: Experimental Evidence from Florida," Department of Education Reform (EDRE) Working Paper No. 2018-08, University of Arkansas, October 2018.

35. Corey A. DeAngelis, Lindsey M. Burke, and Patrick J. Wolf, "The Effects of Regulations on Private School Choice Program Participation: Experimental Evidence from California and New York," EDRE Working Paper No. 2019-07, University of Arkansas, March 2019.

36. Fiona M. Scott Morton, "The Problems of Price Controls," Cato Institute, *Regulation* 24, no. 1 (2001).

37. Corey A. DeAngelis and Blake Hoarty, "Who Participates? An Analysis of School Participation Decisions in Two Voucher Programs in the United States," Cato Institute, September 17, 2018.

38. DeAngelis et al., "Effects of Regulations: Florida," p. 19.

39. Jennifer Oldham, "K–12 Accreditation's Next Move," *Education Next* 18, no. 1 (Winter 2018).

40. Lindsey M. Burke, "Principal Perspectives on School Participation and Non-Participation in the D.C. Opportunity Scholarship Program: An Institutional Theory Analysis," diss., George Mason University, October 2018.

41. Burke, "Principal Perspectives."

42. White, "America's Most Disadvantaged Students," p. 6.

43. Jennifer McMurrer, "NCLB Year 5: Choices, Changes, and Challenges: Curriculum and Instruction in the NCLB Era," Center on Education Policy, July 24, 2007.

44. Hani Morgan, "Relying on High-Stakes Standardized Tests to Evaluate Schools and Teachers: A Bad Idea," *The Clearing House: A Journal of Educational Strategies, Issues, and Ideas* 89, no. 2 (2016): 67–72.

45. DeAngelis et al., "Effects of Regulations: Florida."

46. DeAngelis et al., "Effects of Regulations: Florida."

47. Kisida et al., "Views from Private Schools."

48. Jay P. Greene, "Evidence for the Disconnect between Changing Test Scores and Changing Later Life Outcomes," Jay P. Greene's blog, 2016.

49. Colin Hitt, Michael Q. McShane, and Patrick J. Wolf, "Do Impacts on Test Scores Even Matter? Lessons from Long-Run Outcomes in School Choice Research," American Enterprise Institute, 2018.

50. Hitt et al., "Impacts on Test Scores."

51. Robert C. Bulman, "School-Choice Stories: The Role of Culture," *Sociological Inquiry* 74, no. 4 (2004): 492–519.

52. Eric A. Hanushek, John F. Kain, Steven G. Rivkin, and Gregory F. Branch, "Charter School Quality and Parental Decision Making with School Choice," *Journal of Public Economics* 91 (2007): 823–48.

53. Ellen B. Goldring and Kristie J. R. Phillips, "Parent Preferences and Parent Choices: The Public-Private Decision about School Choice," *Journal of Education Policy* 23, no. 3 (2008): 209–30.

54. Thomas Stewart, Patrick J. Wolf, and Stephen Q. Cornman, "Parent and Student Voices on the First Year of the DC Opportunity Scholarship Program," *Peabody Journal of Education* 82, no. 2 (2007): 311–86.

55 Mark Schneider and Jack Buckley, "What Do Parents Want from Schools? Evidence from the Internet," *Educational Evaluation and Policy Analysis* 24, no. 2 (2002): 133–44.

56. Jill M. Zimmerman and Debra Y. Vaughan, "School Choice Outcomes in Post-Katrina New Orleans," *Journal of School Choice* 7, no. 2 (2013): 163–81.

57. Lynn Bosetti and Michael C. Pyryt, "Parental Motivation in School Choice," *Journal of School Choice: International Research and Reform* 1, no. 4 (2008): 89–108.

58. Atila Abdulkadiroğlu, Parag A. Pathak, Jonathan Schellenberg, and Christopher R. Walters, "Do Parents Value School Effectiveness?," National Bureau of Economic Research No. 23912, 2017.

59. James P. Kelly and Benjamin Scafidi, "More Than Scores: An Analysis of Why and How Parents Choose Private Schools," EdChoice, 2013; Thomas Steward and Patrick J. Wolf, "The School Choice Journey: Parents Experiencing More Than Improved Test Scores," American Enterprise Institute, 2015.

60. Jason Bedrick and Lindsey Burke, "Surveying Florida Scholarship Families," EdChoice, 2018.

61. Corey A. DeAngelis, "Divergences between Effects on Test Scores and Effects on Non-cognitive Skills," *Educational Review* (August 5, 2019): https://doi.org/10.1080/00131911.2019.1646707.

Chapter Ten

1. Matt Barnum, "Does Money Matter for Schools? Why One Researcher Says the Question Is 'Essentially Settled,'" *Chalkbeat*, December 17, 2018.

2. National Center for Education Statistics, "Digest of Education Statistics: 2018," Table 236.55, https://nces.ed.gov/programs/digest/d18/tables/dt18_236.55.asp.

3. National Center for Education Statistics, "Top Stories in NAEP Long-Term Trend Assessment," Nation's Report Card, https://www.nationsreportcard.gov/ltt_2012.

4. John Merrifield, *School System Reform: Why and How Is a Priceless Tale* (Bishop Auckland, UK: Covenant Press, 2019).

5. Organisation for Economic Co-operation and Development (OECD), "What Is PISA?," http://www.oecd.org/pisa.

6. "Nation at Risk Declarations," *School System Reform Studies*, October 2016.

7. Corey A. DeAngelis and Lindsey M. Burke, "Does Regulation Induce Homogenisation? An Analysis of Three Voucher Programmes in the United States," *Educational Research and Evaluation* 23, nos. 7–8 (2017): 311–27; Corey A. DeAngelis and Lindsey Burke, "Does Regulation Reduce Specialization?," EdChoice, March 14, 2019.

8. Corey A. DeAngelis, Lindsey M. Burke, and Patrick J. Wolf, "The Effects of Regulations on Private School Choice Program Participation: Experimental Evidence from Florida," *Social Science Quarterly*, July 4, 2019; Corey A. DeAngelis, Lindsey M. Burke and Patrick J. Wolf, "The Effects of Regulations on Private School Choice Program Participation: Experimental Evidence from California and New York," Department of Education Reform (EDRE) Working Paper No. 2019-07, March 12, 2019; David A. Stuit and Sy Doan, "School Choice Regulations: Red Tape or Red Herring?," Thomas B. Fordham Institute, January 23, 2013.

9. Andrew J. Coulson, "Do Vouchers and Tax Credits Increase Private School Regulation? A Statistical Analysis," *Journal of School Choice* 5, no. 2 (2011): 224–51.

10. This site alleges much scandalous behavior by CPSs: http://charterschoolscandals.blogspot.com.

11. Vice President Al Gore noted in "Reinventing Government" that routine failure is politically insignificant, but scandal is very significant. Albert Gore, *National Performance Review: Reinventing Government*, (Washington: Government Printing Office, 1993).

12. John Merrifield, "Nation at Risk VI, Including a Partial Misunderstanding of the Risk," Institute for Objective Policy Assessment School System Reform Studies, March 2, 2015.

13. Google search conducted September 18, 2018. Short of breaking the law, many activities that reduce costs, including cutting corners on staff, materials, and facilities, may not reduce revenue. Schooling students in a toolshed was noted as a cheap alternative to facility expansion. *Charter School Scandals* (blog) (http://charterschoolscandals.blogspot.com/) also promises "a compilation of news articles about charter schools which have been charged with, or are highly suspected of, tampering with admissions, grades, attendance and testing; misuse of funds and embezzlement; engaging in nepotism and conflicts of interest; engaging in complicated and shady real estate deals; and/or have been engaging in other questionable, unethical, borderline-legal, or illegal activities." All of those, many of which may be ungrounded allegations, are easier to get away with if offended parents are easily replaced from a long wait list.

14. Housing costs more near better schools, and paying for school access through housing premiums creates a much more uniform and less motivated schooling provision than allocation with public-private shared financing of tuition.

15. See Lance Izumi's "Not as Good as You Think" series: https://www.schoolsystemreformstudies.net/wp-content/uploads/Opinion-Forum/Interpretation%20of%20Evidence%20%E2%80%93%20Misleading%20Findings/NAGAYT%20-%20Izumi.pdf.

16. The point is not that money does not matter, though it often does not. It is that socioeconomic status accounts for much more, often all, of the variation in student outcomes. See James S. Coleman, Ernest Q. Campbell, Carol J. Hobson, James McPartland, Alexander M. Mood, Frederic D. Weinfeld, and Robert L. York, "Equality of Educational Opportunity," U.S. Department of Health, Education, and Welfare, 1966; Mark Dynarski, "It's Not Nothing: The Role of Money in Improving Education," Brookings Institution, March 2, 2017.

17. It does not mean that *all* schools are equally bad, only that the vast majority of schooling observations are approximately equally bad.

18. The Program for International Student Assessment (PISA) tests 15-year-olds. The top country PISA scores are about 10 to 15 percent above U.S. PISA reading and math scores. See OECD, "What Is PISA?"

19. Elise Swanson, "Can We Have It All? A Review of the Impacts of School Choice on Racial Integration," *Journal of School Choice* 11, no. 4 (November 2017): 507–26.

20. "Wisconsin—Milwaukee Parental Choice Program," EdChoice, https://www.edchoice.org/school-choice/programs/wisconsin-milwaukee-parental-choice-program.

21. Backed up by a significant flight rate; many more 0-to-4 aged children than 5- to 9-year-olds; Source is author's calculations from the census data embedded in Maptitude. See also Bartley R. Danielsen and John D. Merrifield, "Tennessee Economic Development Zone ESAs: Implementation Considerations and Methods," 2018.

22. John Merrifield and Nathan Gray, "An Evaluation of the CEO Horizon, 1998–2008, Edgewood Tuition Voucher Program, August 31, 2009.

23. Merrifield, *School System Reform*, chap. 2:

1. Central planning can produce high-performing school systems; pricelessness and price controls will not impact the provision of schooling as disastrously as they have impacted everything else.
2. Monopoly—high entry barriers to public school alternatives—is efficiency enhancing.
3. Public funding earmarked for schooling should belong to a particular service provider (the public schools), not the service customers from whom the money was taken through taxation.
4. Incentives don't matter.
5. Specialization within large, uniform conglomerate organizations is better than specialization by organizations.
6. There is one set of best practices for the vast majority of schoolchildren, and the political process will discover them, adopt them, and optimally deploy them.

The newly recognized need for "customization"—no doubt uniformly delivered—"is to be achieved by [further] centralization." Paul E. Petersen, *Saving Schools: From Horace Mann to Virtual Learning* (Cambridge, MA: Harvard University Press, 2011), p. 18.

24. Lance T. Izumi, "Interpretation of Evidence—Misleading Findings," *School System Reform Studies*, https://www.schoolsystemreformstudies.net/ssrs-forums/main-forum-opinion-forum/interpretation-of-evidence-misleading-findings.

25. "The Gold Standard" refers to the reliability of comparisons when "treatment" (such as school choice) is randomly administered, as long as if students given a chance to choose are randomly chosen from a larger set that sought choice. M. Shakeel, K. Anderson, and P. J. Wolf, "The Participant Effects of Private School Vouchers across the Globe: A Meta-analytic and Systematic Review," EDRE Working Paper No. 2016-07, University of Arkansas, May 2016.

26. EdChoice, *The 123s of School Choice: What the Research Says about Private School Choice Programs in America* (Indianapolis: EdChoice, 2019).

27. This statement originated in "Reinventing Government," but a brief search reveals that it is widely quoted. Gore is noting the near political irrelevance of routine failure and the political salience of scandal.

28. Andrew J. Coulson, "The Cato Education Market Index," Cato Institute Policy Analysis no. 585, December 13, 2006; "Andrew Coulson Education Freedom Index," *School System Reform Studies*, https://www.schoolsystemreformstudies.net/education-freedom-index.

29. Cara Candal, ed., "National Charter School Law Rankings and Scorecard 2018," Center for Education Reform, March 2018.

30. "The Education Choice and Competition Index," Brookings Institution, https://www.brookings.edu/the-education-choice-and-competition-index.

31. Samuel Barrows, Albert Cheng, Paul E. Peterson, and Martin R. West, "Do Charters Pose a Threat to Private Schools? Evidence from Nationally Representative Surveys of U.S. Parents," *Journal of School Choice* 13, no. 1 (2019): 10–32; Richard Buddin, "The Impact of Charter Schools on Public and Private School Enrollments," Cato Institute Policy Analysis no. 707, August 28, 2012; Corey A. DeAngelis and Angela K. Dills, "Is School Choice a Trojan Horse? The Effects of School Choice Laws on Homeschool Prevalence," *Peabody Journal of Education* 4, no. 3 (2019): 342–54; Heidi L. Holmes, "Expanding Outcomes in Educational Program Evaluation: Student Outcomes, Systemic Effects, and Policy Implications," University of Arkansas thesis no. 3214, May 2019.

Chapter Eleven

1. Kate McCustion and John McCustion, "Friday Freakout: What Parents of Special Needs Students Say to School Choice Naysayers," EdChoice, February 6, 2015.

2. Rachel Aviv, "Georgia's Separate and Unequal Special-Education System," *New Yorker*, October 1, 2018.

3. "Family of Bainbridge Student Speaks Out about Abuse Allegations," WTXL, Tallahassee, Florida, November 30, 2017.

4. While a child may sometimes gain a certain amount of public school choice through an IEP, proximity to a family's home is a key factor in what school placements are offered.

5. *Endrew F. v. Douglas County School Dist. RE–1*, 580 U.S. ____ (2017).

6. Christina A. Samuels, "A Year Ago the Supreme Court Raised the Bar for Special Ed. What's Happened Since?," *Education Week*, April 27, 2018.

7. Tracy Thompson, "The Special-Education Charade," *The Atlantic*, January 3, 2016.

8. Megan Burgess, "The 5 Don'ts of IEP Meetings," *Scary Mommy* (blog), September 2017.

9. Mark Claypool and John McLughlin, "Why Improving America's Understanding of Special Needs Will Lead to More Educational Choice," EdChoice, August 2, 2017.

10. Claypool and McLaughlin, "Improving America's Understanding."

11. "Cool Schools: This Catholic School Network Exclusively Serves Students with Special Needs," EdChoice, September 24, 2018.

12. Patrick J. Wolf, John F. Witte, and David J. Fleming, "Special Education and the Milwaukee Parental Choice Program," School Choice Demonstration Project Milwaukee Evaluation Report no. 35, University of Arkansas, February 2012; Elizabeth Setren, "Special Education and English Language Learner Students in Boston Charter Schools: Impact and Classification," School Effectiveness and Inequity Initiative Working Paper no. 2015.03, September 2016; Marcus A. Winters, "Why the Gap? Special Education and New York City Charter Schools," Center on Reinventing Public Education, 2013; Marcus A. Winters, "Understanding the Charter School Special Education Gap: Evidence from Denver, Colorado," Center on Reinventing Public Education, 2014; Marcus A. Winters, "Understanding the Gap in Special Education Enrollments between Charter and Traditional Public Schools: Evidence from Denver, Colorado," *Educational Researcher* 44, no. 4 (2015): 228–36; Marcus A. Winters, Dick M. Carpenter, and Grant Clayton, "Does Attending a Charter School Reduce the Likelihood of Being Placed into Special Education? Evidence from Denver, Colorado," *Educational Evaluation and Policy Analysis* 39, no. 3 (2017): 448–63; Marcus A. Winters and Jay P. Greene, "How Special Ed Vouchers Keep Kids from Being Mislabeled as Disabled," *Civic Report* no. 58, Center for Civic Innovation, Manhattan Institute, August 7, 2009.

13. Jonathan Butcher and Jason Bedrick, "Schooling Satisfaction," EdChoice, October 10, 2013.

14. Jay P. Greene and Greg Forster, "Voucher for Special Education Students: An Evaluation of Florida's McKay Scholarship Program," Manhattan Institute, June 2003.

15. Virginia R. Weidner and Carolyn D. Herrington, "Are Parents Informed Consumers: Evidence from the Florida McKay Scholarship Program," *Peabody Journal of Education* 81, no. 1 (2006): 27–56.

16. Jay P. Greene and Marcus A. Winters, "The Effect of Special-Education Vouchers on Public School Achievement: Evidence from Florida's McKay Scholarship Program," Manhattan Institute, April 2008.

17. "Friday Freakout: Some Public Schools Choose Not to Serve Every Child, Block Other Options," EdChoice, May 9, 2014.

18. "School Choice FAQs: Can School Choice Help Students with Special Needs?," EdChoice, https://www.edchoice.org/engage/faqs/can-school-choice-help-students-with-special-needs-2/.

19. Oklahoma Council of Public Affairs, "Chloe—A Lindsey Nicole Henry Scholarship Story," YouTube video, July 6, 2012.

20. Selene Almazan and Denise Stile Marshall, "School Vouchers and Students with Disabilities: Examining Impact in the Name of Choice," Council of Parent Attorneys and Advocates, June 2016.

21. Dana Goldstein, "Special Ed School Vouchers May Come with Hidden Costs," *New York Times*, April 11, 2017.

22 "Children and Youth with Disabilities," National Center for Education Statistics, https://nces.ed.gov/programs/coe/indicator_cgg.asp.

23. "Fast Facts," National Center for Education Statistics, https://nces.ed.gov/fastfacts.

24. Michael Q. McShane, Patrick J. Wolf, and Collin Hitt, "Do Impacts on Test Scores Even Matter? Lessons from Long-Run Outcomes in School Choice Research," American Enterprise Institute, March 19, 2018; Corey DeAngelis, "Divergences between Effects on Test Scores and Effects on Non-cognitive Skills," *Educational Review*, August 5, 2019.

25. "AFT Resolution against Standardized Assessments for Students Receiving Special Education Services," American Federation of Teachers, 2014.

26. Valerie Strauss, "Why It's 'Idiotic' to Force Special Education Students to Take Standardized Tests," *Washington Post*, October 5, 2015.

27. "IDEA Parent Guide," National Center for Learning Disabilities, April 2006.

28. "Why Requiring Public School Attendance to Access School Choice Can Hurt Students with Special Needs," EdChoice, July 25, 2017.

Chapter Twelve

1. Cassady Rosenblum, "Take It from a New Orleans Charter School Teacher: Parents Don't Always Get School Choice Right," *Los Angeles Times*, July 10, 2017.

2. Natalie Wexler, "Six Reasons Why School Choice Won't Save Us," *Forbes*, April 28, 2018.

3. Gail Cornwall, "Why Parents Make Flawed Choices about Their Kids' Schooling," *The Atlantic*, October 18, 2017; Matt Barnum, "A School Choice Quandary: Parents Care More about Who Attends a School Than about Its Quality, in NYC Study," *Chalkbeat*, October 11, 2017.

4. Patricia MacCorquodale, "The Masquerade of School Choice: A Parent's Story," *Washington Post*, April 1, 2017.

5. While policy has been geared heavily toward test scores to evaluate schools, parents often prioritize other things and get better long-term results. See Michael Q. McShane, Patrick J. Wolf, and Colin Hitt, "Do Impacts on Test Scores Even Matter? Lessons from Long-Run Outcomes in School Choice Research," American Enterprise Institute, March 2018; Diether W. Beuermann and C. Kirabo Jackson, "Do Parents Know Best? The Short and Long-Run Effects of Attending the Schools That Parents Prefer," working paper, Northwestern University, 2018.

6. Michael F. Lovenheim and Patrick Walsh, "(Re)Searching for a School: How Choice Drives Parents to Become More Informed," *Education Next* (Winter 2018).

7. Summary of Thomas Stewart and Patrick J. Wolf, *The School Choice Journey: School Vouchers and the Empowerment of Urban Families* (New York: Palgrave Macmillan, 2014).

8. Evan Rhinesmith, "A Review of the Research on Parent Satisfaction in Private School Choice Programs," *Journal of School Choice* 11, no. 4. (2017): 585–603.

INDEX

Note: Page numbers followed by "f" or "t" indicate figures and tables, respectively. Page numbers with "n" or "nn" indicate notes.

ABOUT THE CONTRIBUTORS

Jason Bedrick is director of policy for EdChoice. Previously he served as policy analyst with the Cato Institute's Center for Educational Freedom. He also served as a legislator in the New Hampshire House of Representatives and was an education policy research fellow at the Josiah Bartlett Center for Public Policy. He has published numerous studies on educational choice programs with organizations such as the Heritage Foundation, the Texas Public Policy Foundation, the Pioneer Institute, the Show-Me Institute, and the Caesar Rodney Institute. His articles have been featured in the *Wall Street Journal*, the *New York Post*, the *Boston Globe*, *National Review*, *National Affairs*, and *Education Next*, among others. Bedrick received his master's degree in public policy from the John F. Kennedy School of Government at Harvard University, where he was a fellow at the Taubman Center for State and Local Government.

Lindsey M. Burke is the director of the Center for Education Policy at the Heritage Foundation, where she oversees the foundation's research and policy on issues pertaining to preschool, K–12, and higher-education reform. Burke's commentary, research, and op-eds have appeared in numerous magazines and newspapers, and she is a frequent guest on radio and television shows; she also speaks on education reform issues across the country and internationally. Burke serves as a fellow at EdChoice and on the national advisory board of Learn4Life, a network of public charter schools serving "opportunity youth." She holds a bachelor's degree in politics from Hollins University in Roanoke, Virginia, and a master of teaching degree in foreign language education from the University of Virginia. She earned her PhD in education policy from George Mason University.

Albert A. Cheng is an assistant professor of education policy at the University of Arkansas. His research focuses on character formation, religious schools, and school choice. He is an affiliated research fellow at the Program on Education Policy and Governance at Harvard University and a senior fellow at Cardus. Cheng is also a former math teacher at James Logan High School in Union City, California. He holds a master's degree in education from Biola University and a PhD in education policy from the University of Arkansas.

Virginia Walden Ford is one of America's leading advocates for parent empowerment. As a student, a mother, an advocate, and a grandmother, Walden Ford has spent her life fighting to create new educational opportunities for children and families. A native of Little Rock, Arkansas, and the daughter of two public school educators, Walden Ford and her twin sister, Harrietta, were among the first 130 students chosen to desegregate Little Rock's high schools in the mid-1960s. In 1998, Walden Ford formed a grassroots organization, DC Parents for School Choice, of which she is the executive director. In 2003, with the support of national education organizations and lawmakers, she and her group of parent advocates succeeded in convincing Congress and President George W. Bush to enact the nation's first-ever opportunity scholarship program for low-income children. Walden Ford is the author of *Voices, Choices, and Second Chances* and the subject of the 2019 film *Miss Virginia*. She was a national board member and a founding member of the Black Alliance for Educational Options. She also serves on the DC Advisory Committee of the U.S. Civil Rights Commission. Today she lives, once again, in Little Rock.

Tim Keller leads the Educational Choice Team at the Institute for Justice (IJ), overseeing a group of attorneys who defend educational choice programs in courtrooms nationwide and help policymakers design constitutionally defensible educational choice programs. He served as IJ's lead counsel in *Arizona Christian School Tuition Organization v. Winn*, a U.S. Supreme Court victory that protected Arizona's pioneering tax-credit-funded private school scholarship program. Keller also successfully defended Arizona's Empowerment Scholarship Account Program, a publicly funded education savings account program he helped design. Keller received his law degree from Arizona State University. Prior to starting law school, he worked as a research assistant at the Goldwater Institute, a state-based, free-market public policy organization. Upon graduation from law school, Keller clerked for Robert D. Myers, then the presiding judge of the Maricopa County Superior Court. After leaving the Superior Court, Keller accepted a clerkship with the Honorable Ann A. Scott Timmer on the Arizona Court of Appeals.

Matthew Ladner is director of the Arizona Center for Student Opportunity and the executive editor of the weblog RedefinED. Previously, Ladner served as a senior research fellow at the Charles Koch Institute and senior advisor for research and policy at Excel in Ed and vice president of research at the Goldwater Institute. He has given invited testimony to Congress, state legislatures, and the U.S. Commission on Civil Rights. Ladner has written numerous studies on school choice, charter schools, and special-education reform. He is a graduate of the University of Texas at Austin and received both a master's degree and a PhD in political science from the University of Houston.

Martin F. Lueken is EdChoice's director of fiscal policy and analysis, where he focuses on research and analysis of issues that pertain to school choice bills, current programs, and school funding. His work includes providing expert support and advice for policymakers in helping understand the fiscal impact of current school choice programs and potential fiscal effects of programs introduced in state legislatures. He also conducts data analysis and research on school choice. His research and interests include education finance in general and teacher pensions. He has provided expert testimony and advice about fiscal issues for numerous states that have introduced education choice legislation. His work has been mentioned in various media including the *New York Times*, the *Wall Street Journal*, *Education Next*, *Education Week*, and *The 74*. Lueken received his doctorate in education policy from the University of Arkansas. He also earned a master's degree in economics from the University of Missouri. He received his bachelor's degree in physical education, with an emphasis in sports medicine, from Eastern Illinois University.

Phillip W. Magness is senior research fellow at the American Institute for Economic Research. His research encompasses the two great political problems of the 19th-century United States, slavery and taxation, along with the general economic history of the United States. Magness is the coauthor of *Colonization after Emancipation: Lincoln and the Movement for Black Resettlement*, offering a reexamination of Abraham Lincoln's antislavery and freedmen's policies during the American Civil War, and of *Cracks in the Ivory Tower: The Moral Mess of Higher Education,* a critical examination of the business ethics of the American university system. He has also published several works on the history of education policy, including school vouchers in the civil rights era. His writings have appeared in *Social Science Quarterly, Journal of the Early Republic, Slavery and Abolition*, and the *Southern Economic Journal,* as well as popular outlets including the *New York Times, Newsweek,* and *National Review.* Magness completed his undergraduate studies in political science and economics at the University of St. Thomas and obtained his MPP and PhD at George Mason University.

John Merrifield was a professor of economics at the University of Texas at San Antonio for 32 years before retiring as professor emeritus in 2019 and was the editor of the *School System Reform Journal* and the *Journal of School Choice.* He has published widely on school choice, environmental economics, and public finance. Merrifield has also published *School System Reform: Why and How Is a Price-less Tale, Can the Debt Growth Be Stopped?, The School Choice Wars, School Choices, Parental Choice as an Education Reform Catalyst: Global Lessons, Basic Economic Tools*, 55 peer-reviewed journal articles, and several chapters in edited books in his primary teaching and research fields of education economics, public finance, urban and regional economics, and environmental and natural resources economics. He received a BS in natural resource management from Cal Poly, San Luis Obispo in 1977, an MA in economic geography from the University of Illinois in 1979, and a PhD in economics from the University of Wyoming in 1984.

Ben Scafidi is a professor of economics and director of the Education Economics Center at Kennesaw State University and a Friedman fellow with EdChoice and the Georgia Public Policy Foundation. His research has focused on education and urban policy. Previously he served as chair of the state of Georgia's Charter Schools Commission, the education policy advisor to Gov. Sonny Perdue, on the staff of both of Gov. Roy Barnes's Education Reform Study Commissions, and as an expert witness for the state of Georgia in school funding litigation. He received his PhD in economics from the University of Virginia and his BA in economics from the University of Notre Dame. Scafidi resides in Kennesaw, Georgia, with his wife, Lori, and their four children.

Inez Feltscher Stepman is a senior policy analyst at the Independent Women's Forum (IWF). Prior to joining IWF, she was the director of education and workforce development at the American Legislative Exchange Council. Her research focuses on educational freedom, school choice, and the cultural impact of empowering parents with control over their children's education. Stepman is the author of numerous policy papers, including the annually compiled Report Card on American Education, which ranks the states across six aspects of education policy. Her work has been published in numerous outlets, including the *Washington Examiner*, the *Orange County Register*, *The Hill*, and others, and she frequently testifies as an expert to state legislatures across the country. She is also a senior contributor to *The Federalist*, where she writes on subjects ranging from feminism to fashion, and is the Thursday editor of *BRIGHT*, a women's daily newsletter. She holds a BA in philosophy from the University of California, San Diego, and a JD from the University of Virginia School of Law.

Patrick J. Wolf is Distinguished Professor of Education Policy and 21st Century Endowed Chair in School Choice in the Department of Education Reform at the University of Arkansas College of Education and Health Professions. He previously taught at Columbia University and Georgetown University. Wolf is a coauthor, editor, or coeditor of *School Choice: Separating Fact from Fiction*, *The School Choice Journey: School Vouchers and the Empowerment of Urban Families*, *The Education Gap: Vouchers and Urban Schools*, and *Educating Citizens: International Perspectives on Civic Values and School Choice*. He has authored or coauthored over 180 journal articles, book chapters, book reviews, and policy reports on private school choice, public charter schools, civic values, special education, public management, and campaign finance. Wolf has testified before congressional committees five times and before committees of state legislatures 19 times. He has been interviewed and published in numerous media outlets. A 1987 graduate of the University of St. Thomas, Wolf received his PhD in political science from the Government Department at Harvard University in 1995.

ABOUT THE EDITORS

Corey A. DeAngelis is the director of school choice at the Reason Foundation and an adjunct scholar at the Cato Institute's Center for Educational Freedom. His research primarily focuses on the effects of school choice programs on nonacademic outcomes such as criminal activity, character skills, mental health, political participation, and schooling supply. He has authored or coauthored over 40 journal articles, book chapters, and reports on education policy. His research has been published in peer-reviewed academic journals such as *Social Science Quarterly*, *School Effectiveness and School Improvement*, *Educational Review*, *Educational Research and Evaluation*, *Journal of School Choice*, and the *Cato Journal*. His work has also been featured in outlets such as the *Wall Street Journal*, *USA Today*, the *New York Post*, *The Hill*, the *Washington Examiner*, and *Education Next*. DeAngelis received his PhD in education policy from the University of Arkansas. He holds a bachelor's degree in business administration and an MA in economics from the University of Texas at San Antonio.

Neal P. McCluskey is the director of the Cato Institute's Center for Educational Freedom. He is the author of *Feds in the Classroom: How Big Government Corrupts, Cripples, and Compromises American Education* and is coeditor of the Cato books *Educational Freedom: Remembering Andrew Coulson, Debating His Ideas*, and *Unprofitable Schooling: Examining Causes of, and Fixes for, America's Broken Ivory Tower*. He also maintains Cato's Public Schooling Battle Map, an interactive database of values and identity-based conflicts in public schools, and he is on the editorial advisory board of *The Line*, a journal promoting civil discourse in K–12 policy debates. His writings have appeared in such publications as the *Wall Street Journal*, the *Washington Post*, and *Forbes*, and he has appeared on PBS, CNN, Fox News, and numerous radio programs. McCluskey holds an undergraduate degree from Georgetown University, where he double majored in government and English, a master's degree in political science from Rutgers University, Newark, and a PhD in public policy from George Mason University.

ABOUT THE CATO INSTITUTE

Founded in 1977, the Cato Institute is a public policy research foundation dedicated to broadening the parameters of policy debate to allow consideration of more options that are consistent with the principles of limited government, individual liberty, and peace. To that end, the Institute strives to achieve greater involvement of the intelligent, concerned lay public in questions of policy and the proper role of government.

The Institute is named for *Cato's Letters*, libertarian pamphlets that were widely read in the American Colonies in the early 18th century and played a major role in laying the philosophical foundation for the American Revolution.

Despite the achievement of the nation's Founders, today virtually no aspect of life is free from government encroachment. A pervasive intolerance for individual rights is shown by government's arbitrary intrusions into private economic transactions and its disregard for civil liberties. And while freedom around the globe has notably increased in the past several decades, many countries have moved in the opposite direction, and most governments still do not respect or safeguard the wide range of civil and economic liberties.

To address those issues, the Cato Institute undertakes an extensive publications program on the complete spectrum of policy issues. Books, monographs, and shorter studies are commissioned to examine the federal budget, Social Security, regulation, military spending, international trade, and myriad other issues. Major policy conferences are held throughout the year, from which papers are published thrice yearly in the *Cato Journal*. The Institute also publishes the quarterly magazine *Regulation*.

In order to maintain its independence, the Cato Institute accepts no government funding. Contributions are received from foundations, corporations, and individuals, and other revenue is generated from the sale of publications. The Institute is a nonprofit, tax-exempt, educational foundation under Section 501(c)3 of the Internal Revenue Code.